Norman Handy

K2, The Savage Mountain

Travels in Northern Pakistan

novum pro

www.novum-publishing.co.uk

© 2017 novum publishing

ISBN 978-3-99048-716-7
Editing: Nicola Ratcliff, BA
Cover photo:
Patrick Poendl | Dreamstime.com
Cover design, layout & typesetting:
novum publishing

www.novum-publishing.co.uk

Contents

Introduction – Birth of an idea

I had always wanted to visit the Karakoram Mountains from an early age. I remember reading the Sunday paper magazine supplement in my young teens, with glossy photos of gigantic mountains, huge cliff faces, plunging valleys and the Chinese building the Karakoram Highway (affectionately known as the KKH) named after the mountain range through which it weaves its way up through northern Pakistan and over the Chinese border.

The road was hacked out of sheer cliffs of bare rock. The people and the vehicles in the photos looked like ants and toys against the huge back drop of the mountains. And further to the east is the world's second highest peak after Everest, K2 at 8,611 meters. Just the names of towns and mountains in the area seem to evoke oriental mystery.

The Karakoram Mountain Range is in the Gilgit Baltistan province, in the far north of Pakistan which borders Afghanistan to the west and China to the north and in the east, the mountain range stretches over the line of control into Indian administered Jammu and Kashmir. It was a long way from my suburban life in the London Borough of Bromley.

And I do love the outdoors. I remember with great affection, family summer holidays to the Lake District and trekking up the highest mountain in England, Scafell Pike 978m and marvelling at the scenery, the majestic views, and the sense of adventure and achievement of walking up the path to sit on the summit. In Wales, we headed up their highest mountain, Snowdonia just a little higher at 1,085m.

It was not until I was in my twenties that I attempted Scotland's highest peak, Ben Nevis at 1,344m. This is memorable for me but for different reasons, as there was low cloud, poor visibility, it was cold, windy and lots of rain so I turned back and never did get to the top. It's not surprising it was so wet, as the nearby town of Fort William, is one of the wettest places in the country. It was not much better having turned back as I was camping and was still cold and wet.

Whilst these mountains had great views, they were a long way short of the Karakoram Mountains and the second highest peak in the world, K2 and I knew that there were more mountains just waiting to be discovered for myself.

Pakistan has featured in British history for a long while. It was part of the empire for many years. The area figured in the great game that England played with Russia in Victorian times to gain influence in this geographically strategic area. The Khyber Pass is famous for its place in history and whilst not on the KKH itself, is in the same area and features in several films of the 1960s and not just because of the release in 1968, of the film, Carry on up the Khyber featuring many of the regulars of the Carry On team.

There was a network of ancient caravan routes collectively called the Silk Route stretching from China to Europe that Marco Polo travelled along in the thirteenth century. It wasn't just an east west route but had several spurs for instance north to Russia and south through the Karakoram Mountains through what is now Pakistan to the sea and onwards by sea to the Gulf. For years caravans traded along this route carrying silk, spices, sandal wood, slaves, gems including lapis lazuli, artwork, intellectual ideas and religion.

The conquest of Everest on 29th May 1953, the conquest of K2 on 31st July 1954 and the Apollo landings on the moon on 20th July 1969, when my parents would wake me up, so I could see it live during the night were inspirational in exploration and expansion of man's horizons. And I felt that in that same vein of adventure, I wanted to visit the Karakoram, not necessarily new to mankind but new to me.

The mountains are formed by plate tectonics, with the Indian plate thrusting northwards into the more static Eurasian plate. Where the two meet, the edges are crumpled under the relentless pressure and thrust upwards to form mountains. This is a continuous process but it can manifest itself in sudden movements in the form of violent earthquakes at any time.

There is not one mountain range, but in fact, several ranges and the Himalayas, the Karakoram, the Pamirs and Hindu Kush mountain ranges all meet here. At the same time, the large amounts of rain and snow that fall here feed the rivers that cut deep valleys. Added to this river erosion, despite its southerly position, its latitude is level with the central Mediterranean, due to the altitude, there is snow and ice on the mountain tops and glaciers in the valleys. Some of these glaciers, such as the Siachen, Biafo, Hispar and Baltoro glaciers, are each over 60kms long and are the longest glaciers in the world outside of the Polar Regions.

It is a long way to go and I wanted to do more than just drive up and down the KKH, in short I wanted a purpose other than just to see the road. So after a little research, there were other places of interest to be added to the KKH trip. There was a trek to K2 base camp, a visit to the Kalash valleys, the Deosai plateau, treks on glaciers and a trip northwards over the border into China to visit Kashgar which was a major trading centre on the east west Silk Route.

Obviously this was a trip that was going to take a little longer than could be fitted into a two week summer holiday entitlement from my employer. The idea to visit this area was born but there were practicalities to overcome and not just the holiday entitlement issue. There was planning, the cost and family commitments. Therefore, it was still on my bucket list of things that I wanted to do but it dropped down the list in terms of being practical to undertake.

It was some time later that I found myself divorced, working in London but with a 70 minute commute by train. I loved my job but hated the travelling to and from work. After more than 30 years of commuting, I had had enough. The trains were crowded and there was the noise from people's earphones forcing you to listen to their music, whether you wanted to or not. The train was too hot in summer, too cold in winter and inane half conversations over heard from people on their mobiles.

I had started to devote holidays to ticking items off my bucket list but as fast as I was completing a journey, I would find inspiration to discover something else, so I was adding to the list as fast as I was ticking them off. I also looked at the list and as I was getting older, noted that some of them would require higher levels of fitness and perhaps could not wait for retirement. Therefore, these ought to get priority over cultural visits and cruises before I got too old. I had wanted to reach the summit of Mount Elbrus, Europe's highest peak, at 5,642m, located in the Russian Caucasus Mountains near the borders with Georgia.

I had found a Russian organisation to guide me to the top. I could walk by myself but since the area suffers from a Muslim separatist insurgency, I wanted to be sure that someone knew where I was and could raise the alarm should anything go wrong … whether it was terrorism or an accident. But after filling in a medical questionnaire, it came as a bit of a shock to be told that they would not take me.

Then I discovered Karamkoram Jeep Trek International (KJTI) run by a retired University maths lecturer, who had visited the Karakoram some decades earlier and was inspired to help the locals by establishing a travel company, to guide people on tailor made tours around the area using local guides, local drivers and local hotels. Some of the photos used for publicity were stunning with spectacular scenery and local culture.

This was just what I wanted but given that this is northern Pakistan, there are security issues in the tribal area and it borders Afghanistan, I was always concerned about security. I was assured that where I proposed to go was not a dangerous area, but I had resigned myself to going for just two weeks and squeeze in as much as I could.

I was getting very close to writing a cheque to pay for my proposed trip when on 2nd May 2011, the Americans found and killed Osama bin Laden, near Abbottabad in the Swat valley. The significance of this is that the KKH runs right through the heart of the Swat valley. I decided not to go after all. Later in Mingora, also in the Swat Valley, the school girl campaigning for the right for girls to receive an education, Malala Youzafzai, was shot in the head on 9th October 2012.

Incidentally she survived the shooting receiving hospital care initially in Pakistan and shortly afterwards, flying to the UK for surgery and on 10th October 2013 received the European Union Sakharov prize for human rights and now lives in Birmingham. On 10th October 2014, she was awarded the Nobel Peace Prize becoming the youngest ever recipient.

The Foreign and Commonwealth Office (FCO) gives detailed travel advice and is a marvellous source of accurate and independent travel advice on safety and security. Their security advice at the time was not to travel along the KKH, between Islamabad and Gilgit, the capital of Gilgit Baltistan province, or up the Swat valley. Some of Gilgit–Baltistan was only essential travel but there was no advice against all travel as it was considered generally free of militancy and terrorism.

For the western city of Peshawar, the Lowari Pass to its north and the Khyber Pass into Afghanistan, the advice was against all travel so these places of interest and routes were off the schedule. There was specific advice for the KKH, citing narrow roads and sudden drops, not to travel at night and be aware that there are frequent landslides which is still valid. I might not be going right away but I kept in contact with KJTI as I am an optimist and the situation may yet alter for the better.

Meanwhile, at work, my employer was undertaking a reorganisation and re-sizing the business. This is management speak for reducing costs, a reduction in head count and redundancies. This means different things to different people, depending on their age and aspirations. Some of my colleagues were delighted whilst others were gutted. Some acted that afternoon and signed on with an employment agency. Others were in shock but for me this was an opportunity that I grabbed with both hands and headed for the exit. I had always wanted to retire early so I could travel and this opportunity just came a bit earlier than expected. An added bonus was that after more than 30 years of commuting which I hated, I was finally free.

I got back in contact with KJTI and booked the trip to include everything that I wanted to see and do in Gilgit Baltistan. I had a relaxed start to the schedule so that I could acclimatise to the altitude gently rather than rush straight to altitude and suffer altitude sickness.

In order to avoid the dangerous Swat valley section of the KKH, I was going to fly from Islamabad to Gilgit and would have armed security in the less safe areas to the west of Gilgit. There is an option to get to Islamabad on a long direct flight but I find long flights tedious as you are cramped in your seat for a long time and after you have read the aircraft brochure and scanned through the entertainment on offer of films that you have seen several times before there is still plenty of time left with no distractions.

Therefore I chose to travel via Dubai and have two shorter flights. There was another reason to go via Dubai despite the additional cost. I had heard that there is a lot to do and see so I would take the opportunity to spend some time there visiting some tourist attractions. More importantly for my Pakistan trip, I could acclimatise to the heat in the comfort of a western style luxury hotel in Dubai.

I had visited the doctors and made sure all my injections were up to date and not just the free ones such as against polio but some of the optional ones such as a course of jabs against rabies and hepatitis B. This was despite the cost at £45 a jab. I feel that if there is protection you should have it. After all, you would kick yourself if you were given the opportunity, declined on the basis of cost or dislike of needles and then contract the very disease for which you had been offered and had declined the inoculation.

I had a supply of malaria tablets for when I was in the lower areas (once you are high enough in the mountains there are no mosquitoes). I packed my single bag with as little as I thought I could get away with, to keep the weight and bulk as low as possible and I was on my way to the airport.

Whist in transit, on 22nd June 2013 the Taliban killed 10 mountaineers at the base camp on Nanga Parbat which without even checking, I knew was on my schedule in just a few weeks' time.

Chapter 1

Islamabad arrival – Not so dead of night

The three hour flight from Dubai arrived in Islamabad at 1.20am and I was exhausted. The temperature even at this time of night, was still 29°C and whilst the monsoon was due, it had not yet arrived.

The flight was very pleasant as I had no one sitting in front of me or sitting beside me. Therefore I didn't have every airline traveller's nightmare of the person sitting in front of them who insists on reclining their seat into your lap. Also, having no one sitting next to me meant that I wasn't constantly clashing elbows as we both tried to eat our unimaginative and dull in flight meal.

I had been concerned that the two small girls sitting behind me travelling as UMs (airline language for minors travelling without an adult, literally unaccompanied minors) might make the flight a bit of a chore. However, they settled down quickly enough and the airline hostess made sure that they were alright. They were happy to watch cartoons throughout the flight. Personally, I selected to watch Skyfall, a great film but with aircraft noise intruding through the headphones, it required some concentration on the storyline. Not to mention the PA announcements in both Arabic and English interrupted the film, so I saw the end but with only minutes to spare before the plane landed.

Immigration! What a hassle. There were several lines with large signs above detailing who should join which line, several for returning locals, lines for Pakistanis living abroad, lines for visitors with proof of Pakistani origin, a line for diplomats and UN passport holders and lastly, on the far left, a single line for foreigners who didn't fit any of the other categories. This line was the longest. And it was also the slowest moving.

Whilst the other lines slimmed down steadily, ours was moving ever so slowly. Eventually, the other lines were duly processed and emptied. And when the immigration officers had cleared their lines completely, they waved us over. So what was the point of separate lines?

I needn't have worried about the delay, for once we were through the doors, towards the baggage reclaim area, everyone who had disappeared through those doors ahead of me, were standing about waiting for the baggage on the still empty carrousel. Then the carrousel started moving and there was anticipation in the crowd. The crowd was five deep and it was difficult to see the belt through the bobbing heads.

I have always been amazed at the volume of luggage that some people take with themselves. For this particular trip I had 12kg of luggage in one bag, and no hand luggage (I had packed my small day rucksack into my main bag). I take the view that if I have my passport, money and credit card on my person, everything else can be replaced if the worst case occurs and the airline loses my bag, or if I have left something behind that really is essential. It also means I don't have to lug around heavy baggage around the airport, finding a trolley without any wonky wheels, what to do with it when you want to use the toilet etc. It is so much easier to move about without extra baggage.

I saw one gentleman with a trolley with some bags on it but it was obvious that he was still waiting for more items. He already had a trolley with three big bags on it and I was aware of him bobbing left and right behind me to get a better view through the throng of people in front of us to look at the bags on the carousel as they came past. He pushed past me and scooped up a bag. But it wasn't until he had filled his trolley high with five big bags, all wrapped in plastic, plus a cardboard box with the top and corners covered in gaffer tape plus a small bag over his shoulder that he tried manoeuvring his load laboriously towards the exit. I am so glad that I travel light.

Finally, after more than 30 minutes of watching the carousel go round and round, I was delighted to see my black waterproof bag with the logo and words on the end prominently displaying 'Mountain Equipment', one of my favourite brands which I scooped off the belt and headed for doors, above which was a sign welcoming you to Pakistan.

I was being met by my guide Karim, a compact five foot six in his mid-forties who spends his time between his home town of Karimabad, in the Hunza valley in summer and Paris in winter. I had met him five months earlier, in London, and was confident I could pick him out but I was not prepared for the huge number of meeters and greeters, all waving their boards with the name of the person they were due to pick up. We saw each other at the same moment, shook hands and headed out to the car.

Leaving the bustle of the airport at the dead of night, I expected the roads to be quiet, so I was surprised at how busy the roads actually were. It was the middle of Ramadan, so for observant Muslims, night time is when they can eat and drink but that didn't wholly explain the number of people, not just driving, but also gathered in small groups on the roadside and even walking along the edge of the busy motorway, heading towards Islamabad city centre.

This was my first visit to Pakistan and I was fascinated by the lorries. Each driver customises their vehicle with colourful paintings, mirrors, lights, carvings and ornaments. They looked more like fairground rides than lorries. Also, many of the lorries have an extension projection up and over the drivers cab, and extensions jutting out from the front and back bumpers. There are also chains dangling from the extended bumpers that jingle as they bump along the road surface.

We turned off the motorway and made our way through the dark streets. I sensed we were close, as we drove through an area of large detached houses with well-tended gardens behind high walls with large gates. There were a few people about but those I saw, all wore uniforms of private security companies, anti-terrorist squad or police and all were armed.

We turned off the road and the side road was barred with a three bar barrier with a big counterweight at one end plus coils of barbed wire either side blocking what would have been the pavement, between the barrier and high walls of the corner properties. A guard stood by the barrier, dressed in black with the words anti-terrorist squad on his back armed with an AK47.

His colleague sat behind some sandbags, under a canvas tarpaulin to give protection against both rain and sun. Even in the dim light under the canvas, I could make out the outline of a mounted machine gun jutting out above the top row of sand bags. We were asked for our IDs and a barrage of questions, who we were, where we were going, the number of the house, the name of our host, whether we were expected … in short, a thorough interrogation. My name was found on a list, cross checked with my passport and we were allowed through.

We drove 100 meters down the road and pulled up in front of a pair of solid metal gates and the driver hooted his horn several times until the night watchman opened the gate. We were welcomed in and I was given a cold bottle of water and shown to my room. It had been a long journey and it was after 3am and breakfast time was only a few hours away so I collapsed on the bed and went to sleep.

I was due to meet Karim later that morning at 11.30am. I hadn't set the alarm as it refused to work but in the end I didn't need it, as I didn't sleep well and I was awake at 7.30am. On arrival I was too tired to take much note of my surroundings so I took the chance to look around. This was the Hunza Embassy Hotel, a grand name but in reality, it was just a large house. The furniture wasn't new, or non-descript institutional but looked like a collection of items that any family might have collected over the years.

The bathroom had hot and cold running water, a basin, a western toilet and a shower above the bath although there were rusty marks where the taps had dripped over the years. The window was set high in the wall, overlooking a small light well and it was a bit dim in the room as there was vegetation growing thickly over the window.

Last night I had put the bottle of water in the fridge which curiously stood by itself in the middle of the room, beyond the end of the double bed as if it were a feature. In the light of the day, I now noticed that the fridge wasn't making any noise and wasn't cold … it didn't work. Beyond the fridge there was a fireplace and a gas fire in the hearth which seemed incongruous, given the outside temperature. I opened the curtains to look out over a small concrete covered yard with high whitewashed walls which was home to some broken furniture.

On one of the walls of the room, set high almost touching the ceiling, there was an air conditioning unit and a control unit on the wall. It hummed quietly away, on a low setting, which I left unaltered. Underneath was a dressing table and on it there was a menu detailing breakfast menu options, sandwiches with various fillings, burgers (obviously geared towards western tastes) and a selection of curries and side dishes catering for local tastes.

There was also some details of this hotel and I discovered that it was part of a chain of hotels which were locally owned, one hotel in the capital and a selection throughout the northern Gilgit-Baltistan area, all with their pictures and a brief description. Many were located in places that were on my schedule and I realised, I would be staying at several of them over the next few weeks.

The hotel itself was similar to a large semidetached house, two storeys high and there were probably fewer than twenty rooms for guests, a small neat garden at the front, with a handkerchief sized lawn, a drive up the side of the house and walls all the way round the perimeter. One of the heavy double doors, through which we had come during the night was open. The road outside was straight, perhaps 200m long with security barriers and armed guards at each end. The opposite side of the road was a 3 metre high wall, stretching the length of the road behind which I discovered later was a school. All the houses on the road had large gates and a number had their own security guard together with a little hut for their protection against rain and sun.

The breakfast menu was a simple affair. There was a choice of continental breakfast, basically fruit juice, tea or coffee and toast; American, being continental plus cereal and eggs, any style or Pak Nashta. This caught my eye and needed a bit more investigation. Luckily all the staff spoke English as my Urdu is rudimentary. It consisted of lassi, best described as a yoghurt drink, Pak omelette, an omelette with vegetables in it, paratha, an unleavened flatbread and a choice of coffee or tea. On the basis of 'when in Rome' and travelling is an adventure and a chance to experience different cultures and cuisines, I opted for the Pak Nashta with green tea.

On the advice of my doctor, for a healthier fat free diet, there are a number of foods that I should avoid or at least reduce such as red meat, cheese, salt, fat, sugar, fried food, etc … I can't remember all the details but fish and vegetables are definitely okay. It's a shame as some of my favourites used to be salted roasted peanuts, bacon sandwich and blue cheese. This you may think might make me a fussy eater and I do adhere to the dietary advice at home. But whilst on holiday the strict regime goes to pot and I will try anything that is on the menu, especially if it is a local dish.

I am always interested in sampling different cuisines and if something is eaten locally that I have not had before I will always try it whatever it may be. Ultimately you may not like it, but it is not poisonous as the locals eat it and how would you know whether you like it or not if you don't try it.

There is only one food item that I know I will refuse to eat … tripe. I had heard about this as a child and asked my mother to cook it for me. She duly cooked it and I hated it but since she liked it, I was allowed to leave it on my plate and she ended up eating it. When I was working in Madrid, as an adult, many years later, I saw los callos, Spanish for tripe, on the menu. It had defeated me as a child, but as an adult, with different taste buds and experience of a range of cuisines, I tried it again. Same result. It was still horrible. I tried several mouthfuls but couldn't believe that I still couldn't eat it. I left most of it and ordered something else.

It appeared that I was the only guest having breakfast that morning as other than staff, I saw no one else. The result of the Pak Nashta that I had ordered was that I liked nearly all of it but lassi is not to my palate. I finished the whole glass but made a mental note for next time when I order a Pak Nashta for breakfast to change the lassi for a fruit juice.

After breakfast, I went for a walk up the junction with the main road. I smiled at the guard who was the same guard who had interrogated me just hours earlier but I was allowed out without any problem. Much easier to get out than it was to get in. On the main road in the morning light I noticed that many of the side roads also had barriers and guards. Several of the houses both down the side streets and on the main road, had guards with small huts for them to sit in or tents with canvas awnings and sandbags.

At the end of this road was a dual carriage way and on the opposite side, a large arch proudly declaring it to be the Zafar Gate of the Navy Head of Command and yet more security, this time armed military personnel in camouflage fatigues. I looked around and saw no signs forbidding photography but remembered details of my security advice not to take photos of anything sensitive. This included a long list, detailing such things as security force personnel, military camps, police stations, bridges and women which were all considered sensitive. The arch was distinctive and I was tempted to take a photo but decided to have the rest of my holiday in freedom, rather than getting thrown in jail and waiting for the High Commissioner to get me out.

I was reading an English language local paper to catch up with local news, when Karim and a driver turned up early at 11am so we set off to Rawalpindi. We were heading for some shops to buy a couple of shalwaar chemise for me. This is the local dress that both men and women wear in the area. The shalwaar is a pair of baggy trousers, held up by a drawstring. The chemise is like a standard shirt with a few buttons at the neck and put on by pulling over the head. The difference compared with western shirts, is that the shirt tails are extended to the knees and worn outside the trousers.

Pockets are fitted into the seams of the shirt at hip level. There were two reasons why I was getting these. One, is that they are very practical in hot climates and I had been assured that they are remarkably cool, which having worn them for several weeks I can confirm that this is absolutely correct. The other, was security in an attempt to fit in to local crowds, thus drawing less attention to myself but also to allow fewer barriers between me as a foreigner and the ability to interact with the locals.

I had a choice of only a few simple colours, such as white, black, khaki, olive, brown and tan and wasn't offered any brighter colours or patterns. Indeed, in retrospect, I saw no bright colours and very few patterned materials used for men, throughout my time in Pakistan. On the basis that both white and black would show the dirt and that we would be camping at times, I opted for one olive and one brown.

Karim had two female clients to pick up from the airport the next day and there would not be time to shop before flying up to Gilgit so he had an idea to buy them shalwaar chemise on their behalf, so we headed off to a dress shop. Unlike shalwaar chemises for gentlemen, the ladies' versions came in all sorts of colours and patterns, ranging from quite traditional colours and patterns to some very modern avante garde looking designs.

Had the two clients been men, I would have had more confidence in selecting a colour for two people that I didn't know, as the choice for men was quite restricted. But in the dress shop there was far too much of a choice and I voiced concern that we were dicing with death as our choice could be very wrong. Therefore Karim agreed it might be better to take them to a shop in Gilgit on arrival there.

I needed to exchange some money so we went not to a bank but to the money changers. This was a row of several shops in a three storey building, most of whom seem to be money changers. In front and up the side of the building were rows upon rows of armoured security vans, with different logos belonging to the different shops in front of us. Around the vehicles were numerous uniformed armed guards and as we went up the steps there was another guard waving his shotgun around and smiling at us as we passed. There were thick bars tightly spaced on the doors and windows and we went through the open door.

Once inside though, there were none of the armed guards to see, nor very much in the way of security. There was a table with a teller and next to him, another teller, but with bars reaching up to head height. On the table were stacks and stacks of notes, mostly well-worn and grubby and not being familiar with the currency, I had no idea how much was neatly stacked up on the tables.

I handed my sterling to Karim who counted it and handed it to the first teller, who counted it twice and calculated its value in rupees. He handed it to the second teller who counted it twice and re-calculated the rupee amount. Then, he counted out the rupee amount twice and I saw my bundle of rupee notes make the return journey through different hands being counted several times, until Karim had finished counting it and handed it me. I didn't bother to count it.

Walking around the streets was an eye opener, as there didn't seem much differentiation between pavement and road. It was chaos, with people pushing or pulling barrows with cars, motorbikes, lorries and pedestrians, all using the road at the same time. Traffic was thick and slow but there didn't seem to be any road rage between the different road users, as they inched their way past each other.

The streets were also full of rubbish of all sorts and I regretted wearing sandals as I followed Karim, whilst at the same time as trying to walk around or stepping over rubbish and foul looking puddles of muddy water, which covered who knows what beneath their surface. Looking up above the chaos, there was a mass of power cables and telephone wires criss crossing the sky above the street. It looked like chaos up there as well.

One feature of the traffic that surprised me was how few bicycles there were as I had expected great crowds of them on the streets. This was countered by the throngs of mopeds wherever you went. The road rules were obviously different or perhaps not adhered to in the least. Very few of the drivers or passengers had helmets, as if this was an optional extra that people didn't appreciate was for safety. Lady passengers sat sideways on the back of the mopeds which I have never tried, but I imagine that the co-ordination and balance must be an art.

And when referring to passengers, I mean one moped and several passengers. Why stop at one passenger when there is room for more? It was a common sight to see two passengers plus the driver and I started to count and look out for more. My best sights were a driver, two adult passengers and a child and a driver with four children. I never saw a woman driver.

We stopped at a local restaurant for lunch. There were the usual beef, mutton, chicken and vegetable curry dishes, dahls, different rice dishes and side dishes that you would expect in any Pakistani restaurant back home. I chose chicken tikka masala, since it is one of my favourites and I was curious how it might compare with what I am familiar with in either my local Pakistani restaurant or shop bought ready meals. Karim was happy to eat his meal with his fingers carefully scooping up the food with a piece of pitta bread. This was a skill that I had yet to acquire and I was hungry, I wanted to eat it rather than play with it and push it around my plate so I went for the knife and fork option.

The first difference that I noticed was that I am used to large chunks of filleted meat whereas the dish in front of me had clearly been made from a small and scrawny chicken. There were a few scraps of meat, clinging to small bones which had to be prised apart and having found some broken bones, I was cautious about what lurked in the sauce as I didn't want to break a tooth or lose a filling on a piece of bone. So it looked like I was going to play with my food after all. Taste wise I was surprised, as the flavours were not as strong as had been adapted for western palates at home. It was neither highly spicy nor burning hot. As I like spicy hot food, I was both surprised and rather disappointed at the real thing.

That afternoon we headed for the Margalla Hills National Park just north of suburban Islamabad and the Daman-e-Koh viewpoint that overlooks the city. The road twisted and turned up a steep hillside to a large car park which has a short walk to the viewpoint. There was a slight breeze which was a relief, after the hot sticky city. On a clear day, the view would be great but there was a haze from the heat and pollution.

At independence in 1947, the capital was Karachi but this was felt to have too much association with the colonial past, as control was wielded from that city. Other factors supporting a relocation, was that it was at one end of the country on the coast and subject to enemy naval attack, rather than a central location. Also its location so far south made it subject to a tropical climate, monsoons and cyclones.

Moving the capital to its current location was also nearer to the economically important Punjab area and army headquarters. Hence, it was developed in the 1960s as the new capital, laid out on a grid pattern and the government moved to its new home in stages, throughout the first half of the 1960s. The grid pattern is clearly discernible from the vantage point, high above the modern city.

The nearby Faisal Mosque with its unconventional design was clearly visible, not surprisingly as it was the largest mosque in the world named after King Faisal bin Abdul-Aziz of Saudi Arabia who financed its construction. It lost its pole position as being the largest mosque in the world, with the completion of the Hassan II mosque in Casablanca in 1993 and with the expansion of the mosques in Mecca and Medina in Saudi Arabia, it now lies in fourth position. Beyond the mosque in the mid distance, the tall modern buildings of the business district and Rawal Lake were indistinct through the haze. Anything further was too blurred to make out.

That short walk between the car park and the view point was full of the usual street vendors selling ice creams, snacks, sweets, drinks and souvenirs. In front of me was a well-dressed family with a young daughter, perhaps five years old, flanked by mum and dad who were both looking down at her, as she looked up at one and then the other accompanied by a torrent of Urdu.

The daughter had been treated to a packet of crisps which she was tucking into as they walked along. When she finished, she simply dropped the packet, rubbed her hands together and made a comment at which point, the whole family laughed. The packet was caught by the gentle breeze and was wafted across the path and into the foliage to join loads of other wrappers and rubbish.

They walked on as if nothing had happened. I noticed that it wasn't the lack of litter bins as there were plenty of them. I might have expected some rubbish in the crowded city market but in a tourist site, advertised as a scenic view and in a national park, I was deeply disappointed to see that littering everywhere was considered normal.

Back in the city we headed to a local well renowned Afghan restaurant, for our evening meal. Outside was a giant barbeque on which were cooking skewers of meat, tended by a very busy chef with great clouds of smoke billowing across the street, assisted by a small electric fan blowing across the top of the glowing coals. I didn't recognise any of the dishes so took pot luck and had a local dish of chicken and a soft drink.

As we left the restaurant, what we hadn't eaten was packed up and put in a bag for what I discovered later was in effect a tip for the driver who had sat in his car waiting for us whilst we ate. The journey back to the hotel was illuminating. It was dark by now and there were few street lights with most of the light flooding from the shops and buildings, lining the road and other vehicles.

I prefer to sit in the front so I get a good view of what's happening. The driver eased his car into the flow of traffic. After a few hundred meters, where there was a darker section of road and almost as an afterthought, the driver switched on his lights for which I was relieved. However, looking about from the vantage point of my front seat I could see that several other road users seemed to be on the road, without lights. Plus a bicycle, with a passenger on the back happily cycling down the middle of a dual carriage way without lights or reflectors.

Finally, nearing the hotel on a wide but quiet boulevard we were going down on our side of the road and coming towards us, admittedly with his lights on, was another vehicle. Our driver gently swung across the road to avoid a collision and carried on without a word, as if it was an everyday occurrence, which it probably was. So I was glad to get back to the road block, go through the identity questions again and get back to the safety of my hotel.

Chapter 2

North by Pakistan International Airlines

Today was an early start to get to the airport for a 10am flight from Islamabad to Gilgit. I was leaving before the usual start of breakfast, so I had arranged for an early breakfast to be available. I guessed that there might be an inflight meal so something light was all I needed, so the night before I had ordered some toast and green tea. I got served black coffee and buttered bread.

It wasn't quite what I'd ordered but I wasn't going to starve. Rather than send it back for what I had originally ordered the night before, which could mean a possible delay, during which, the car to take me to the airport might arrive and I might end up with nothing, so I drank and ate without complaint.

Heading down Faisal Avenue and on to the Islamabad Expressway I was still looking to see whether I could improve on my maximum number of passengers on a moped score. In the early morning rush hour traffic, there were plenty of examples of multiple passengers but I didn't see more than two.

We turned off the expressway at the airport exit and joined a long row of slow moving traffic to get to domestic departures. There were plenty of armed soldiers about and as we approached the security barrier, there was a knot of soldiers looking inside all the vehicles, as they slowly inched past. Then my heart sank. Coming towards us, on the passenger side of the vehicles in front of us, was a soldier pointing a device at the vehicles as he passed, that I can only describe as, a brass handled steel divining rod. This was their version of a bomb detector.

My thoughts turned to Gary Bolton and James McCormick, two British business men who had recently made the headlines for their convictions. Independently of each other, they had sold fake bomb detectors to unsuspecting buyers, including the Afghanistani and Iraqi governments, with the full knowledge that they were in fact, utterly useless.

Unless there was some Eastern mysticism at work, of which I was unaware, I suspected that this divining rod had the same chance of working as the fake bomb detectors. There was an outside chance that this was some form of sophisticated bluff that worked along the lines, that if a terrorist thought it was effective, in which case, it would work as a deterrent. Either way, I was not reassured for my security.

I pulled my bag out of the boot and headed through the doors to domestic departures where the security was then more familiar with x-ray machines for the luggage and metal detectors for passengers. I made my way to departures and waited for Karim who was at international arrivals to greet his two guests from London Heathrow.

It was in domestic departures, that I finally met Judith from Lincolnshire and Etso who lives in London, but was originally from Japan. Both ladies were a similar age to myself and obviously had a sense of adventure to travel independently to northern Pakistan.

We had a few moments to introduce ourselves and start to get to know each other before it was soon time to board the aircraft. We headed through the doors to board the bus and out to the aircraft. This is always a moment of apprehension for me, as there are certain standards for air travel in Europe that airports and airlines are forced to follow. Further afield standards are different.

I remember travelling in Russia some years previously and the international fleet was well maintained but the domestic fleet had a poor reputation for air safety. The state airline properly known as Aeroflot was known jokingly as Aeroflop. I was making an internal flight in Siberia and had been assured that the plane would be an airbus. So I was surprised to be confronted with a Tupolev, a Russian aircraft and whilst aircraft recognition and specification is not my primary area of expertise, it was obviously rather old. I sat next to the emergency exit and there was a constant, very cold draft, around my feet coming from the door where the seal should be.

Back on the aircraft apron at Islamabad, the bus pulled up at our aircraft and I was relieved to see that it was a new European built ATR 42, an aircraft that I know well, which is known for its excellent short runway performance. Just as a book should not be judged by its cover, just because the plane was new and I recognised it, doesn't eliminate pilot error or poor maintenance, but it was reassuring.

We taxied towards the take off point and came to a halt at right angles to the main runway. There was a queue of aircrafts, to take off ahead of us, a couple of PIA airbuses and a military Hercules. The two airbuses took off, followed by the Hercules and then we rolled forward on to the runway, turned and without pausing we took off some 25 minutes late. The aircraft banked hard and gained height.

After a short while, the pilot come on over the intercom and made an announcement in Urdu. I won't say that I speak Urdu but when I travel I do like to have a few words and phrases of the local language before I arrive. I usually start with the basics such as greetings, numbers, food and directions and build on this. I didn't understand what the pilot was saying but I did pick out several inshallahs which translates as 'if God wills' or 'God willing'.

Then he made the announcement in English, which was the usual pilot announcement regarding the flight, warning of some turbulence and details of the weather on arrival at Gilgit being patchy cloud and a cooler and more pleasant temperature of 22°C. But he continued to use inshallah such as 'flight time is one hour inshallah' and 'landing at 11.25am inshallah' as if there was some real uncertainty in the safe outcome of the whole flight. It's lucky I am not a nervous flyer.

The plane would be cruising at 18,000ft (it's operational ceiling is 19,000ft) which seems high but en-route, we would be flying right past Nanga Parbat which is the 9th highest mountain in the world at 26,660ft (pilots still seem to use feet but for those who use metric measurements we are flying at 5,486m and the mountain is 8,126m … still a bit of a difference in whatever measurement that you use).

Nanga Parbat is at the western end of the Himalaya range and has a very prominent peak. Its name in Urdu means 'naked mountain' as an acknowledgement to one of its faces, the Rupal face which is the highest face in the world which rises straight up for over 4,600m from its base. It is so steep that snow can't settle on it, hence the name 'naked mountain'.

Flying regulations here require that the pilots can see the ground, so as to avoid flying into the mountain. Therefore, weather conditions must be good in order to fly. When weather conditions are patchy clouds, as they were on this flight, the plane must fly around or under the clouds so as to maintain visibility, hence there was a lot of manoeuvring and turbulence so the seatbelt sign was on for the whole flight, but I didn't mind as I always have a window seat and spend the whole flight looking out of the windows at the scenery below.

It was all very worthwhile, as the view of the mountain as we went past, was spectacular, revealing bare ragged rock slopes ending in pinnacles of rock and patchy snow on the summit. It was an odd feeling to be flying in a plane and to see the ground rising above you. If the cloud cover gets too thick then planes are either grounded before take-off or must return to their departure point.

Soon, we were descending and flying up the upper Indus valley. As we were so low there was a great view of the mountains, the Indus River, the KKH below and you could pick out the individual vehicles moving along the road. We flew over the confluence of the Hunza and Gilgit rivers and after a few turns landed at Gilgit airport.

This airport is one of the world's top ten most dangerous airports. Flat land in this mountainous area is hard to find and the twisting valley approaches are thwart with danger. The runway is fairly short so large planes can't land.

The runways eastern end is above the steep banks, down to the Gilgit River and faces the confluence of the two rivers and a tall bluff at the confluence point. At the western end, the valley bottom starts to rise steeply towards high mountain peaks. Only planes that can manoeuvre in tight turns and undertake steep ascents and descents on their approach can use this airport. Again, visual flight rules apply and if visibility is poor at the airport, flights can and often are cancelled.

We landed without incident and disembarked. I noticed that also on the ground was the Hercules with the same aircraft recognition number painted on the fuselage that had taken off ahead of us in Islamabad which was powering down its engines. Then I realised that we had our own military escort for the journey and wondered whether we really were at risk from terrorist anti-aircraft missiles, or whether it was just a coincidence. I asked Karim and he just said that it was always happening.

We collected our bags and jumped into jeeps for the short drive to the local PTDC hotel for lunch. The PTDC, which stands for The Pakistan Tourism Development Company, is a government sponsored organisation which as its full name suggests promotes tourism to both local and international tourists. Its aim is to provide quality accommodation at a competitive price in areas where private companies may be reluctant to invest. It operates more than twenty hotels, mainly in the north and north west of the country.

Two notable exceptions are the Flashman's Hotel in Rawalpindi and the hotel at Wagah, not that the hotel is exceptional but because Wagah used to be the only road crossing to India and the soldiers on both sides, some with giant handle bar moustaches and all in full dress uniform perform a spectacular blustering ceremony at the closing of the border at dusk.

The hotel in Gilgit was off the main road, down a quiet side road near the river, where the main road crosses the river. It was set in its own grounds, surrounded by a wall and gates at the entrance. Inside was a well-kept garden with shade trees and a lawn surrounded by flower borders. The main facilities were housed in a single storey building, opposite the gates with a few rooms off a long veranda. More bedrooms were provided at each end of the main building in modern concrete framed two storey extensions.

Painted on the wall outside of the door to reception was a map with the heading 'Wildlife of Northern Area', two metres long and a metre high. It had the outline of Gilgit Baltistan, with major towns, roads and rivers marked. Scattered all across it were images of the heads of the wildlife to be found in those areas. The key on one side showed the English and Latin names of the animals such as snow leopards, bears, ibex, marmots and eagles. Also depicted by little coloured circles was whether the animal was common, rare, vulnerable or endangered. There were only a few green circles indicating common, and far too many orange and red indicating vulnerable and endangered.

We relaxed after the flight with green tea at one of the tables in the garden. It was like a pleasant English summers day, and a lot cooler than Islamabad. From the garden looking up between the trees, we could see the valley sides stretching hundreds of metres up towards the sky and their bare rock faces. And to the north over the Gilgit River, was the Karakoram mountain range. But my trip to see them would have to wait as we were due to head west first which has the most security issues. I wanted to visit there first and get it out of the way, so I could enjoy the rest of the trip without the nagging concern of security.

It was a little early for lunch so we headed off to town to get Judith and Etso their shalwaar chemises. The main shopping street was a busy bustling place with crowds of shoppers with small traders showing off their wares on the pavement or hanging from the front of the shop. It was colourful and noisy after the stillness of the garden at the hotel.

One of the girls, as I affectionately thought of them, chose quickly and settled on plain simple colours similar to a gentlemen's version, both in a light pink but in different shades. So similar that you could only tell them apart when you saw them both together.

Etso was harder to satisfy, trying on several different choices. The colours were wrong, the stitching wasn't good enough, the cut was too tight or too loose and in short, nothing was quite right. We headed off to another shop and the same thing happened, the design too modern, the pattern too busy. Personally, I couldn't see a problem, as these were what the locals wore and might just be worn for the time that you were on holiday anyway and were included in the price so the cost was immaterial. Finally, we headed back to the first shop and made a purchase. It was more than two hours after starting the shopping trip that we left the shop and headed back to the hotel for lunch.

Our bags had been tied to the back of the jeep and covered with a tarpaulin, to protect them from the dust. I sat in the front, next to our driver Matu, whilst Judith and Etso sat in the back and Karim perched on the edge in the back. We set off from the hotel and headed down to the river and turned left to follow the road along its edge heading west out of town.

We were heading for Chitral in the west, not far from the Afghanistan border. I didn't have any detailed maps but I'm used to looking at a detailed map such as an Ordnance Survey map and measuring the distance and knowing it was fairly accurate. That assumes good tarmac covered roads but here in the far north of Gilgit Baltistan province, outside of the towns some of the roads are just rough tracks. Frequent landslides and wash outs also hinder progress. At a guess, Chitral is about 360kms from Gilgit and luckily most of this road is tarmac but it would still take us three days with the first overnight stop near Gupis.

The houses gave way to farmland on both sides of the road on the valley bottom, hemmed in on both sides by bare rocky slopes rising steeply to the mountain tops. Beyond the fields on our right was the Gilgit River which was out of sight, as it flowed between high steep banks.

We rounded a corner and on the side of the road, was a large canvas tent and a barrier across the road with several policeman standing about. Behind the tent was a large satellite dish pointing skywards. Karim got out and showed our papers to the policeman in charge. He seemed to be answering a lot of questions and an animated conversation ensued with the policeman.

After a few minutes, he exchanged a few words with Matu and returned to his conversation with the police, pulling out a packet of cigarettes and offering them to the policemen. Matu pulled over to the side of the road and switched off the engine. It seemed that this wasn't a straight forward formality of checking papers and being waved through. It was because we were foreigners and there were security issues. In contrast, a local drove up to the barrier, flashed his ID card and almost without stopping, was waved through the barrier. Obviously no security issues for the locals.

I got out to stretch my legs. On the far side of the road was a simple shack selling crisps and sweets, amongst other items, to passing travellers. There were a number of locals milling about and some of them wandered over and stared at us. They weren't threatening, begging or trying to sell anything to us, they were just curious and just stared, standing too close for comfort.

They didn't seem to have that self-consciousness where if you are caught staring you would look away or realise that they are too close to someone's personal space and back off. I wandered up the road and they followed me. But they were well within my personal space so I thought it better not to go too far and went back and sat in the jeep with some people standing right next to the jeep, staring at us.

Finally our details were taken down in a book, name, nationality and other passport details. Karim got back into the jeep, together with our first guard and a policeman, armed with a Kalashnikov. He squeezed into the front and sat between me and Matu resting the butt of his gun on the floor between his knees.

We set off again up the valley on the dry dusty road. It seemed that we hadn't gone far when there was another police check point, a barrier across the road and a canvas tent. This time Matu pulled over and switched off the engine. Karim, the guard and I got out and walked over to several policemen sitting around a table. Another book was pulled out and our details entered into it.

There was another conversation but this time it was a lot quicker and our guard was replaced with another.

The system seemed to be that at every road block, our details were taken to record who was travelling on the road and roughly where we were at any given time. The guard would travel with us to the next checkpoint where he was relieved by another guard. He then stays at this post until there is a car going back towards his original post so he can hitch a lift back.

I wasn't sure that having the guard was effective as a deterrent or reassuring. He was only one person. His gun was resting upright on the floor and if we were ambushed, the attackers would have their guns out and our guard would not have time to level his weapon let alone use it. As he was armed, if there was some shooting, from an attackers point of view it would be best to shoot him first and he was right next to me. And having a guard is bringing attention to the fact that there must be foreigners in the vehicle, almost advertising the fact.

But orders are orders and all foreigners must have an escort. I reflected that perhaps his role was to alert the authorities after we had been kidnapped. One of our guards that day was a surprise to me. Most of them were young with typical Pakistani type features with dark skin and black hair. One particular guard had ginger hair and fair skin and I half expected to hear a Scots accent. These was definitely not local genes and I quietly speculated whether somewhere in his background there may be some relative, perhaps a soldier from Scotland, as the area around here had been garrisoned by the British for a long time and there were a lot of Scotsmen in the British army. I know it's a stereotype that Scotsmen have ginger hair, as other people do as well but like I said, it's a stereotype.

Our progress was not helped by the unstable nature of the environment that we were going through. In several places water had poured down the mountain side and deposited a lot of mud and stones across the road. This didn't look recent and judging by the tyre marks, it was common practise to just drive over them. I noticed that where the deposit was mostly stone free and just mud that local farmers had brought wheelbarrows or carts and were taking the soil away to spread on their fields.

This far up the valley there are only occasionally fields. Most of the landscape near the road is open mountainside, rough ground with few plants or trees and steeply sloping. Looking at the few fields that there were on small patches of flatter land, there were quite a lot of stones in them, and although it was hard work scooping up the mud, it was a good way of improving the soil.

Only rarely did I see a mechanical digger being used to tackle the larger fans of debris across the road. At one spot where the debris was particularly big both deep and wide, a large yellow digger was busy cutting through it to expose the tarmac again. We bumped off the road down to a flat area which floods when the river level is high and followed a deeply rutted rough track for 300 meters. The track had recently been created to get around the debris and the digger and back onto the road. Four wheel drive vehicles are essential, if you want to get around in this terrain.

Where the road gets close to the fast flowing Gilgit River and its brown muddy water, brown due to the huge amounts of silt and mud that it carries, there is another problem. The power of the river erodes the river edges and undercuts the riverbank which collapses. And with the collapse, the road collapses into the river. Where this happens, a new track is created further up the slope to get past the collapsed section of road with another bumpy diversion.

The area is not good farmland being so mountainous and in places is sparsely populated so no one complains when a new route is hacked out of the steep slopes above the collapsed area. A digger comes along and scraps away at the slope until a flat area, wide enough for at least one vehicle is created. The largest rocks are removed and if available, smaller rocks are tipped over the top to fill in the larger holes. But the rough track created is not smoothed off with a scree of gravel so is still very bumpy. Therefore, although this section of road is designated as having a tarmac surface, lots of it has a rough surface and for comfort can only be traversed at a low speed.

We had been following the Gilgit River upstream westwards until we reached a point where there is a large bend in the river. The rivers source is to the north and it heads south until this point where it bends east but we were heading west so we turned away from the main river to follow a tributary up into the hills to the town of Gupis.

Gupis lies in the Hindu Kush mountain range on a tributary of the Gilgit River, more than 20kms west of the large bend in the main river. We stopped at a police station just outside the town and whilst the police took down our particulars, I had a chat with Salmon, one of the police on duty at the gates to the police compound, armed with an ancient looking bolt action rifle.

He was a young man, fit, lean, immaculate light brown trousers and black shirt and he spoke excellent English. It turned out that he was a university graduate and former English teacher. I was surprised to learn that he thought being a policeman was a better occupation than being a school teacher citing better pay, prospects and a career ladder. Even after I pointed out that the police are targets for bandits and the Taliban, he still felt it was a good job and I half expected him to add inshallah just for good measure.

In turn, he questioned me on whether I felt safe in the area. I pointed out that I was here and although I was aware of security issues, I wouldn't be here if I was that worried about security. I told him I had come to visit, despite these concerns and was sure the police would look after me if something happened. He gave me a genuine broad beaming smile. That was my diplomatic answer, whereas my quick honest answer, which I didn't vocalise would have been along the lines of 'yes I am concerned but I had always wanted to come and if I waited for better security I might never get to see the Karakoram and the spectacular scenery'.

We picked up our latest guard, Aksan and headed into town. After the empty landscape that we had passed through earlier in the afternoon, here was a contrast with lots of shops, people, houses and other vehicles. Beyond the main shopping streets were more houses and roadside shops consisting of a single room opening straight onto the road. There were plenty of recently built buildings and other buildings under construction.

Our hotel for the night wasn't in the town but several kilometres outside. We left the outskirts of the town and were back in the countryside. There were animals in the fields and noticeably more trees. The road started to ascend up the side of the valley and the valley sides closed in.

The river was off to our right in a deep gorge. The area is heavily glaciated and has plenty of features associated with glaciation. The ability of the glacier to erode the valley floors and sides depends partly on the resistance of the rock. Where there is a rock that is resistant to erosion lying across the valley, the outcrop acts like a dam and temporarily holds the glacier back. Ice builds up on the upstream side but the glacier continues to push down the valley from its source. This increases erosion on the upstream valley side as the ice and rock within it builds up against the outcrop.

The glacier will eventually rise up and over the obstacle and will erode the valley downstream of the blockage. When the glacier finally retreats, as it melts faster than new ice can form, it leaves a jumble of rock on the valley floor.

As the glacier melts, the resulting melt water forms a river that reworks the jumble of rock left by the retreating glacier. At the resistant outcrop, a lake may form upstream as the river flow is blocked by the outcrop acting as a dam. The lake will build and deepen until the river flows over the top of the obstacle. As it flows over the rock, it will cut a deep gorge as it erodes the rock.

Upstream the river becomes a lake until the outlet is cut through the rock and the lake drains. Until this happens, the sediment in the river settles on the bottom of the lake resulting in a wide flat rock free area ideal for farming.

This was exactly the scenery that I was looking at now. The deep gorge to the right of the road and a steep slope stretching across the valley in front of us up which we were heading. And from the top of this outcrop, looking upstream, was a steep slope down to a lake. This vantage point high above the valley floor was an ideal position to give a wonderful view downstream to the town or upstream across the lake. And looking down from the edge of the resistant rock, stretching across the valley that had held up the glacier, the calm surface of the lake narrowed and became turbulent white water as it rushed down the steep narrow gorge that the river was cutting through the barrier.

This was also the site for our overnight stop at another PTDC hotel at an elevation of circa 2,300m. This was a recently built construction in local stone and timber with a pitched corrugated iron roof surrounded by a wall built on top of the outcrop without any other building nearby. There was a grand central building with reception, dining rooms and kitchens. The guest rooms were in a couple of separate blocks to one side.

There was a power cut when we arrived so I made sure I knew where the candles and matches were kept that were thoughtfully provided in each room. I memorised the room layout and where the candles were kept, in case I needed them in the dark.

The room was clean and spacious. The furniture was modern and in the bathroom, a shower and toilet. There was also a large red plastic bucket full of water that struck me as odd until I tried to take a shower. No power meant no water, hot or cold so I washed in cold. Next to the bucket were the necessary accessories for doing the job, a small plastic container like a jug and a plastic teapot. I soon learnt not to waste water as the toilet wouldn't flush without water. So that's why there is such a large bucket of water in the bathroom.

It was getting late and dusk wasn't far off. It was over cast with a slight wind and the temperature was dropping. There were occasional patches of snow on the mountain sides high above us.

I donned a fleece and went past reception where Aksan would settle down to sit all night and I went out into the grounds of the hotel. After that, I walked down the road on both sides of the hotel and looked around at the local scenery. Plenty of trees and several large boulders large enough to hide behind along the roadside.

I was researching my immediate surroundings and scouting for paths. This was part of the routine I planned to follow, to ensure my security. If there was a need to get out quickly in an emergency, I didn't want to run madly into the dark and fall off a cliff or plunge down the deep gorge that the river had cut to one side of this obstacle in its path. I would rather take a chance at escape than just stand still and be captured by terrorists or bandit's intent on violence so this recce would improve my chances if I knew beforehand where there were paths to follow and dangers to avoid.

There was a sheer drop at the back of the hotel and on the far side of the road down to the river so those routes were out of the question. The only routes away from the hotel were down the road either side of the hotel or a narrow path leading up the valley side away from the hotel. I investigated this carefully so that I might recognise it in the dark, if there was a moon or some bright stars.

Chapter 3

West via Shandur Pass polo pitch to Chitral

We had a long way to go so it was an early start with breakfast at 6.30am and a departure time aimed for 7am. We loaded our bags into the jeep and set off up the valley. Along the lake shore there were fields of wheat and potatoes, some grazing animals and trees, mostly poplars. We passed the end of the lake and the valley narrowed again, the trees thinned and soon there was bare rock and steep valley sides with no signs of any human activity other than the road weaving its way up the side of the valley.

In places the road had been hacked out of the sheer cliff face. There was so little traffic it was novel to see another vehicle. At mid-morning we came across a group of locals milling about on the road. Beyond them and out of sight had been a major landslide. The debris from the landslide had been washed down a tributary and had partially blocked the main river. This had caused the river to change course and washed away the road.

We had known about this, as it had happened several days before, but we had an alternative plan. A new diversionary road had not yet been made further up the valley side. The road was impassable to vehicles but there was a narrow path up and along the steep slope above the washout which then re-joined the road. At the far side of the washout, there was another jeep waiting for us. Our luggage would be carried by porters which is what Karim was negotiating with the waiting locals. They had a sense of an opportunity for paid work and hung around waiting for portering jobs.

With the price agreed, a number of porters started heaving our bags onto their shoulders and we set off up the path. Matu turned the jeep around and went back down the road to find somewhere flat and safe to leave it for the next week or two.

I followed the porter who was carrying my bag as I wanted to keep an eye on it. After about 20 minutes of walking up the valley side, the path levelled out and after a scramble over and around some large rocks, we were heading downhill. I could see a number of vehicles waiting for passengers and a number of porters waiting for business in the opposite direction.

There were some people coming the other way but I was surprised by one particular group. There were five people man handling a motor bike over the rocks with some difficulty. It was obvious that a landslide, a washout and a rugged mountain trail was not going to stop this particular owner from getting to his destination.

We got to our new vehicle, another jeep driven to the washout to pick us up by its owner. We waited for all the porters to catch up and reload our bags into the new jeep. Looking downstream the tarmac of the road dipped and disappeared under water. On either side of the road was a row of trees and the tops of trees sticking out of the water marked where the road had once been. They headed towards the base of a newly formed steep cliff plunging into the river with white water bursting over boulders at its foot which was where the road used to be.

Looking upstream the road turned and changes into a rough track, heading uphill away from the river. Below was a steep bank down to the river where another section of road had been washed away and the bank looked fresh as the river continued to erode its base and threaten valuable fields just above it.

We set off again up the road then turned off it between fields and finally we came to the debris washed down from another landslide up the valley of the tributary and a collection of fresh rocks with a rough track over the top. This was the landslide and flood that had altered the course of the river below and buried the original road under several metres of debris for a length of several hundred meters.

It was a relief when we left the rough rocky surface of the diversion and got back to the original road and its tarmac surface. We headed onwards towards Phander Lake and the village of Phander.

This new vehicle was a different ride to our previous vehicle. Although it was the same make, an American Willey Jeep, it was designed to take more people and luggage. Consequently, it had a harder suspension which meant it was a harder and bumpier ride.

Sitting in the front I noticed that the water temperature gauge, the engine temperature gauge, the fuel gauge and the speedometer didn't work. The spare tyre didn't have any tread (nor did any of the tyres I would notice later). It also had a hole, a gash a finger length long which seems to have been repaired with a section of another tyre stuck on from the inside.

It was around here on the road that the amount of vegetation was changing noticeably. In the valley bottoms where there was water there was green grass, crops and trees. Just a short distance up the side of the valley the land was sparsely covered with increasing amounts of bare rock and scree slopes exposed. There were strips of snow on the more shady parts of all the mountains around us. We headed away from the river for a gentler ascent, away from the steep slopes near the river.

Stopping on a promontory high above the valley floor, we could see the river where it entered a narrow deep gorge to drain the lake. On one side was Phander Lake, with its dark calm waters reflecting the mountains around it and the blue sky above. On the other side we had a view of the flat valley floor with its patchwork of fields stretching up the valley with occasional trees. Though the middle of the fields snaked the calm water of the river, flowing slowly past the fields.

We descended to the valley floor and dropped Aksan at the police post on the main street of the village. Just behind the police station, was a restaurant painted bright pink, run by the owner of the jeep that we were borrowing, where we stopped for lunch on the patio. Looking around I noticed that the trees all had bundles of thorns tied around the base from the ground to chest height. This was to stop hungry animals chewing the bark.

Some clusters of trees had fences of thorns around them for the same reason. It was becoming a common sight.

I had mentioned earlier that at home I largely ate fish, fresh vegetables and fruit so our host went out of his way to cook us a fish dish. I had no idea what type of fish it was but it tasted great, although there were a lot of small bones so you had to take care.

Here was our first experience of a non-western or squat toilet. This consists of a piece of porcelain set into the floor with two raised footprints set either side of the hole. There was no cistern and no paper but there was a tap above a large bucket, together with the necessary accessories. This was something that I would have to get used to. I always checked my pockets as I was ever fearful of dropping something and it disappearing down the hole never to be seen again … and even if I could see it, I didn't fancy fishing it out.

We sat outside on the patio of the restaurant and waited. At length, our new guard wandered down the road to the restaurant to find us. He greeted everyone at the restaurant, it was a small place and the police tend to be recruited from the local population so like in any village, everyone knows everyone. We said our goodbyes to the restaurant and jeep owner, climbed back into his jeep and with Matu driving, we turned back onto the main road.

Just out of town the tarmac finished and we were on to unmade road as far as the eye could see and it would be unmade or rough gravel tracks for a long way. Down in the valley bottom on the good farmland there weren't too many stones and the surface wasn't too bumpy. This area had some local traffic on it and was maintained to a good standard but the further we progressed away from the village, the worse the road became.

The vehicle's mechanical integrity I noted was not to the same level as our previous vehicle. The fuel cap didn't quite fit sufficiently snugly so with every bump, petrol slurped up to the cap and leaked around the edge. Liquid leaked down the side of the vehicle and due to the position of the running board below the cap, this also was covered in petrol.

Getting in and out left a deposit on your shoes that followed you about. That was resolved with a handful of sand spread on the running board. But it didn't solve the petrol slurping out from around the cap or the smell.

The exhaust was not at the back but on the passenger's side perhaps a foot from the front seat. The fumes were noticeable without a strong wind which denied me of the opportunity of smelling the clear fresh mountain air. Going down narrow enclosed roads between fields, surrounded by stone walls was also not ideal for the passenger, as the fumes were more concentrated.

Further up the valley, the steep valley sides were closing in and there were fewer fields and much less farmland between the wide gently flowing river and the steep valley sides. A bit further on upstream, the fields abruptly stop to give way to a steep rocky barren mountainside, with the river emerging from a narrow gorge. The road curves its way up the face of this mountainside and eventually goes over a high pass into the Swat valley. At this bend, the main road turned away from the river and snakes up the side of the valley. We took this road which leads towards the Shandur Pass.

The Shandur Pass was one of the sights that I had wanted to see. It is the site of the highest polo match field in the world situated at the top of the pass that links Gilgit with Chitral at a height of 3,720m. It hosts an annual match between local rival teams and is reputed to be a great event pulling crowds of people, teams, supporters and vendors. There is also dancing and other cultural displays over three days and it is usually held in early July.

This year it had been postponed and postponed. The washout on the road that we had negotiated earlier, meant that the teams from the Gilgit side couldn't get their horses to the event. The authorities had said that building the diversion around the washed out road would start soon but the diggers hadn't arrived. It had been estimated that it would only take a few days to improvise a diversion but work had been delayed, thus postponing the polo matches. It had also started to rain, thus reducing both visibility and temperatures so my view of the area wasn't ideal.

The road hair pinned up the valley side to follow a small tributary of the main river. Here there were no fields, only a few stunted trees and bushes growing near the river with bare rocky hillsides. The road surface was rough but where the road crossed tributaries, there were substantial concrete bridges with their footings protected against flooding. Signs at the end of the bridge warned that the maximum load was 40 tons which gives an indication of how strong these bridges had been built. Despite being quite remote and the unmade road, there had been some significant investment and these bridges were built to last.

At the top of the valley the road levelled off and the steep rocky mountainsides seemed to retreat. Here there were no trees or bushes at this altitude, just grass spread across the wide shallow valley. The snow-capped mountains seemed to be much further away. Water flowed almost imperceptibly in narrow shallow channels through the undulating pastures. There was the occasional sheep or goat, quietly grazing the mountain meadows.

I was surprised at the extent of the polo match site at such a remote site. The polo pitch is shorter and narrower than a normal polo pitch, but there were substantial white washed grandstands surrounding the pitch on three sides. Beyond there were numerous other substantial buildings. Even now with yet another postponement there were some vehicles and more than two dozen tents.

At the side of the road was a sign for the Shandur Natco Hotel with an arrow pointing up the side of the valley. Looking up the slope was a whitewashed single storey stone built building covered in graffiti. It was a former shepherd's hut used as a base for summer grazing which consisted of two rooms with a large tent pitched to one side with chairs outside. We went through the main door to shelter from the persistent light rain.

We had stopped for some green tea. It was run by a one armed man and his son. They cooked on a single gas fired stove, served refreshments and slept in the same single room. The other doorway led to where the animals were kept. I sat on the bed and drunk green tea from a chipped cup. It was a comfortable temperature inside and at its raised position on the valley side, it had a great view over the polo pitch on the valley floor below, but I wasn't looking forward to staying here overnight, as temperatures plunge at night at this altitude but it would be snug in the small single room of the shepherd's hut.

Further down the road there was a wide shallow grey lake reflecting the grey cloud overhead. On the side of the road, were work crews building protection for the road against waves wiped up on the lake by winter storms.

The road reached the end of the pass and started a steep descent down to the next valley. Rolling pastures gave way to more rocky steep slopes, with precipitous drops on one side of the road as it twisted its way down the mountain side. The grass only appeared in patches and didn't look as green as it had on the pass above us.

As it neared the valley bottom, greenery reappeared with fields and trees. There was a scattering of farms, all with shiny red corrugated iron roofs. There was a check point but it was manned by only two policeman. Its role was to regulate traffic, closing the pass in bad weather so we didn't change our guard but continued down the valley.

When we got to the bottom of the valley, the gradient levelled off and we started to pass between fields growing wheat, fodder and potatoes. At one point on the road, there was a scar on the mountainside which looked fresh as it had not been weathered and darkened like the rock face around it. Below this scar was a giant boulder more than ten meters across.

Around this boulder were the remains of houses. The giant boulder had fallen off the cliff face and crushed some buildings below. These had subsequently been abandoned which were the remains seen from the road. This is evidence of the active nature of the landscape that these people live in and that natural disaster can strike at any time.

We changed guard at the next police check point. Instead of a policeman we now had a surly quiet member of the anti-terrorist squad, as per the letters on the back of his all black uniform. I had noticed that some of the guards were happy to chat, some would answer questions in a civil but functional attitude but didn't want to engage in conversation. This chap from his glares followed by his one or two word answers obviously didn't want to talk.

We had crossed the water shed and were now heading downstream towards Mastuj. This valley was much like the others we had gone through. It had green fields and trees where the gradient on the land was gentler and where water could be used to irrigate the crops. Otherwise, it was steep rocky and barren with snow on the mountain tops.

The road had a tarmac surface but only in places, mainly though villages and on gentler slopes. Half of the road between the Shandur Pass and Mastuj was rough track, and on steep slopes there were diversions around or over landslides. Where minor tributaries had flooded and flowed over the road, they had washed away the surface leaving a bumpy crossing. From mid-afternoon until we reached our destination it was just a rough track.

The PTDC hotel at Mastuj is a single storey bungalow with a large open porch under a corrugated roof. As it had been built on a slope, one side had a lower storey. Rooms were either in the lower storey or in several separate buildings enclosing a square courtyard and a patch of ground that had it had more greenery might have passed for a lawn but looked more like an overgrown sandpit.

My room was in one of the separate buildings. It was the shape of a large rectangle, had a table and chair at one end and a bed and bedside cabinet at the other. On the table was a candle and a box of matches just in case of power cuts. In a side room was the bathroom having a shower, a basin, a western toilet and a large bucket of water. There was electricity but no hot water.

I went to reception to meet Karim, but as soon as I went in, I was hit by a thick fog of smoke from cigarettes, which I find hugely offensive so I turned around and waited outside. We decided to go for a walk and we headed down a path towards Mastuj Fort.

We stopped outside and knocked on the door. An elderly gentleman opened the door and Karim asked whether we could see the fort. We were told that it was not open to the public but looking at me, and noting that despite my shalwaar chemise, I was obviously European, he asked what nationality.

English he was told. And in reply he turned to me and in English with a glint in his eye, he said 'In that case we are open to you'. From a brief look at him, you might think he was well past retirement age, but he was the manager of the fort that also hosted a hotel. He welcomed us through the door. He walked with a stick but his back was straight and his step was measured, not showing his age at all. I doubted he really needed the stick for short distances.

The fort may not be open to the public but within the grounds are some modern chalets with hydroelectric power (HEP) generated electricity with hot water that are available for renting. Through the garden, passing under apple, walnut and apricot trees, we followed the manager and stood outside the front of the fort.

There had been a fort here for centuries but this one dated from 1883. There were frequent earthquakes in the area and the fort has had to be remodelled several times in the past. It is still owned by the Mehtar or King of Chitral. Although the princely state was incorporated into Pakistan in 1969, and he has no political power, the Mehtar continues to live in several properties in the area and takes a keen interest in local issues.

The walls are arranged in a square, built of stone with horizontal wooden struts at intervals with a total wall thickness of more than 2 meters with large towers at each corner. The whole edifice is covered in mud.

It was both an administrative centre and a strategic military position. The fort lies at a confluence of the tributary that we had followed since descending from the Shandur Pass and the Yarkhund River at an elevation of 2,359m. To the north up the Yarkhund River less than 80kms away is the Baroghil Pass 3,804m which leads into the Wakhan Corridor part of Afghanistan.

Little survives inside and there's not much to see. It's now laid out as gardens. We could only peer through a doorway in passing as this area is the Mehtar's private residence and he and his family were expected shortly.

By dinner time the power had come back on and I ordered soup, okra and rice. Half way through the meal the lights went out. This didn't seem to bother a large local party behind me, who seemed happy to carry on talking as if nothing had happened. In no time at all, staff appeared with gas fired lights and put them on the tables.

Breakfast this particular morning was at a civilised time of 7.30am consisting of scrambled egg and green tea. I bought some bottled water to fill my Camelbak for the journey and loaded my luggage onto the jeep. It looked to be a nice day, so we took off the canvas top and had an open topped jeep, to get a better view of the scenery.

We headed back to the village and turned onto the main street where we picked up a new guard and continued to the local garage. Filling up with petrol is fairly mundane and would not normally warrant a sentence, but this is the Hindu Kush. The garage had a hard standing surface and a single pump. The office was a small hut on the far side of the site from the road. The petrol pump was the usual shape that I would expect but without the cover, therefore exposing the electric pump. The attendant pulled on the fan belt on the exposed side of the unit and the electric pump spluttered into life! No guards for the fan belt or the spinning wheels, although, I noted the attendant still had all his fingers. I also thought that petrol fumes and electric sparks didn't mix, but I am still here to tell the story.

Another unfamiliar aspect, was paying. This was paid in cash, in the open, to the attendant and some change was required. The attendant pulled out a bundle of bank notes, two inches thick and peeled off the necessary notes. Walking around some of the more dubious areas back home with that sort of money would get you mugged, in no time at all. Here in the mountains, it is a much more respectful environment.

We left the village and crossed the Yarkhund River, by a substantial concrete bridge with supports sunk deep into the bed of the wide shallow meandering river. On the north side of the river, the road was another rough track which turned left to follow the river downstream.

The valley on one side was a steep sided slope, with bare rock, dissected in places by small streams, either with water or dry but full of water when it rains. Conversely, on the other side, the lower slopes were a gentler gradient, with green fields and trees. At a point perhaps 100 meters above the river level, the fields ended and there were no trees and above that line, the slopes were as steep and bare as on our side.

I don't have a good head for heights at times, but after some of the previous routes we had taken, I was getting braver. In places, the rough track was just a single vehicle wide, with a sheer drop on one side. In places, the road was so narrow that had the jeep stopped, I would not have been able to get out on my side of the track, without falling hundreds of metres.

I began to appreciate that Matu was a real expert, because I wondered how he knew that he could negotiate the track and at times, the tyres were just inches from the edge of the cliff. I was also getting reassurance on the road builder's skills, as despite the closeness of the tyres of a laden jeep, the edge didn't crumble and plunge us to our deaths, a long way below.

After a certain point, it doesn't matter how far you fall, as you will have reached terminal velocity, at which point hitting a hard surface will give such a low probability of surviving that death will be highly probable. Around here the access problems are so difficult that even if you survive the fall, you will die of injuries before help can arrive. Even if medics can reach you quickly (I hadn't seen any ambulance stations) the nearest hospital is hours away, whether by road or air as there are so few helicopter accessible sites.

Trying to remember back to my school physics classes, I seem to remember something about weight and height and the influence of the probability of fatal injury, given the number of variables. I gave up and guessed five stories or 15 meters is bad. Add five meters for safety (or given the ghoulish nature of the issue should I say margin of error?) to give an approximation of twenty meters. Given the rough terrain and absence of medical assistance, within at least 30 minutes, the probability of survival plummets. The prospect of survival with serious permanent disability was not appealing as an alternative. We were way above 20 meters so on an intellectual level I should stop worrying about falling over the edge and enjoy the scenery. I was safe from the scenario of survival but with serious permanent injury, inshallah.

This was a really dangerous mountain road, narrow, steep, drops to one side, solid rock cliff faces to the other side, tight bends, unable to anticipate what was coming ahead of you, risk of avalanche and not to mention accident or mechanical failure. And what do you do if you meet a vehicle as there are few if any passing places? At least that was the driver's worry and not mine. I decided that if he was to reverse I would get out and walk. Luckily, this was a quiet section of road and we encountered very few vehicles and where we did meet oncoming traffic, there always seemed to be a wider section of road nearby.

Despite the poor surface of the road, we came across one of those highly decorated lorries, with a load towering above the cab that meant it must have been over loaded. The driver was standing with the bonnet up, leaning in trying to effect a repair. It was the first time I'd seen a breakdown but it was odd to see a lorry on such a dirt track.

Later, we were to come up behind another lorry, trying to climb a steep gradient in its bottom gear. It was going at less than a walking pace and throwing out clouds of black exhaust smoke. I wondered whether we were stuck behind him for the rest of the route but a flatter and wider section appeared and the lorry inched to one side and we bumped onto the even rougher surface, at the side of the road, to overtake and get back to our normal speed.

I looked over at the speedometer out of interest and noticed that it didn't work and I looked at the other dials. Speed zero, engine temperature cold, revs zero, amps zero and petrol empty. None of them worked. At least the engine and steering worked and the tyres held their pressure, despite the hammering they were getting on the bumpy road.

As a treat, we had some individually wrapped sweets which we offered about occasionally. We offered some to our guard who chose one and tore off the wrapper. The sweet was popped into his mouth and to my outrage, the wrapper was thrown out of the jeep to litter the countryside. I was so deeply disappointed to think that I was here to marvel at the wonderful scenery and that the locals treated it with so little regard and were not looking after it. In poorer rural communities, there was less rubbish than in the towns but perhaps more affluence brings more litter. I glanced at Judith in the back, with a shrug of her shoulder, I knew she knew what I was thinking about the locals littering their environment.

Judith called our first photo stop of the day. We had discussed this previously, over a meal in the hotel. Left unrestrained, I would be calling for a halt every 100 meters and then spending several minutes walking up and down to get the right camera angle or waiting for a vehicle or animal to come into shot, to give an idea of size and perspective. It would take ages to get to our next stop before nightfall if left to me.

I had decided to take shots from the vehicle as it was moving and only ask for a stop where the scenery was particularly impressive. I was trying to restrict the number of stops that I called, to a similar number as my fellow travellers.

We had stopped at a point opposite, where a tributary on the far side of the valley joined the main river. It was a hanging valley that drained the higher mountains and joined the main valley down a sudden descent. We could see a road hair pinning, back and forth to get up the slope. Looking up the valley, were great mountain peaks capped with snow. The river below occupied a wide flat riverbed and split into several separate ribbons of muddy water as it made its way slowly down stream across the debris that filled the valley floor.

It had rained overnight although it was warm and sunny now. Surface water runoff had brought debris down on to the road to form fans of debris across the road. There were occasionally muddy bits and puddles but we pressed on regardless.

The valley widened, the slopes become less steep and farms and fields reappeared. The road descended and we were near to river level. Here to my surprise were paddy fields, flooded with water and the green shoots of the rice plants sticking out of the water. The river bed was wide but as the spring melt was not in full flow the river was still split into many separate channels.

There was a police station where we stopped and our guard got out. There was time to stretch our legs because we had learnt that changeovers were never quick. There was a bridge next to the check point across the river where the river had narrowed significantly to flow through a narrow gorge. The river roared in the narrow space deep below the bridge.

Apparently, we didn't need a guard despite having left Gilgit Baltistan province and entered Chitral province, and its numerous passes and hundreds of kilometres of its northern and western areas bordering Afghanistan. Except for landslides and washouts the road was largely tarmac and smooth. The valley was wider here and although there were rocks beside the road, making farming impossible, the terrain was gently undulating so the road were straighter and you could see quite a distance.

We set off again without any guards. We took a left turn, crossed the river and followed it westwards on the southern bank. We came to an army post, barrier across the road, high walls to our right, with pillboxes and narrow slits for lookouts and weapons.

There was a commotion as Karim negotiated with the army guards and there was a lot of exchanging of views with frantic arm waving and shouting into mobile phones. In short, the army controlled the road ahead and would not let us pass without a guard whereas the police that would have provided a guard hadn't/wouldn't/couldn't provide a guard. I never did find out a plausible explanation. We were told to reverse away from the check point at least a hundred metres and wait.

The army rule here and the police had to provide a guard if we were to go forward. This ensured a long wait of more than an hour, although it seemed longer, but at least we had the shade of the trees, to avoid the hot sun. Then around the corner roared two new shiny police Toyota pickups each with two armed police in the cab and two armed guards in the back. We approached the army checkpoint again and having already given them our details during the first encounter, we were waved through now that we had an escort.

They were in a hurry to get through this section and kept up a pace, faster over the rough road surface than we had so far experienced. It might be comfortable in a long wheel based pick up but in the smaller jeep, we were jolted around more than I would have chosen.

Part of the road had suffered a landslide and a new road was being carved out of the mountainside high up to our left and there was a diversion down towards the river. The temporary road was right down by the river and hundreds of metres long before climbing back up the bank to re-join the tarmac. Despite the rougher surface, there was no difference to the speed at which the Toyotas sped forward.

They were obviously in a hurry. Topping a rise after fording a small stream, the lead car pulled over and indicated we should pull alongside. The man in charge, I can't remember how many stripes or other marques of authority he had, but after his driver stopped, he leant out of the window. Apparently, the next police post had sent a car to meet us so he was turning round to head back, as this was the extent of his patch.

We carried on and after a few kilometres, we came across a police vehicle slewed half way across the road. On seeing us the driver flashed his lights a few times, the officer sitting in the passenger seat waved an arm indicating us to follow and the driver swung the vehicle in a large circle and set off down the road ahead of us although at a steadier pace than the previous police vehicles to the outskirts of the town of Chitral where he pulled over and waved us on.

Chapter 4

Chitral to the Kalash Valleys

The road was descending steadily and there were more trees, fields and houses. Eventually the road had flattened out and there were nonstop fields, trees and lots of houses. We were approaching a bridge across the river which we took to get to the north side. There was a bus station to our left and in front of us was Chitral's main shopping street. Part way up this road we took a left hand turn and after a hundred metres we took another left turn into the courtyard of the Tirish Mir View Hotel (although I have also seen it spelt Terishmir).

It was after 2pm and we hadn't stopped for lunch en-route. So we ordered lunch first and then checked in at reception. I noticed that the fans weren't working and sure enough there was a power cut. Whilst waiting for lunch to be served I had a look around the hotel.

The hotel was single storey, modern in style and faced the road, but was built on a steep slope so there were several lower floors at the back. From the bridge a kilometre up river that we had crossed earlier it looked like the hotel was five storeys high and I was to discover that it had more than 75 guest rooms.

The garden was well kept with a large lawn, with some shade trees surrounded by flower borders. Wandering along the edge of the lawn and looking at the flowers, I recognised many of the species which were the same as you would find in an English garden. This was not surprising, since rich Victorians would sponsor expeditions to travel the world in search of new exotic plants for their gardens.

Looking around the garden I could name a lot of the plants. There were fuscias, geraniums, roses, chrysanthemums, privet, marigolds, antirrhinums, tomatoes, daisies, pansies, red hot pokers, wall flowers, dahlias, marigolds, hollyhocks, grapes, runner beans, ivy, dandelions, primulas, fig trees, acers, walnut, maples and a host of other plants that I recognised, both plants and weeds but I didn't know their names. I am not a keen gardener but there was a mass of plants that I recognised but couldn't name.

On reflection, this familiarity with so many of the plants was not so unusual and despite being so far from home and high in the mountains, my familiarity was due to those Victorians. Many expeditions would set out to find new plants and bring them back and now people claim that they are local and many are widespread but their origin is actually miles away in far distant lands.

Beyond the garden walls were fields and the Chitral River, some 200 meters distant so the garden was peaceful and secluded. Looking up the valley from the garden was an uninterrupted view of the snow-capped peak of Tirish Mir 7,708m, after which the hotel had been named. Although high by UK standards, it is only the 33rd highest mountain in the world but it is the highest mountain in the Hindu Kush.

What we were served for lunch wasn't what we ordered but we were hungry so we ate it anyway without complaint, but it would become a recurring theme, ordering one thing receiving something different. After lunch we wandered up the road to register with the police. Inside the police station on the wall, was a chart of all the nationalities of visitors who had visited Chitral Province since 1997. There were 69 countries represented but more than half only had a few visitors.

The most represented country since 1997, was the UK with 3,175. The next most represented countries, in decreasing order, were Japan 2,562, Germany 1,380, and USA 1,108. Foreign tourist numbers from around the world annually, easily exceeded 1,000 until 2009. Since then the numbers have collapsed to circa 500 a year. I didn't see any other foreigners west of Gilgit for the whole trip so I suspect the number is continuing to fall, due to security concerns.

Our new guard was Abdul, who would be with us for several days whilst we were in the Chitral area. At night, the hotel had its own armed security. At least two men dressed in traditional local dress and hats holding AK47's. So whilst we were staying at the hotel, Abdul could go home to be with his family overnight.

Late afternoon, after the heat from the sun was waning we went for a walk up the main street. It was a hubbub of activity, mainly men, and working their way slowly through the crowds, were cars and lorries, squeezing past each other down the narrow street. There were dozens of shops selling their particular specialities, fruit and vegetables, pots and pans, carpets, knives, tailors, spice grinders or mobile phones.

We stopped at a smoothie shop for refreshments. Fresh mangoes and bananas were peeled and put in a blender, together with mineral water (tap water was the standard but we paid extra for the mineral water version to try to avoid stomach upsets) plus ice scraped from a large block of ice covered by a cloth. The ice was cut from the glaciers in the surrounding mountains and carried down by mules to be sold in the market.

The smoothies were wonderful, fruity, cool and refreshing. On reflection, although we had paid extra for mineral water, I pondered on the fact that they rinsed the blender, the knives, the chopping board and the glasses in tap water and wondered whether stomach upsets would still be avoided after the smoothie but only time would tell.

At the top of the main street we crossed a bridge over a ravine and passed the polo pitch for the town and next door to it, the football field where a match between local rivals was taking place. The players weren't wearing any discernible kit, although several were wearing white tops of different designs but not a full team of eleven. The players seemed to know who was on which side and both the players and the scattering of spectators were having a good time.

We skirted a poorer part of town and I sensed that Abdul was suddenly nervously looking about and tense. If my guard was happy, I was happy and obviously if he's nervous, I was nervous. It was time to head back, so I suggested we walk back up the road towards the centre of town. We walked purposefully and determinedly, away from that particular area and I sensed that Abdul had calmed down somewhat.

We took a side street to avoid the bustle of the main street. It passed the court house on one side and the prison on the other. Passing in front of us was an inmate literally in chains. He had manacles around both his wrists and ankles which were chained together by a short chain, allowing him to take only small steps and another chain connecting his hands to the foot chain. I had seen these in museums but never thought I would see them used in real life. He was escorted across the road in front of us to face his sentence in the courthouse.

Arriving back in the hotel, we ordered our evening meal from the menu and would dine at 7pm. The electricity had come back on so we rushed to our rooms to take a hot shower before the electricity failed again. Our meal was served on time and unlike lunch, it was what we ordered.

The next morning, I got up before the alarm went off. I had had a disturbed night and I was wide awake. I was woken in the night by the muezzin calling the faithful to prayer and in the stillness of dawn I imagined I could hear the river rushing past so I decided to go for a walk before breakfast. I tried the light switch but there was a power cut which also meant there was no hot water again.

I left the hotel turning left towards the river, passing the mosque next door to the hotel. The next building was an elaborate gatehouse to the fort but not open to the public. The road ended at the edge of a stand of trees and beyond that, I could just see the river bank. I was passing a small house on my right, when a gentleman came out and greeted me. His name was Ahvad and he was a teacher at the Langlands School.

I had read an article about the Langlands School, just the year before. The school was founded by Major Geoffrey Langlands who arrived in Pakistan with the British army during the Second World War and he had never left. After the war, he was an instructor for the new Pakistani army and later was a maths teacher at the Aitchison School, the Pakistani equivalent of Eton. In 1979, he founded the Langlands school to educate both boys and girls up to 18 years old. Lessons were originally taught in English but due to the lack of English speaking teachers, some lessons are now taught in Khowar, the local language.

He continued to run it and raise funds for its continuance and only retired aged 94 in 2012 and moved to Lahore, where he continues to raise funds and act as a trustee for the school. It takes a lot of money to run a school and parents pay fees. However, the fees are modest and many parents plead poverty so get reduced fees or free education for their children. Finance is always stretched and fund raising could be a full time job but education is a worthy cause to support. The school is located on the airport road, north of Chitral and is now run by Carey Schofield, a journalist and author amongst many other achievements, who is originally from London.

Ahvad walked with me to the river. He told me a story from his youth that he used to swim the river to the other side. I looked at the angry raging torrent of the river which was a grey colour laden with silt. He explained that the river level is highest in the morning as the melted water from the previous days sunshine takes all night to get to this part of the river. He acknowledged that he might enter the water here but ended up much further down the river on the other side. In order to avoid the very long walk to the bridge further upstream for his return journey, he would walk upstream and swim across whilst being swept down aiming to get out at the place where we stood.

I wanted to take some photos of the fort. This fort was about 70m square with an 8 meter high wall covered in mud. Ahvad guided me past the gardens and liaised with the watchman. He knew the Mehtar's family, the same family that owned the Mastuj fort and I was invited to look inside the gate.

The walls were 2.5m thick. There was a square between the river and the building used to house guests. This was brick built, two storeys high, with a colonnade on both ground and first floors.

Pointing out between some of the ground floor columns were three cannons, the same ones that were used by the British army in 1895 to defend the fort from besieging local tribesmen for six weeks until they were relieved.

Finally Ahvad pointed upwards and there on the skyline high above the town I could see another substantial building. That was the Mehtar's summer palace, a cooler place able to catch the breeze to avoid the summer heat experienced on the floor of the valley. I thanked Ahvad for his time and details of local history and headed back to the hotel for breakfast.

We packed our luggage onto the jeep and as soon as Abdul appeared we set off. One of the bridges across the Chitral River had been washed away and another had been weakened and could not take vehicles, so we followed the old road southwards out of town. The tarmac finished at the edge of town and we were back to rough track.

Our side of the valley was barren and rocky. From our road, high up the side of the valley, we could see over to the other side of valley where there were trees, fields and farms until the slopes were too steep to farm and transitioned to bare rock. There was also a tarmac road on the other side but our side was the more scenic route.

After an hour on the rough track, we entered a village. This was previously a Kalash village but over time it had expanded with Muslim families moving in and Kalash families moving out so now there were only three Kalash families left. There was a bridge over the river connecting our side to the main road on the other side. As the track descended towards the bridge, the tarmac re-appeared. We turned right away from the river and headed up the hillside up towards the Rumbor valley road. The tarmac finished and the track zig zagged across the steep slope, forever gaining height.

We soon left the fields behind and entered a deep gorge with the river flowing swiftly to our right. In places, the valley floor was so narrow that the road had been cut into the cliff with rock below us, a rock wall to our side and a rock roof. The colour of the water in the river was very different. Unlike the grey swirling water of the main river, this water was blue with water crests of white foam where it swirled around boulders in its path. In some parts, there was an irrigation ditch running along the side of the road taking water from the mountains to the fields in the valleys below.

We met a wedding party in a convoy of cars coming towards us, all decked out with tinsel instead of our customary white ribbons. We bent our wing mirror inwards and pulled over as far as we could, next to the vertical cliff face whilst they drove as close as they dared to the edge.

We inched past each other with a lot of waving of hands and shouting from helpful male relatives or guests eager to help and not be too delayed. We were inches from scraping the paintwork, whilst they were inches from falling off the edge. I noted that the women had stayed in the cars for this perilous manoeuvre and had I been a passenger, I wouldn't of had the nerve to stay in the car, so close to the edge. I expected to see it plunge to the floor of the valley far below, at any minute, but they all made it past safely and we continued without mishap.

We came to a bridge, over the river, which ended in a choice of turning either left or right with a police check point and a barrier across the road on the bridge. We went through the well-practised checking of documents routine before being allowed to pass and carry on. We didn't change guards and Abdul stayed with us.

Around a corner we met a policeman guarding a short section of road. The edge had been washed away by the river and was extremely narrow and I got out and walked up the road to the far side of the washout. Vehicles had come down the road, so we knew it was passable but only with extreme care. I could see concern on Matu's face as he inched the vehicle forward in a low gear.

I could barely watch as the front offside wheel dipped off the road into air, with stones falling into the river below. Matu revved the engine and inched forward ever so slowly. The wheel gained some grip on the edge of the chasm only for the back wheel to lurch into nothingness. There was a gut wrenching moment as the back of the jeep lurched downwards and the diagonally opposite front wheel lifted into the air, but Matu revved the engine again and got some momentum, and we were soon back onto solid ground and safely past the washout. We all sighed with relief when he was safely past the hazard and got back on board.

We went past our first Kalash village which was noticeably different from other villages. There were only a dozen or so buildings, all wood, usually two storeys perched on the side of a hill above the track. I glimpsed a few people in the village, the men were dressed in the standard shalwaar chemise, some with Chitral hats, and one with a waist coat.

The women were totally different from those that I had seen to date. Gone was the scarf and the head and face coverings worn by Muslim women. They had uncovered faces, with distinctive elaborate and intricate ornamental beaded head dresses and thick coils of beads around their necks. The dresses had waistbands of colourful material tight around the waist and the dress billowed out to a large hem. Their ankle length dresses were largely black with brightly coloured, handmade, embroidered patterns on them. And some of them, especially the children, smiled and waved as we went past.

The Kalash are a unique population with their own culture, their own language, which is Kalasha and their own religion. They live in just three remote valleys, high in the mountains and were unknown to the outside world until late in the last century. The total population number circa 3,000 although up to double this number speaks Kalasha as some were converted to Islam. Converts are not allowed to live in the traditional Kalash villages and are shunned thus preserving the cultural integrity of the villages. The religion has multiple deities and sacrifices for instance of milk or goats are made to the gods. The economy is based on agriculture, with crops of wheat, maize, grapes, apples, walnuts, apricots and mulberries. Livestock includes cattle, sheep, chickens and goats.

The valley above the village widened out and there were fields and a few buildings, farmhouses in the main although there was an opened sided saw mill and a recently built medical centre provided by the government. We were nearing our destination, the village of Balanguru in the Rumbor valley. We crossed a rickety suspension bridge to enter the village, passing the temple on our right on one side of a square with a large mulberry tree in the middle of the square.

We arrived at the guest house and unloaded the jeep. The hotel or guest house consisted of one single storey building and a two storey building, facing each other across a square lawn with a small irrigation channel running underneath both buildings and across the middle of the lawn. There were two rooms in the smaller building and four rooms in the two storey building. Access to the upper two rooms was by an outside staircase, leading to a common covered wide walkway in front of the two upper rooms.

My room had two single beds and two bedside cabinets. I tried the lights but they didn't work. Through an open doorway was a bathroom area consisting of a basin, a shower or rather a shower head at the end of a piece of metal piping above a bit of sloping concrete floor that led down to an outlet that disappeared through the floor. There was a western toilet and the usual bucket. Looking out of the bathroom window was the flat roof of the neighbouring house, with mulberries and herbs laid out on the roof, to dry in the sun.

One side was bounded by a privet hedge and the other was open, looking out across the river to the far bank. There, perched on the edge of the river bank, was a small stone shed with a pipe running into it from an irrigation channel. This was a small HEP plant but some of the equipment had been damaged when the river had flooded and they were waiting for spare parts. Above the channel was natural landscape, a rocky steep slope and a scattering of trees.

We sat in the garden drinking green tea waiting for our lunch. On the opposite bank there was a constant trickle of rocks, rolling down the slope stirring up dust. Initially I thought this was a landslide, but on closer inspection there were men up there. Our host, Yassir, explained that if you want to build something, you go up and help yourself to the stone that you need. The men were quarrying stone and wheeling it away in wheelbarrows. The stones rolling down the hill were off cuts that they didn't want, or chunks they had prised out but had fallen over the edge.

Yassir took us for a walk around the village in the afternoon. On the far side of the road opposite the hotel was a small field, perhaps a hectare in area. There was a fence around it built of branches pushed into the ground. On top of the fence was washing hung out to dry providing a splash of colour. The farmer had just started to harvest the crop by hand, using a hand scythe and leaving the cut wheat in small bundles, to be collected at the end of the day. Further down the valley the crop had already been harvested but up here the winters linger thus delaying the spring planting so harvesting is correspondingly later.

In winter, the passes are filled with snow and the whole of Chitral province used to be cut off for months at a time. A new tunnel, over 8kms long, through the Lowari Pass to the south has recently opened and hopefully will provide an all-weather road link to the south, parallel to the border with Afghanistan towards Peshawar 300kms to the south.

There was a single road running parallel to the river running through the village which was spread out along the road with outlying groups of houses connected by footpaths. In the square we had passed through earlier was the temple and there were two small shops. Although dusty, there was no litter. Other than our jeep parked under a tree, I saw no other vehicles and there was no passing traffic.

Walking up the road, the next building we came to was a 4m square, single storey, stone built building with timber struts and a flat roof. Inside was a mill stone powered by the irrigation channel that later flowed through the guest house. The farmer would leave his grain with the miller who would grind the ears of wheat and take a modest cut of the resulting flour as payment for his efforts.

We followed Yassir through a doorway in the stone wall next to the road and found ourselves in a small courtyard with a grape vine growing over a pergola, providing both grapes and shade. Underneath, were some bed frames and children playing on the beaten earth floor. One side of the courtyard overlooked the road. On the left was washing and toilet facilities, on the right was a kitchen area, and in front were four rooms.

This house was shared by four brothers and was home to 18 people. Two of the four wives were at home, dressed in traditional costume, looking after the children. Although we had not knocked and were unannounced, the ladies didn't seem surprised, as if this was a common occurrence and were happy for us to look around and answer our questions with Yassir translating.

Across the road were sheds built of wood on stilts, with three or four steps going up to a small door and no windows. These were used for storage of crops and fodder for the winter. Around a corner, we came across a much bigger and substantially built house. This is where Akiko Wada lives. She was originally from Japan but whilst backpacking throughout the Hindu Kush on holiday, she fell in love with the simple lifestyle and the village. In 1987, she left behind her cosmopolitan urban lifestyle and moved to Balanguru. She became a Kalash, following the religion, speaking the language and marrying a local man. She has published a book, titled Kalasha with many glossy photos of the Kalash lifestyle.

We moved uphill to a collection of houses, built on the slope of the valley side. The flat roofs of the house at the base of the slope, served as a patio area for the houses further up the slope where fruits and herbs were spread out to dry in the sun. The houses were all of a similar style built of stone with wood struts and flat mud roofs. There was a storeroom below with a small door and no windows and the room above where the family lived.

We looked inside one of the houses where two girls were looking after two of their younger siblings. There were four beds on a raised dais against the wall, a table with chairs, a hearth used for cooking with a collection of kitchen utensils and some personal items hanging on the wall. They didn't have much but it is a simple lifestyle and this was all that they needed. This might be functional for summer but I wondered what it was like in the depths of winter with snow on the ground.

We headed back down the valley but took a footpath further away from the river and past more fields and came to the village square. We had a look inside the temple. It was a large room with some carving on the wooden pillars and dust floating in the air, irritating my eyes. The only light came from the hole in the ceiling open to the elements.

It was empty with none of the usual statues, paintings and decoration that I usually associate with religious spaces. Yassir mentioned some of the ceremonies in general terms and I was fascinated but didn't take any notes at the time and didn't want to intrude by asking a hundred questions. However, the explanations seemed comprehensive with the gist of the ceremonies and their symbolism being explained.

Crossing the bridge we passed more houses and on the edge of the main village was the menstruation house. This is where all the women go when they are having their period or giving birth. They are considered unclean so must leave the home and stay here. They undergo a cleansing ritual before returning to the home.

Down towards the river, set in its own grounds with flower borders, was a large modern building. It was a lofty single storey building and looked new although it was built in 2002. This was the local primary care centre, staffed by a single nurse but it was shut at the time that I visited. I emphasise that this is only for primary care, for anything more serious people have to travel to the hospital in Chitral.

We crossed the river by a rope suspension bridge. On the far side, on the river bank, was another mill with its own small mill race. We walked through a wheat field and started up a long flight of steps. I started counting them but lost interest somewhere beyond a hundred with still a long way to go as I concentrated on breathing in the thin mountain air.

The flight of steps turned a corner under a walnut tree, reaching the crest of the slope and the terrain levelled off as we approached a group of houses with an irrigation channel flowing under more walnut trees. At the start of the growing season in April there had been a lot of rain and the temperatures were lower than usual. This bad weather had affected the blossoming fruit trees with apples, figs and apricots doing particularly badly. But for some reason walnuts were doing very well as were the mulberries, despite the bad spring weather. It is the typical multi-crop farmer's lot, that whatever is bad for one crop is good for another.

It seemed to be wash day for this small group of houses. There were a number of women and girls washing clothes in an irrigation channel and chatting away as they worked. There was another group sitting under a tree, in the shade chatting. Nearby, we were shown what was alleged to be, the oldest house in the village. There was no way of verifying this fact short of dendro-chronological testing but looking at the possible sites in my view this would have been the first choice.

It was built on the edge of a crag, sticking out of the surrounding terrain with breath-taking uninterrupted views down and across the valley and catching the morning, midday and afternoon sun. During the summer, families tend to spend more time outside rather than inside. The wide veranda jutted out over the cliff and between the floor boards were gaps through which I could see the ground far below.

On this veranda were chairs, remains of a fire used for cooking on a slab of rock, cooking utensils and assorted boxes and bags. The lady of the house was sitting with her back to the low wooden wall, just knee height that separated the veranda from the abyss. I thought about the health and safety implications and how easily a trip or stumble could result in a death fall.

Also on the veranda was a hand operated Singer sewing machine, at which sat an 11 year old girl. She was embroidering a black dress with a yellow thread to make a shape like an ash leaf. All the dresses and their intricate patterns are designed and hand-made at home. I never saw the same pattern repeated on another dress. This girl had been making dresses for two years and she manoeuvred the material and wound the sewing machine with obvious skill. And I didn't see a pattern or template, it was all done by eye.

I am getting better with heights and big drops and the gaps between the floor boards, but with the ground a long way below was still unnerving so I was happy to move on. Our next stop was a local carpenter and sculptor. He had a malformed foot and moved with difficulty but he had great skill with wood. He was delighted to show some of the toys and carvings that he had created. He was currently working on a full sized deer with real horns.

We settled down for tea with Yassir's aunt, who was one of the women we had met earlier, at the irrigation channel. We sat on the veranda and drank green tea. Yassir's aunt had a problem and she was haranguing Yassir who being a local headman, had some influence and she was seeking a favourable outcome. It concerned access to some land whose ownership was disputed but I didn't press for the technical details.

Two of her daughters were also on the veranda. The eldest was doing her homework and the younger daughter was hand feeding a minah bird. The bird was kept in a covered basket hanging from a rafter overhead. At one point, the bird escaped and flew off to a nearby shade tree. The two girls rushed after it, recaptured it and put it back into the basket.

We followed Yassir's lead when he got up to leave and followed him off the veranda into the open. His aunt wasn't taking this as the end of the conversation though. She insisted on walking with us and was still talking, even as we walked away, until she finally said goodbye and returned to her home. We got to the irrigation channel and walked along the edge around an outcrop of rock and down back towards the road bridge.

We re-crossed the road bridge and headed up the hill. This hill is a steep sided pointed rock protrusion, sticking up from the valley floor with several houses built up its sides. Like the earlier oldest house in the village there were verandas with small walls or rails with long drops below. Families spent their spare time on these verandas and there were toddlers crawling along the boards. My safety concerns were reawakened and I asked Yassir how many accidents had there been. To my surprise, especially given that the hand rails were so low, he said that no one had ever fallen over the edge.

At the top of the hill was a spring festival religious site with a flat festival area constructed with donations by the Norwegian and Dutch embassies, as per a brass plaque at the edge of the area. There were carvings of heads of animals like sheep, goats and cows. Above was a large boulder which legend has it, was washed up here by a large flood and so sacred that only men could go up to it. To me it would seem improbable that a flood could have washed it up here, given its size as it towered above me, and that it is 80m above the current river level, but I couldn't explain how else it got there as it was made of granite and the surrounding bed rock was slate. (A more scientific explanation might be that it was probably an erratic, a giant boulder, brought here by a glacier from a long way away and left here when the glacier retreated but I didn't want to spoil the local legend).

That evening, back in the guest house, whilst passing time waiting for supper, I met a number of local dignitaries. One was Temour Shah, who claimed to be the advocate for the Kalash peoples at the UN and the engineer in charge of the HEP project being installed just up the valley. My ears pricked up on the prospect of discussing a topic, in which I was really interested. A local headman, Bezaingi, an important local and village elder, was also introduced to me. He was involved in the committee overseeing the project, as was my host Yassir.

I am a keen supporter of HEP and sensitive economic development. Although not an engineer by profession, I keenly follow developments in this field and a career in economic development would have been my second choice of ideal careers. That aside, my first ideal choice of career as a child was to be a farmer. After working in agriculture on and off from aged 15, experiencing the early starts, the long days, the cold, the rain, the loneliness, the vagaries of the weather and the catastrophic financial effects on your crop if you had one left at all, after working hard all year made me alter my sights a little. I thought it better to have an alternative income and become a gentleman farmer. I could have breakfast at a sensible time and meet my farm manager occasionally, to discuss strategy and work on the farm when I wanted whilst he had the job of worrying about the crop and getting jobs done or being fired.

I quizzed Temour at length to get the full details of the HEP development project. He said it was a 500MW power station on the far side of the valley, to provide electricity for the Kalash valleys. It was funded by international donors including USAID, the UN and partly funded by the community themselves.

Some 70 % of output would be consumed locally and the project would obtain an external funding stream from exporting the surplus 30 % to Chitral. Generating costs would be 4.5 rupees per unit and sold on for 5 rupees against an existing current price of 10.5 rupee.

I queried the planning and design time stream suggesting 3 to 5 years. "No," he proudly said with a smile, and continued to tell me, it had taken just a single year and waving an up stretched digit in the air and repeating just one year from conception to completion. The project consisted of a five foot wide and five foot deep channel over 4,800ft long taking water from the river to a tank on the valley side right above the power station that would house the turbines and generators. He boasted that they had built a bridge over the river to give road access to the site and as the project was progressing well that transformers would be delivered within a fortnight.

I wondered about whether a lorry would be able to negotiate the nearly washed out road that Matu had had trouble getting the jeep past. Also, I wondered whether the bridge that we had crossed several times during the day would take the weight of a transformer on the back of a lorry and also of how a large vehicle would negotiate the narrow streets and one particularly tight corner around a building, just the other side of the bridge. I guessed that if it was delivered in parts, it could be assembled on site but I had no notion to question the plan.

Given the rock conditions, steep slopes, the mixture of scree and solid rock in the valley, the unstable slopes and potential of earthquakes, I questioned him about the difficulties of building the channel. He mentioned the name of one of his workmen and said he was the best rock driller in the area, giving me the impression that the channel had been freshly carved out of the rock. I was fascinated and asked whether I could see the site tomorrow, to which the response was affirmative. We had been due to walk up the valley the next day but the schedule was flexible so the walk was shortened and I was set to visit the HEP site the next afternoon.

That evening we sat in the garden and our meal arrived. And I do mean arrived, as there are no cooking facilities in the guest house, the food is cooked up the road and carried down the street to the guest house. It was getting dark so candles were lit.

We had a treat with our meal of the local alcoholic drink, made from mulberries that was called a wine which is quite novel, given that this is predominantly a Muslim country. The best description I can manage, is that it was rather like effervescent cloudy raspberryade. I doubt it was very alcoholic and it wouldn't be to everyone's taste, but personally, not liking sugary fizzy drinks which were so typical of the area, it made a change to having water.

After the meal, we chatted for a while and then I went up to my room to bed. Abdul lay down on a bed frame in the courtyard in the open with just a blanket. He would sleep in the open whilst guarding us in this remote but pleasant valley just a few kilometres from the border with Afghanistan.

Chapter 5

Mismanagement in the mountains

The plan was to walk up the valley and for the jeep to drive up and collect us, to get us back for lunch so that I could see the HEP site in the afternoon. Etso didn't want to walk anywhere, so she would stay with the jeep. Judith, myself and Abdul set off on foot through the upper village and Matu would drive Etso and Karim plus another policeman as their guard to meet us higher up the valley later in the day. The extra security was required as we were very near the border with Afghanistan. Chitral was 45kms from the border, here we were perhaps less than 15kms from the border.

The sky was blue without a cloud in sight and the temperature was rising. We passed the last house in the village and soon the fields ended and the valley returned to its natural state. The track was little more than two parallel tyre marks on the rough ground, stretching up the valley. There was an occasional tree, some shrubs and lots of rocks.

From a bend on the track, to negotiate a promontory, we saw the river below to our left. Upstream there was a newly built suspension bridge that started on our side on a cliff high above the river level, with a ramp on the far side to get the road down to the valley bottom. This location was chosen to allow the bridge to be above likely flood water levels. There was also a sign detailing the cost of the project, the contribution of the community and various details and indicating it to be 250MW not the 500MW mentioned the day before.

The track descended to cross a small stream. At the side of the stream, was a large wild mulberry tree, providing some shade where we rested for a while. The tree was in fruit so we helped ourselves. The mulberries that I was familiar with at home are red but these were white. They were small but sweet and so fresh that they were a pleasant and refreshing addition to our morning break.

We could see the river occasionally as we neared a small hamlet and there were a few small fields surrounded by stones and a farmhouse. A couple of long thin tree trunks had been placed across the river to act as a foot bridge. In places, there were great baulks of timber that had been washed downstream by a flood and left high and dry on the river bank. These appeared to be basically tree trunks that had been cut to a length and squared off by removing the outer sections of bark and recent growth to produce a short rough cut length of timber, square in cross section that had been washed downstream by the river in flood.

After more than two hours of walking we saw ahead of us on the slope of the far side of the valley a collection of buildings comprising the next village up the valley. This was Nekrator, a wholly Muslim village. This was where two rivers meet and the valley widened out and the ground was more suited to farming. There were few women about and the few we saw, wore veils.

We were invited into one of the houses for tea, located in perhaps the third or fourth tier of houses, up the slope, giving a view of the river and fields below. Terraces of fields stretched up the opposite slope with a scattering of farm buildings. Men from the village were manhandling great baulks of timber down by the river to reinforce the river bank and protect the houses above the bank from further erosion.

We headed back across the bridge, to where the jeep was parked and piled in for the trip back to the guest house, together with two lads from the village, who were hitching a lift down the valley. The track was narrow but all the time we had walked up and on the ride back we didn't see any other vehicles and I didn't remember seeing any vehicles parked in the Muslim village of Nekrator.

I met Yassir after lunch and we headed off up the valley again up the same road that I had travelled that morning. After a short while we cut off the track and headed down hill towards the river. Here was another footbridge that I hadn't seen from the track above constructed of a few planks nailed onto a couple of tree trunks spanning a narrow part of the river.

We walked through fields and trees and came to the site. It looked like the workers were living rough with bundles of clothes, blankets and sleeping bags scattered about, some litter and the cold remains of an open fire. There were a couple, of what I assumed to be workers, wandering about, seemingly doing nothing.

At the far side of this temporary camp was a small single storey building built of local stone with a corrugated iron roof. This was to be the powerhouse for the turbine. It had a skim of concrete on the floor to give a flat surface to receive machinery. A large square hole in the wall on the mountain side of the building allowed it to accept the pipes that would bring the incoming water to generate electricity. There was a smaller hole in the opposite wall, for the discharge after powering the turbine. A large hole at the front, the size of double barn doors, was to enable the large parts of the turbines and generators to be able to gain access to the inside the building. There was also a normal sized doorway for people to ingress and egress the building.

Noticeable by their absence, there were no pipes to carry the water to the turbine. There was no spillway to take the water back to the river, having generated the power. There were no foundations to receive the transformer and no sign of any cables or pylons, to take the electricity away.

Yassir and I scrambled up the hillside, to where the channel would bring water from the river to the powerhouse that we could just see through the trees, directly below us. There was a square tank with a hole on the downhill side, where the water would flow into a pipe down to the powerhouse. There were a couple of workers there. It seemed that they had just finished pouring concrete, judging by the fresh darker coloured concrete drying behind the roughly sawn wooden shuttering.

I had expected a newly made channel but this was actually a former irrigation channel that had provided water to the fields further down this side of the valley. I could see the now dry channel, disappearing round a corner, towards the fields I had seen earlier, on the far side of the valley from the hotel.

The original channel did not have the volume required for both irrigation and power generation so the section between here and the intake from the river, further up the valley had had to be widened.

The channel upstream of the concrete tank was made of local slate. We walked up the channel using the base of the channel as a path. Despite the rough stone, the whole effect was a neat flush finish built by master craftsmen who knew exactly how to handle stone. The neat geometry of the flat base, equal distant parallel walls snaking away was a delight. However, it did not seem to be five foot deep by five foot wide, which I had been told the day before; we could not walk side by side but the wall was no higher than waist height.

In places, the walls looked like they were finished, with the inside faces ready for lining either in mud, as was the local traditional method of holding water in the channel, or by cement which I had seen in other modern and refurbished channels.

In other places the walls were non-existent. Around one particular outcrop, there was no wall at all and there was barely a two foot wide path between the cliff face on my left and a precipitous drop to my right. I inched my way along, with my back to the wall, trying not to look down. One section was cut into the cliff and I had to stoop to carry on. Luckily, it was quite short.

Yassir was happy to walk in his flip flops and chat over his shoulder without a care in the world, about the possibility of plunging to his death just inches away from the narrow rough path. Now I had lost sight of him, around another section with a low rock roof above. I was ready to turn around and I shouted out, hoping my voice would carry around the bend. He came back into view and I explained that I had had enough of the nearly non-existent paths above dangerous drops. He promised it was not much further, before the path widens and the retaining walls begin again.

The further along we go the less the drop is, but anything higher than 5 metres is enough to get my nerves tingling. It doesn't make much difference if the drop is thirty meters or fifty meters. When the path is narrow, and I have no distance from me to the precipitous edge to reassure me, it's still too much for comfort. I carried on and tried to put the thought of the return journey, out of my mind.

The channel reached the point where water from the river entered into the channel. This particular area ended in bare rock with hardly a scrape left of the former irrigation channel. There was a concrete structure of the original intake, but it seemed more work was still required, in order to get water to be diverted into the channel. And I saw no evidence of any drilling or blasting on both this area, and the section where I had nearly turned around and both areas would need a lot of hard work, to create the necessary channels.

Also, Yassir's insight was interesting. The planning and design had taken longer than the one year I had been told the day before. The construction completion timescale that had originally been agreed, to take place between June and November 2012, was already a year behind schedule. The winters are so harsh that construction can't take place over the winter so if it couldn't be completed this season, it would be yet another year before completion.

On the return journey, we stopped and talked to three labourers who were building the walls we had seen. It turned out that they hadn't been paid for months and they were very angry. They saw me as a foreigner and must have thought I had some leverage associated with the funding of the project. One man had a court case in Chitral but as he hadn't been paid for months, he didn't have the money to pay for the bus fare so he had missed his court date. He thrust a note book in my face and pointed to dates worked and pay due. His two colleagues chipped in that they hadn't been paid either. They couldn't leave as they had no money for bus fares and so had carried on working with the hope that they would eventually be paid before winter set in and would have to return to their homes.

On the return journey, when we got to the concrete tank, instead of retracing our steps and heading straight down the hill, we carried on along the dry irrigation channel. The fields and trees on this side of the valley looked very different compared to those on the far side.

There had been about 20 families on this side of the valley. The farmers had been told that construction would be June to November 2012 so they may have to forego water for irrigation during construction. Harvests are from July onwards so the interruption would not be too disruptive, if water was to be available for the next growing season. In return for electricity and a short disruption to irrigation water, towards the end of a single season, it seemed a good trade off. Now the project was a year over due and if it wasn't completed this summer, another season would be lost and it seemed the farmers had been sold short.

The fields here were dry, dusty and bare. The trees didn't look in good condition and the fruit trees were dying. Without water, these families could not grow crops or water the fruit trees so that they had moved out to live in overcrowded houses with relatives on the other side of the valley. In my opinion, there was so much work still to do that the project would not be ready before the coming winter. The picture painted to me by Temour the day before was so far from the realty. I was outraged that a project for good could absorb so much charitable money, over run for so long and potentially destroy the livelihoods of these families through so much delay and mismanagement.

The next morning, we were waiting for the jeep to be loaded, when a lorry came down the road laden with timber, and I was struck, that despite the guest house being on the only road through the village, I had not heard any vehicles going past, all the time I had been here.

The great baulks of wood which I had seen up the valley, were basically tree trunks that had been roughly sawn, to make them into a rough baulk and square in cross section. The ones I had seen earlier, had obviously been in the river, as their surfaces had the same eroded faces and rounded corners that we had seen on the timbers by the river the day before.

Due to the lack of heavy equipment, few lorries being available, and the poor access to the forest for vehicles, the original freshly rough cut timber from the forests, higher up the valley, are dragged to the river's edge and left. When the river floods, the timber is washed downstream. When it has been washed down near enough to where it is wanted, it is then man handled from the river bank, back towards the road. Then a lorry or jeep is borrowed to pick it up and deliver it to the local sawmill. The sawmill just below the village was a simple affair, a few baulks of timber, a pile of chips, sawdust and off cuts, a saw pit and perhaps, a circular band saw under a roof but no side walls.

We were leaving the Kalash valley to head back through Chitral to the hot springs at Garam Chasma west of Chitral. Yassir's sister hitched a lift with us to visit a friend in Chitral. The washout where we had got out, to leave just Matu to drive past in the jeep on his own was being repaired by a couple of labourers, using hand tools. Large rocks had been rolled into the river to fill in the hole left by the river undercutting the bank and a retaining wall was being built using local stone and no cement. We continued to descend the Rumbor valley road and came back to the town on the main Chitral River where the tarmac started again.

In Chitral we checked in at the police station and to pick up another guard. Abdul was a pleasant young fellow and easy going. Although he didn't seem to speak English, he was a nice chap so we asked whether we could keep him. It was agreed to give him time to go home, change his uniform and say hello to his family before picking him up again after lunch.

We had stopped off at the Tirish Mir View Hotel where the fans and lights weren't working due to a power cut which had become a common event and hardly worth mentioning, as it seemed to happen so often. We ordered from the menu and sipped green tea in reception until lunch was ready.

After a short while, we were told our meal was ready and on entering the restaurant we noted that we were the only customers. We had ordered pasanda curry, qeema vegetable curry, rice, salad and yoghurt. The rice, salad and yoghurt arrived as ordered but the two main dishes served were meat in spinach and beef curry. The waiter assured us that this was what we ordered. After previous mishaps we had written down our order and handed it in at the reception and he couldn't have mixed up the orders especially if no one else was in the restaurant. We didn't argue but smiled as we ate, knowing full well it wasn't what we had ordered earlier at reception.

The jeep wouldn't start, so we pushed it up and down the courtyard in front of the hotel entrance until it coughed into life. We weren't going to risk breaking down in the middle of nowhere, so our departure was delayed whilst the starter motor was fixed in a local garage and the tyres were checked and pumped up.

We headed for the bridge but instead of crossing it, we carried straight on towards the airport and past the Langlands School. Beside the road was an unusual sight of a PIA aircraft with a brick wall built around it. It had crashed when it over shot the runway, some years before. Rather than take it all away with the associated difficulty and expense, they had only salvaged the engines. The airline had bought the plot of land, on which it stood, from the local farmer and built the wall all around it and had left it there behind the walls. It must have been a good piece of land and cost a lot, as there was an impenetrable jungle growing up around the abandoned aircraft.

The tarmac finished and the fields disappeared, as we headed up the valley with the river on our right, carving a deep narrow gorge. The road hugged the small strip of land between the river's edge and the steep valley sides. All the way up the road, there were small groups of workers clearing landslides or cutting back the steepness of the slope, to reduce the risk of falling rocks. In one place, they were building avalanche protection for the road looking like a tunnel with the side opposite the river, just pillars holding up the roof with large gaps like windows looking out over the river. There was the occasional field and farmhouse but the valley was too narrow to allow enough flat land to make a living for more than a single family.

One of the tyres on the jeep was slowly deflating and no surprise, given the hefty bashing they were getting from the rough road. Luckily, it was mid-afternoon and we were approaching Hotel Innjigaan, our spa hotel in Garam Chasma which means, 'hot spring'. We unloaded our bags and signed in as Matu drove away the now empty jeep to find a garage.

The hotel was a modern built, single storey, purpose built hotel with the guest rooms built on three sides of a square. The rooms were well appointed with new furniture. The lights worked and there was hot water. On one side of the hotel was a large swimming pool, with steam rising from it with a faint whiff of sulphur. At one end, there were steps going down into the water that stretched all the way across the width of the pool. It didn't have tiles, it was just plain concrete. This was Garam Chasma or the hot springs.

The water seemed very hot but I eased my way in slowly and sat on the top step. As I got used to the temperature, I eased myself in, further down the steps just like easing yourself into a hot bath. Soon I was floating and the water was deep enough to be unable to sit on the steps due to the buoyancy so I set off and swam several lengths at a leisurely pace.

I relaxed by the edge of the pool and looked around at the mountains towering above us. Wishing to make the most of this opportunity, I went for a few more lengths of the pool. Sitting on the side, drying in the sun, I reflected on the spa and whether it had done me any good. I am usually sceptical about paying a lot of money for spas and have never read any scientific research proving their benefit, but I was sure that my skin really had benefitted from the mineral rich dip. And there had been no baths in any of the hotels, just showers, so the long hot soak ensured that I was really clean although there was a slight whiff of sulphur, even after I was dry.

We had time to kill before dinner, so I went off to find Karim and Abdul so I could wander about the town centre. Etso didn't want to go for a walk but Judith joined us. Heading up the main street, off to one side, was a football pitch with a game just about to start, between the town and another local side. One team in red shirts, the other in green. It looked a lot more organised than the match I had seen in Chitral.

There were the usual array of small shops selling hardware, agricultural hand tools, toiletries, a tailor with a Singer sewing machine, a grocery store where we bought bananas and mangos and one particular shop, where I bought myself a Chitral hat to complement my shalwaar chemise.

A Chitral hat or pakol is very popular throughout the Hindu Kush and neighbouring areas. The lower part is made of woollen cloth, wrapped in a coil to resemble a rope to encircle the head. The upper part has a flat top with a small peak all the way around, starting from behind the coil, coming up to cover the coil to cover the outer edge. Each valley has a particular design and those in the know can tell where you are from, just by the hat. They also have other names depending on where they were made, such as Hunza hats from the Hunza valley.

We walked up the road and crossed the river. The road ascended steeply, parallel to the edge of the river, as the water cascaded over rocks. Looking back towards the far bank of the river, there was a channel high up the mountainside, with a pipe down to a powerhouse. This was the local HEP station so I doubted there would be any reason for power cuts here. The power cuts were becoming so numerous that I had stopped remarking on them.

We continued up the road towards the pass into Afghanistan, a few kilometres further on. We passed small fields of potatoes, wheat and maize. One particular field caught my eye. It was planted with wheat but had two varieties mixed together, the majority of the crop was a short variety with large ears of grain whilst the other was taller and thinner with widely spaced ears and made up perhaps a fifth of the total. The taller more exposed variety was gently swaying in the breeze as we continued our ascent.

We had left the town a long way behind and the fields were getting smaller, as the valley narrowed and had become too rocky to cultivate successfully. After more than an hour, we turned round and retraced our steps back towards town. We passed the shops we had stopped at earlier and picked up our goods that we had bought earlier and left behind the counter, so we wouldn't have to carry them up the valley and back.

We took a different route through the town to get back to the hotel, walking along the edge of the river until we turned away from it to get home. We came across a garage. There was no sign outside, but it was obvious what it was, judging from the oil stained ground and an assortment of various car parts, scattered along the side of the road.

A mechanic had a welding torch and was doing some welding work to the front of an old battered lorry. He had no eye protection and the sparks were arcing and landing around his bare feet. Amongst the various rusting bits of vehicles, was our jeep. It had been jacked up on one side, resting on a rock with one wheel removed. There was a lot of banging and shouting coming from the dark interior of the garage, as other mechanics undertook repairs. It seemed that a hammer giving something a bash to repair it, was the preferred method over the use of a screwdriver and a replacement part.

I took full advantage of the spa and had another swim before breakfast. I had the pool to myself again. Business wasn't good for the hotel as there had only been us and another family of four, the night before and although my room looked out over the pool, I never saw or heard anyone else use it.

We loaded the repaired jeep and headed down the road which was as dusty as ever. Despite being early on a Sunday morning, there was still traffic on the road heading into town. The road crews were at work again, building retaining walls, loading stones onto trailers, quarrying sand and mixing cement.

We got back to the Tirish Mir View Hotel in the early afternoon and we all ordered vegetable curry and salad which unlike earlier experiences came as ordered except the drinks. The three bottles of water and a glass of mango juice were replaced with one bottle of water and three glasses of mango. It just wouldn't feel quite right if we got everything we ordered.

We sat in the garden to let the heat of the day pass. Despite being in the centre of town it was quiet, except for the noise of the river rushing past beyond the walls and the occasional squawking of some minah birds. It was pleasant to sit in the shade of a maple tree and benefit from the gentle cooling breeze that gently moved some of the leaves on the tree. The majestic Tirish Mir peak in the distance was a little darker as more of its snow had melted and the snow line was noticeably higher up the shoulder of the mountain.

We got back into the jeep and headed back up the same road towards Garam Chasma past the Langland School and the abandoned crashed aircraft. The area beyond the town is part of a nature reserve of 20,000 hectares and we were here to see deer that come down to the river bank, to drink at the end of the day.

We pulled off the road and parked at a spot, looking over the river to the far bank. There were a few trees near the edge of the river and above them, rising straight out of the river, was hundreds of metres of virtually bare, rocky steep slope. As the sun dipped towards the horizon, the deer started to come down the opposite slopes to the river. Firstly the males, followed shortly afterwards by the females, with some calves following.

The braver animals jumped around on some of the rocks in the river. Others were walking their front legs up the tree trunks, to reach the more succulent leaves higher up the tree. One deer had jumped into one of the trees and was happily eating the leaves at the top of the tree.

Two calves had managed to climb on top of a massive slab of rock, but were having difficulty getting down. Several times they got to the edge and had prepared to jump only to back off again thinking that the drop was too long. They spent quite a while rushing back and forth until finally one jumped, landed on all fours and run off to find its mother. Having seen the first one jump, the second calf also jumped and run off. Altogether, there were more than a dozen deer on the far bank. Exact numbers were hard to judge, as they kept moving about and their light brown colouring made excellent camouflage against the bare rock making them hard to count.

Other drivers had stopped to watch and those of us with binoculars, were happy to pass them around to other travellers. There was a park ranger who had come to check on the deer, who was happy to advise those watching, on the habits of the deer and pass his binoculars round the gathering crowd.

I was startled by a man standing next to me, addressing me in excellent English, nodding towards the deer and asking me whether I was enjoying the spectacle. We exchanged greetings and he introduced himself and he welcomed me to Chitral. It turned out that he had been a student at the London School of Economics and after graduation and gaining some experience, now worked in finance in Dubai. I was intrigued as to how he spoke such good English and equally why he was interested in my reasons to visit this remote and inhospitable place, not least because of the security situation.

He was visiting family who turned out to be the owners of the construction firm, who were improving the road between Chitral and Garam Chasma. I mentioned that this would seem to be a never ending job, as there would always be work here to improve and maintain the road. He was happy to leave this work to the family company, whilst he pursued a career in finance in Dubai.

Back in the hotel, we ordered pea pulow and pasanda curry, especially as we'd had it here before. I am sure they do their best, but following earlier experiences, it was no surprise when we got served mutton curry and mutton biryani. The waiter, again, assured us that this is what we ordered. There was another power cut. This came as no surprise, as we were now seasoned travellers. We ate by the light of a single hurricane lamp, in the centre of the otherwise empty and dark restaurant.

Chapter 6

Up the Hunza valley

I was woken up in the middle of the night, by the muezzins calling the faithful to prayer. As they need electricity for the loud speakers, it was not annoyance at being woken up that I felt, but relief that the electricity was back on again. I made the most of it and took a warm shower, although it was the middle of the night.

We were having an early start going east back through Mastuj over the Shandur Pass and on to Gupis. We had done this section of the road a week earlier in three days, but now were due to do it in just two days, via the same PTDC hotel, outside Gupis that we had stayed in the week before.

The alarm went off, I pulled myself out of bed and tried the light switch. Nothing. Yet another power cut. I shaved in cold water, in the bathroom with no windows in the early morning gloom, before dawn so that the flickering candle on a shelf was doing its best to counter the gloom. I had a cold shower to wash my hair that I had not washed during the night before. It was not a shower as you might expect, but more precisely, standing on the concrete floor and pouring cold water over myself using the small jug dipped in the large bucket of water.

We left Chitral after filling up with petrol before leaving the town. We hadn't been going for an hour, when we pulled into a garage to check the tyre pressures and fill up with air. There must be real problem with the tyres as we seemed to need to fill up much more often than I would expect. As there was no electricity to work the pump, a foot pump was produced and with a lot of effort, some air was pushed into the tyre and we carried on. We had only borrowed this jeep and we would get back to our original jeep on the other side of the washout just beyond Phander later in the day. As long as it could hold out until Phander, we would be alright.

Just short of the bridge, over the river to Buni, we took a mid-morning break. We sat drinking tea in a quiet garden, forming part of The Golden Inn, under an apricot tree, whose gardens and pergola, also supported a grapevine.

We didn't cross the bridge but kept to the left taking the road to Mastuj. We re-visited the PTDC hotel at Mastuj for lunch and were the only guests. Here, we visited the police station and said goodbye to Abdul, who had looked after us for several days in Chitral, the Kalash valleys and Garam Chasma. He had looked after us well and received a good tip for his efforts. He would now wait for the next vehicle which needed a guard heading for Chitral, which meant a wait of maybe a day or two, as tourists were few and far between.

On the Shandur–Mastuj Road, near Harchin, a week before I had wanted a photo of a particular area where there was a dramatic drop from the edge of the rough track that was the main road down to the river. The area was made up of weak unconsolidated glacial debris where the runoff had carved deep gulleys descending from the road at a very steep angle, down to the river, a long way below. My earlier attempts, taken from the jeep as we passed were either too blurred or I had pushed the button a second too late so missing the shot I wanted. Therefore, I asked that we stop at a convenient spot nearby and I walked back and forth to get the right shot.

The reality was spectacular but the resulting photos did not do justice to the reality. It would be a memory of an event, unsupported by any photographic evidence. As is so often the case it is hard to capture the magnificence of a situation against a two dimensional photo. The best shot would have been from the other side of the valley a bit further along and looking back with a tele photo lens to capture the height and the angle. Taking a shot from the top of the gully just didn't capture the grandeur.

By mid-afternoon, we were well on our way to the Shandur Pass. We needed air again for the tyres so we stopped at Sor Laspur, the last village before the ascent to cross the pass. There was a light on in the garage so they had power. We pulled in and stopped in front of the garage. I got out, treading on the running board as usual. And it creaked as usual.

The policeman who had been sitting next to me, followed me out and tumbled to the floor with his Kalashnikov clattering across the concrete. He ended up in a heap on the floor and I learnt my first local swear words. That creak of the running board as I got out was the last straw and it had snapped off as he had put his weight on it.

The enterprising mechanic took all this in his stride, checking the tyre pressures and filling up the tyres as necessary. He then got out a welding torch and crawled underneath the jeep to weld the running board back on. And this welder used his welding mask. This was a very different experience compared with that at home. If this had happened at home, my local garage would have taken a look, told me they'd need the car all day, and would try and fit it into their schedule, a week next Wednesday! In total contrast, in less than ten minutes, the tyres were pumped up and the running board welded back on and we were on our way again.

In the Shandur Pass there is the Shandur Lake. The weather the week before when we came through it was overcast with patchy rain. Today it was a clear and bright blue sky. This showed off the lake at its best and instead of a rather grey rough foreboding surface, it was calm and a brilliant blue azure colour. The rain had filled the lake and its edges had expanded to flood some of the surrounding grasses, whose fine tips were pushing through the surface of the calm blue water.

We reached the polo grounds and its associated buildings. Karim suggested that we stop at the Natco Hotel but it was getting late, we had a long way to go and the shadows were lengthening and noticeably so. However much faith I had in Matu's driving skills, I didn't want to be negotiating mountain roads in the dark. I also didn't know whether the lights on the borrowed jeep worked and by now, I wouldn't be surprised if they didn't work and therefore I voted that we pushed on.

On our descent, on the far side of the pass, there was a horrible bang and hissing sound as our left hand rear tyre was punctured. We got to a flat section and pulled over. The old wheel came off and the replacement wheel with the large gash in the tyre and suspect repair was put on. Despite my scepticism, it worked and we set off again.

We descended to the valley bottom and here there were more animals, scattered horses and a herd of goats being driven along the road. The river to our right had attracted a couple of fishermen. We stopped and called them over, with a view to buying their catch, but they'd had a bad day and didn't have any to spare. Despite offering way over the odds for their fish, they refused to trade.

Nearing the bridge over the next river and the police post there was more activity although the local village was still 5kms up a side valley. Some youngsters were playing football which we watched for a while, whilst the police took our names and checked our permits.

Five young girls, wearing brightly coloured clothes without veils, approached us, giggling and pointing. They ran away when a camera came out and as soon as it was put away, they came back and continued to point and giggle. I think we were a novelty for them, as I doubt they get to see many tourists up here.

Further down the valley, we came to a sudden stop and Matu jumped out. He bent double over an irrigation channel scooping water up in his cupped hands and started throwing it over the radiator. Despite the temperature gauges not working, he knew that the engine was overheating. Karim joined him in splashing water over the radiator. Any lingering faith in this particular jeep was fading fast with every new problem.

After splashing on water to cool the radiator, using the hem of his shalwaar chemise for protection against steam and heat, Karim took off the cap of the radiator. Using cupped hands and plenty of round trips between the irrigation channel and the radiator, the radiator was refilled. I didn't think you were supposed to put cold water into a hot radiator, but then Karim was the mechanic with the knowledge. The sun had disappeared behind the mountains as we set off again.

In Phander, we picked up the owner of the jeep and dropped off our police guard. This was only a small police station and they could only provide a guard for the route towards Gupis up to the washout but not beyond. We would have to continue afterwards without a guard.

We got to the washout and hired porters to take our equipment and luggage over the rough footpath. Since our last visit, a large digger had arrived and was clearing a route around the washout, but it looked like it would be yet another week to get a route around the washout that four wheel drive vehicles could negotiate. We said goodbye to our police guard and to the rather unreliable jeep, to re-join our original jeep.

It was almost with a sigh of relief that we got back into our more reliable original jeep. Further down the valley, we came across two fishermen walking alongside the road carrying their catch home. There were a dozen or so fish, each the length of a man's hand. After our earlier unsuccessful attempt, we offered a good price and bought the lot.

We were still on the road as it got dark but ahead we could see a lot of lights of a procession marching our way. There had been some football tournament earlier in the day and the successful team and their fans were walking back to their village, holding the cup above their heads, celebrating their victory with singing and chanting.

At the PTDC at Gupis, our new guard was waiting and welcomed us, introducing himself as Kamal. Our rooms had been reserved but as they were the few rooms with running hot water the manager and the assistant manager had taken them over for themselves. Karim was brilliant, insisting that they move out which after some resistance, they picked up their things and moved out. The power was on so we had hot showers and air conditioning. The chef cooked the fish and in a deserted restaurant we had fresh fish, salad and rice for our evening meal.

It was another early start. We dropped our police guard, Kamal, in Gahluch to pick up another guard. As it turned out, Kamal's shift had finished and as he lived near the next police station and needed a lift home, we dropped him at home and met our new guard at the next police station. We drove out of town and headed off towards Gilgit.

On the outskirts of Gilgit there was an army checkpoint where we were flagged down. Karim got out and showed our permits and passes to one of the senior officers. Whilst he was doing this one of the soldiers approached us and asked to see our IDs. I pulled out my passport and handed it over. He took it and looked at the front and back, then opened it and scanned it page by page.

This was an old style passport, with the picture and details at the back. He started leafing through from the front and was confronted with page after page, of visas and stamps from all over the world. He turned eventually to the page with the Pakistani visa but when he turned it sideways to read it and held it upside down, I realised he might be able to read local script but couldn't read English. Before he had got to the picture at the back of the passport, the officer handed Karim our papers, waved us through and I got my passport back from the soldier. Karim told me never to hand my passport over to anyone, without him saying it was okay to do so.

At the final police checkpoint, a bit nearer to the centre of Gilgit, we dropped our last guard and headed for the PTDC for a late lunch. After lunch I met my new driver, Koshal, who would be driving me up to Karimabad and we headed out of town over the Gilgit River by a rather rickety bridge towards the KKH. There were two jeeps, two drivers, Karim our guide and three guests. We took a circuitous route which when I queried, was explained to me that it was to avoid traffic and guard posts. Judging by the amount of traffic, everyone else was doing the same thing. We crossed the Hunza River and crawled up a muddy slope before going through a village and joining the tarmac of the KKH.

Finally, we were on the KKH which was the main aim of the trip. This road was immediately and noticeably different, from those other roads that I had encountered to date. It had a good smooth tarmac surface, was wide enough for at least two vehicles plus some hard shoulder on either side. The gradients were gentle as were the curves. For the first time on my travels in the area, I noted that in places it had railings or crash barriers, often in good repair.

After a while though, I did also notice that the barriers were inconsistently placed, with some sections having steep or vertical drops without barriers, whilst other seemingly less dangerous sections, had newly built barriers. There were a number of partly built, but unfinished barriers, indicating that this was a work in progress, even after all these years. Construction had started in the 1960s, but was obviously undergoing continual improvement.

The valley was wide and the river was a long way off to our left. There were occasional farms and fields and patches of trees but mostly the valley was bare rocky scrubland and too rocky to cultivate.

We stopped on the KKH at a point on the opposite side of the river to the village of Nomal, at the mouth of the Naltar valley, by a monument, built to remember some of those who met their deaths whilst building the KKH. There is a memorial in bright yellow, resembling a rock drill bit plus not more than thirty graves of local workers. The numbers actually killed during construction are not certain, as there were no comprehensive central records kept but of the perhaps more than one thousand deaths, over 80 % were Pakistani, the balance being Chinese.

I was tired and we had seemingly been travelling for days on end. The journey was interesting but nothing stood out as memorable, until we reached Rakaposhi. At 7,788m, this is the 27th highest mountain in the world and the name means snow covered.

We stopped at the side of the main road and Karim pushed some notes into a slot in the top of a metal box located next to the pavement. I asked about the money that Karim had pushed into the slot. This was an offertory box and it is a habit in the area, for travellers to make a donation to the local deity in order to ensure a safe journey. We crossed the road to sit down at the Rakaposhi View cafe located on the side of the KKH, so called, as it allegedly has a marvellous view of the peak itself.

It was mid-afternoon and therefore about time for tea. The cafe is situated at the mouth of a valley that headed up into the hills but the weather was not in our favour. There was low cloud and we could only see the lower slopes and the peak itself was completely obscured by cloud.

We stopped for green tea and hoped that the cloud might blow away but we were unlucky. We would be coming back this way later, so I hoped to get ahead of the planned schedule so we may be lucky enough to stop here again on the way back and perhaps trek up the valley. We lurched back onto the tarmac and further conversation about the box was difficult as Karim was in the back and I was in the front. Later, I discovered that the money goes to the local community to help fund local projects.

The road this side of the river was being upgraded in places with substantial concrete retaining walls and avalanche protections being built so we picked our way through the works avoiding diggers, drilling machines and cement mixers and all the paraphernalia associated with road building.

We crossed the river and followed the road up the side of the valley. A kilometre ahead there was a massive retaining wall being constructed. Some of the weak jumble of rock, comprising the valley side had been dug away and a 40 meter high wall was being built. Workers were pouring concrete into shuttering on a 20 meter high section, which was more than 10 meters thick. They had another 20 meters to complete before reaching the road level above them. The cement powder was delivered in sacks and poured into big mixers on the side of the road. Gravel gathered from the hillside, was added and after mixing it, was then poured down a chute straight into the shuttering in a 24 hour operation.

There was traffic beginning to back up on both sides of this activity which was unusual, as at other sites, the traffic continued to flow despite the road construction activity. The difference here was that an accident had occurred just moments before.

One of the mixers on the side of the road was toppling at a crazy angle on the edge of the cliff above the shuttering below. Every now and again more rocks and dust would fall as the cliff edge crumbled under the weight of the mixer.

Some quick thinking workers had chained the mixer to a digger but whilst it was stopping the mixer from tumbling over the edge, the digger didn't have the power to pull it back from the edge. Meanwhile, the cliff continued to crumble. The foreman was trying to get an even bigger digger from further along the road to provide assistance. Until it arrived, the digger holding the mixer from crashing into the shuttering below, was blocking the road. I noticed that the driver was not sitting in his cab.

We waited for an hour but no bigger digger arrived and there was no progress made to pull the mixer back from the brink. Traffic continued to pile up on both sides of the blockage, and there was no prospect of getting through anytime soon.

Karim hatched a plan using his local knowledge and contacts. We left Koshal, Matu and the two jeeps to follow us later, when the road was open again. We carried our hand luggage past the digger holding the mixer back from oblivion. Several people were standing between the digger and the mixer. I preferred to squeeze past the back of the digger and the rocky bank. We found our new vehicle and driver that Karim had negotiated, a large four wheel drive people carrier so that we could continue our journey.

We arrived at the Hunza Embassy Hotel in Karimabad in the middle of a power cut but we were assured that the hotel had a generator which would be switched on at dusk. This hotel was built on a steep hillside high above the river with store rooms on the ground floor, reception on the first floor accessed up a flight of steps and the guest rooms up a staircase on another level. It was on a quiet road with access to left and right and as I was to discover later, it had a back door leading to a flight of steps, up to the main road, higher up the mountain.

The guest rooms were arranged on two levels, overlooking a courtyard on three sides. The fourth side was open, facing south across the Hunza valley with a view of the Altit fort and the KKH bridge over the river, the junction of the Hopar Nager valley opposite, and the rest of Karimabad to our left.

That evening, we sat outside on the top floor, overlooking the courtyard and I had a treat. I had got some beer in cans, a rarity in a predominantly Muslim country and I hadn't had a beer for weeks. It tasted good but at over $9 dollars a can, I would not be getting any more.

We were due to head up the Hunza Valley to stop at Passu, with the ultimate aim of visiting the Khunjerab Pass. This pass is the highest international border pass in the world at 4,693m and is a strategic point on the KKH route between Kashgar with its railway terminus in China and Gilgit and then on to Islamabad and ultimately the Indian Ocean on the Pakistani coast. This is so high that snow cover in the winter forces the road to shut for six months of the year between November and May every year.

After breakfast, we waited until another guide joined us at the hotel, Mohammad Karim, a local who had lived in Karimabad since childhood and knew the Hunza Valley area well. We headed down and out of town, to cross the river and head north up the valley. We were in a convoy with two jeeps, two drivers, Matu and Koshal, two guides Karim and Mohammad, no guard and just three guests, myself, Judith and Etso. We had needed guards going west from Gilgit but this area, going north and east, was considered safer so guards were not required.

On the road up the valley, we passed a deserted factory with a tall chimney. This was previously a brick making factory built by the Chinese. It is surprising that they ever thought they could make money out of this enterprise. Both the clay to form the bricks and the fuel to fire the furnaces to bake the bricks had to be transported hundreds of kilometres to this remote site.

Counter this with the local tradition that if you wanted to build anything you would just go to the river or the mountainside and help yourself to as much stone as you wanted and could carry for nothing. It was difficult to imagine who, therefore, would pay for expensive bricks, compared to the option of getting building materials for nothing. No wonder the factory was now abandoned.

The valley narrowed and the way ahead, was up a steep jumble of rocks that stretched across the whole valley, with the road snaking up across its face. The rocks were fresh grey coloured, jagged, untouched by weathering and with no vegetation. Near the summit was a line of more than a dozen diggers, lined up, facing down the valley belonging to the Frontier Works Organisation (or FWO), a section of the army responsible for engineering in the northern areas.

This was another marvel that I had specifically wanted to see. In January 2010, the local villagers had noticed that a crack had developed high up the valley side stretching for hundreds of metres. They feared that an avalanche was imminent and had started to evacuate.

The crack widened further and the whole side of the valley collapsed in a massive avalanche that destroyed and buried the village and fields under millions of tons of rock and blocked the river by the debris, to a height of hundreds of metres. It was truly cataclysmic.

The natural rock dam interrupted the flow of the river and water started to build up behind this dam, flooding villages and fields up stream. This is Lake Attabad named after the village that the avalanche covered. The fear of a sudden bursting of this dam by the build-up of pressure behind the dam, forced the evacuation of thousands of people below the dam to higher ground for safety.

The entire community of Domaki speakers located in the village of Shishkat near the upstream end of the lake, a historically marginalised community who only existed in this one valley were displaced by the rising flood waters. Altogether, more than 25,000 people were displaced and they have little prospect of ever returning to their own homes in the foreseeable future. Unfortunately, there were 20 deaths from the avalanche and the ensuring floodwaters that slowly swelled and creeped upstream as more water flowed into the lake but had nowhere to go.

The FWO started digging a channel, hundreds of metres long, through the natural rock dam to release the pressure and get the river flowing again. It was not until June that the river started flowing again, over the dam and down the spillway that the FWO had created reducing the lake level. Meanwhile, it had inundated farmland and villages upstream for more than 25kms.

Although this is a massive dam, it is only the second largest natural dam in the world. The largest natural dam is in Tajikistan, formed in 1911 by an earthquake which is more than 550 meters high and formed the Usoi Dam and Sarez Lake behind it, which is more than 55kms long.

The Usoi Dam is different, as the rock fall left enough gaps between the rocks that water doesn't spill over the top but the water under pressure from the weight of water in the lake, is forced through the jumble of rock that forms the dam. This is equally dangerous, as the water could erode the dam from the inside and this erosion, or another earthquake, could destabilise the dam and cause massive flooding downstream. As with many valleys in these mountainous areas, they are narrow and steep sided which would maintain the devastating effect of a wall of water, bursting down them and not only through Tajikistan but further downstream would be affected, through Afghanistan, down the border and further into Pakistan.

After cresting the summit we descended to a small port, no more than where the road met the water's edge. There was no infrastructure at all. The brightly painted boats tied up against the rocks and a boarding plank would suffice to get people and goods from the boat, to the waiting lorries and vice versa. There were a number of colourfully painted and decorated lorries. They were here to pick up loads from the boats either pre booked or just hoping to barter their services plus dozens of hopeful porters also waiting for a chance to earn some money.

There is a bespoke ferry service available, to transport lorries, but it is unreliable and costly. Therefore, loads are manually unloaded from lorries and stacked high on the colourfully painted boats.

Cars are sometimes taken on the boats rather than the vehicle ferry. Two stout planks are placed across the boat, resting on the gunwales and two more form the ramp to allow the car to drive from the road on to the boat. I saw several brave owners taking their cars over the lake in this manner, but the boats looked rather top heavy for safety and I wondered how the boats would cope on a windy day.

I asked how many accidents there had been but got a non-specific reply and pressed for a better response. All the response that I got was "… accidents happen … a boat will sink if it is over loaded … no statistics are kept … no one likes to mention it as it is bad for business …" All of which I could believe but left me with no hard facts or insights into the danger of travelling across the lake. I knew that this was a seismically active area, with devastating earthquakes a real possibility, so I tried to shut that out of my mind and the consequences of a landslide falling into the lake, creating a mini tsunami to capsize the boat or of an earthquake destabilising the dam and emptying the lake with us still on it.

We said goodbye to our drivers and with our two guides, we loaded our luggage onto our boat and set off up the lake. The boat was built of wood and had been carried up the KKH by lorry from the Punjab over a thousand kilometres away by road. It was wide with a shallow draft. It was more than 15m long but not more than 3m wide, with low gunwales in the middle but with high symmetrical prows at the front and back. Propulsion was provided by two engines mounted on either side, on a plank stretching across the mid-section of the boat with long propeller shafts that could be raised or lowered into the water.

It was a damp overcast day with a light drizzle falling from the clouds overhead. Not the sort of weather conducive to sightseeing, and the ferry journey up the lake took about 40 minutes. I was happy to gaze at the granite formations, streaked through with quartz veins whilst everyone else huddled in the bottom of the open boat trying to keep dry and out of the cool breeze.

There was no evidence of any human habitation along the sides of the valley. The fields and houses were under water over 100 metres below us and the valley sides at water level were too steep, rocky and barren to even provide pastures for goats.

High on the hillside, to my right going up river, I could catch glimpses of construction works. The Chinese were building a new section of road to get past the new natural barrier of the lake. They had tried to cut a road into the valley side, but it was too challenging, so they had opted to build tunnels around the more geological and from an engineer's viewpoint, challenging sections of the valley side. Needless to say, this would take years but they are keen to invest in this transport link for the long term. Until it was complete, the dam and lake would impede the free flow of goods and people up and down the valley and ultimately international trade between China and Pakistan.

We approached the end of the lake and I noticed the colour of the water. The water in the lake was still and it had dropped its load of silt so it was a clearer blue colour. In contrast, the water rushing into the lake from the river was heavily laden with silt and was a grey colour. The two different bodies of water were mingling with the heavy silt laden water from the river swirling and sinking beneath the lighter clearer blue waters of the still lake.

Looking upstream as the lake narrowed and became a river, there was another port on the other bank. This had the usual array of lorries, waiting to load or unload goods and a collection of boats, moored at the edge of the lake next to the road, likewise waiting for their next load.

But unlike the port downstream, where there were no buildings, here there were a number of small huts erected out of anything that was available to construct a hut that were selling tea, curries, biscuits, bottled water and anything else that a traveller might wish to buy or sit inside out of the rain or sun, whilst waiting for their boat to depart. The main village was on the far side of the river. There had been a bridge between the two sides here and the supporting pillars still stuck out of the lake but the road bed had disappeared. The only way across was by boat so this port served ferries crossing the river as well as ferries plying the length of the lake.

Our captain shouted to the people on the shore and he was directed to a position to moor. Ropes were thrown and we were moored against a jumble of boulders. A plank was laid from the gunwale to a rock and we disembarked carrying our hand luggage and we waited for the porters to unload our main luggage.

Karim found our new driver and introduced him as Nassir, a large jovial chap with impossibly black hair given his suspected age. Our luggage was loaded onto the jeep and we set off to our hotel in Passu. Our route took us along back roads, high above the former outskirts of the village of Gulmit that had looked over the river before the flood.

The lake levels have fallen from their peak to reveal the devastation wrought by the water. There was a thick layer of grey silt covering everything in the valley bottom. There were leafless dead trees standing eerily out of the silt. Everything was grey and plants had not yet reclaimed the area so it was lifeless. Large boulders stood out of the silt which had been washed down steep ravines above the village.

All the roofs of shops and houses had collapsed or floated away. In places, the debris was so thick that a former bridge over a ravine was barely visible as the ravine had been filled and only the railings were visible. The valley beyond Gulmit was unaffected and there were green trees and fields with crops.

Despite the green fields, there were other consequences for the community. People had been evacuated so there were fewer people around to support the local shops that had reopened. The close community of the rural village had holes in the fabric of life as friends and neighbours had not returned. Schools had been destroyed and why would they be rebuilt when there were no students.

The extra cost and inconvenience of crossing the lake meant less passing trade for cafes, restaurants and guesthouses. Petrol stations were abandoned due to the difficulty of obtaining supplies. Not to mention, there were fewer vehicles and less trade.

Merchants had moved away and were now building their businesses elsewhere. It would take years to get back to any form of normality. It had the air of a ghost town.

We worked our way along the valley and finally got back onto the original KKH road and a tarmac surface. The valley bottom was narrow, cultivated where it was flat enough and free of boulders to support farming. The sides of the valley were bare rock and stretched skyward, for hundreds of metres to craggy peaks. Great fans of debris starting high up on the valley side cascaded down towards the valley base. The river was wide, but in places, it was so choked with debris and the valley floor so flat, that the river braided or split into multiple channels, as it gently wound its way downstream. The large quantity of silt carried by the river coloured its surface to a muddy grey colour.

This was flat land but was not used for agriculture. The irrigation ditches looked like they were in need of repair but there was little point if the fields were abandoned. The ground was very stony so being marginal land this would be the last to be cultivated whilst there was better land elsewhere.

Chapter 7

Khunjerab Pass

Two kilometres outside the next village, we turned into the courtyard of our hotel, the grandly named Passu Ambassador Hotel. This was a recently constructed concrete purpose built hotel set back from the main road with a central block containing restaurant, reception and TV room. There was ample parking in front and the whole hotel, garden and courtyard was surrounded by a concrete block wall, built to waist height. The guest rooms were in separate blocks to the right and behind the main central block. It had running hot and cold water, clean bedding and floors but no electricity as … guess what, there was a power cut.

We signed in, dropped our luggage and Nassir drove us back down the valley for a walk up the Passu Glacier which cascaded down a side valley to join the main valley. We headed up a narrow road, past some small green fields surrounded by a wasteland of grey boulders. We passed Borag Lake, a small nearly circular lake with clear deep waters that reflected the blue of the sky and darker hillsides around it on its mirror like surface.

We parked the jeep and Nassir sat down on a nearby rock. Karim stayed with Etso as she didn't want to go walking, so Mohammad Karim led Judith and myself up the valley side. There were a selection of weirdly shaped rocks with smooth curves and holes. This is the result of sand particles being blown by the wind, gradually eroding the rocks into these strange shapes.

The bare rock exposed on the side of the valley showed striations from the passage of the glacier. These are lines etched in the rock by a harder rock embedded in the ice scraping along the surface of this now exposed rock face. It is a good indicator of the previous height of a glacier and its direction of travel.

We came across an irrigation ditch, taking water from the glacier to the fields a long way below us and walked along the edge of this ditch towards the glacier. We crossed a lateral moraine made of debris from the glacier and stopped at its crest.

Below us was the Passu Glacier. It had little debris on the surface so displayed a lot of white ice crisscrossed with darker lines. These darker lines are made of fine debris that had fallen into crevasses which had reclosed, leaving a dark line of debris running through the otherwise white ice of the glacier.

From our vantage point, high above the glacier, we could see down to the terminal moraine where a lake had formed from melt water seeping out of the glacier. In the distance we could see the overflow cutting a channel down to the main river in the far distance.

Back at the hotel, there was time before our evening meal, so I went to investigate the surrounding area. There were some houses and fields with crops but the irrigation ditches needed attention and some farms looked abandoned. The petrol station was empty, a wayside store abandoned and a large stone building set well back from the road, nearer the river had lost its windows but it was unclear what its former use might have been.

At 7.30pm the electricity came on and the meal was served. I discovered later that electricity came from an HEP station in the next village up the road. Water is plentiful around here so the outage wasn't to save water but there was no explanation as to the cause of the outage. It happens so regularly that locals don't even comment on it.

I was woken around 1am by the sound of heavy rain beating on the roof. I looked out of the window and it was pitch black, no moon, no stars, no lights, just clouds and heavy rain. And made darker by another power cut. I heard voices and some shouting and banging. I was up and dressed in no time fearing the worse. I eased the door open and just down the path, I could see the door to reception. It was some late night guests, waking the owner, to get a room for the night. Perhaps it wasn't the rain that woke me but the sound of their vehicle drawing up. I went back to bed, re-lieved that it was just late arriving guests and not anything worse.

Today was another early morning start, with the alarm going off at 6am. At breakfast, I found out more about the late night guests. They had been coming down the valley when it had start-ed raining. They had come across a landslide where rocks were still tumbling down, so they had sheltered in an avalanche tun-nel, until the rocks had stopped rolling down the hill. Heavy rain makes the hillsides less stable and more prone to landslide so is an additional hazard in the mountains.

We were due to visit Khunjerab Pass. This is the highest in-ternational tarmac border crossing in the world at 4,693m and the highest point on the KKH. I had wanted to cross the border to travel to Kashgar and return across the border but on applica-tion for a visa I had been refused. No reason was given but due to Chinese sensitivities of their relations with Pakistan and the situation in nearby Afghanistan, so much could be read into the decision but would be speculation.

It was still raining, although lightly, but the cloud level was low and obscuring the nearby peaks that I had seen from the ho-tel just the day before. It was uncertain what the weather con-ditions were like, up at the pass and being so high, it may have snowed overnight at that altitude. I might get cold but the view would be worthwhile it if the weather conditions were favoura-ble. Security was always an issue but I had taken precautions and hoped for the best. What I was not used to, was trying to assess the landslide danger and this is where I had to trust my guides.

Nassir arrived and we had a meeting to assess the risk. Nassir, a local from up the valley was perfectly happy to drive and didn't seem to worry about conditions. We decided that we wouldn't know for certain, until we had seen it with our own eyes and talked to travellers on the road so we set off, not knowing wheth-er we would get to the pass or not.

Judith asked a few questions and decided to stay at the hotel and Etso wanted to know when we were starting and I suspect, wanted to go whatever the hazard. I doubted that she had understood the dangers or the gravity of the situation, more due to her limited English than an understanding of the situation from a position of knowledge. The rain had eased off so the worst of the danger may have lessened by the time we got to the more dangerous upper reaches of the valley. As a last resort, if I didn't want to go on I could always get out of the jeep and wait for its return back to the hotel. So we set off in the jeep with the group comprising Etso and myself driven by Nassir plus our two guides Karim and Mohammad Karim.

We passed a brightly painted lorry, parked at the side of the road. It seemed an odd place to park, unless it had broken down. It was only when we drew level with it that I could see the whole front of the vehicle had been stoved in. It looked like a head on collision with another vehicle, but it was here all by itself.

The road was crossing a rugged but open area. After more than an hour on the road the solid dark clouds had changed to light grey, it had stopped raining and there were small patches of blue sky trying to break through the cloud cover. The road followed the easiest route across the bare rocky ground with some spectacular views of distant peaks.

We stopped at a garage in Sost to get petrol and enquire about road conditions ahead. There were stories of minor landslides but that traffic was still coming through, so it was passable but with difficulty. Awaiting repair at the garage was a Chinese truck with obvious damage to its cab from falling rocks. One side of the cab had a dent in the metal work of the roof and a smashed windscreen. Our jeep with its canvas top, would provide no protection and I wondered whether I had made the right decision to continue up the valley.

Although we were more than 75kms from the official border, the customs post was set on the outskirts of town and there was a line of large Chinese lorries, awaiting clearance for official entry into Pakistan. Many had goods covered with tarpaulins, giving no idea of the nature of the cargo but a sizeable number had cement bags on the back, no doubt heading towards the road improvements being implemented by the Chinese, as intergovernmental aid on the KKH further down the valley.

At the side of the road we came across a World Wildlife Fund project site. Here, there was a snow leopard cub that had been rescued in the winter before. A mother and her two cubs had been crossing a frozen river when the ice gave way and one of the cubs had fallen in. Luckily for the cub, it was rescued and had been held here until it was ready for release, back into the wild.

It was very well camouflaged and even up close, it was hard to distinguish it from the background. If approached too closely it would snarl and hiss but it knew the cage would not let it escape nor allow visitors to harm it. Despite our closeness to it, the snow leopard stayed curled up with no movement other than the snarl to warn us to keep our distance.

Also here, was a giant of a bird which I was told was a lammergeyer, a German word meaning lamb vulture. It was a bird of prey standing as high as my thigh, with large eagle like hunter's eyes, a dark pupil surrounded by a yellow iris and a sharp beak and wicked looking talons for ripping at flesh. It had had a broken wing and was staying here for recuperation, restrained by a tether to one of its legs. It hardly moved but its eyes were alert and I was not tempted to go closer than 4 meters, broken wing or not.

The valley sides closed in to form a deep gorge which narrowed to no wider than the road and the river with steep sides so closed in on the road that I couldn't see any peaks except the brightening sky right above us. The river was a mass of white water thundering over boulders in the depths of the narrow gorge. Here and there in the road were rocks that had fallen from the cliffs above. My confidence wasn't boosted when I noticed that as Nassir drove, he spent nearly as much looking up for falling rocks as looking at the road.

Around a bend there was a large digger in the middle of the road. Ahead of it, was an avalanche protection tunnel with its river side having a series of pillars supporting the roof, built to protect the road from debris, falling down the valley side. Above it, was a massive scree slope stretching high above the road. It appeared that the tunnel had not been built quite long enough as the fan of debris was longer than the tunnel and debris from above had half blocked the entrance. We could see a couple of vehicles on the other side of the partial blockage in the tunnel waiting for the digger to clear the road.

The digger's driver and a workman were 30 metres short of the blockage and looking up the slope. There was a constant trickle of small rocks rolling down the slope each leaving little trails of dust marking their descent. Bigger rocks would disturb smaller rocks which joined their bigger brother to roll down the slope adding to the danger. The digger waited for a while and backed away. It waited for a bit longer and when it didn't seem likely that the fall would stop any time soon it turned around, picked up the workman who hung on to the outside of the cab and they disappeared back down the road. This small blockage would be cleared but when was another matter.

We had nothing else to do so we sat and waited to see what would develop. I wondered whether this was the place where the nocturnal guests that had disturbed my sleep that morning had taken shelter. Perhaps it was too dangerous to go on but I would give it an hour before agreeing to turn around.

Little by little the flow of rocks slowed. Inside the tunnel we saw that drivers and passengers were rolling rocks to the open side of the tunnel and throwing them into the river below. We walked quickly up the road, one eye on the slope above and joined them inside the tunnel and started shifting stone. Every now and again a larger rock would roll down the slope and we all jumped back from the mouth of the tunnel waiting for it to hit the road or roll right over it and into the river. The noise of its passing echoed in the confines of the tunnel. Once the dust had settled, if there was no more sounds of falling rocks, someone would sneak a peek up the slope to check for further danger before we all went back to work.

We had a four wheel vehicle so our aim was just to flatten the mound to give us sufficient clearance under the roof of the tunnel and at a sufficiently low slope across the road so as not to tip us over onto our side.

Nassir was satisfied he could get through so he went back to the jeep, engaged four wheel drive, revved the engine and bounced across the blockage. The surface was very bumpy and the jeep rocked from side to side and it could not have been a comfortable ride for the driver or passengers. There was a cheer from all those that had been shifting rock, as the jeep stopped on the tarmac beyond the blockage, in the safety of the avalanche tunnel. I got back into the jeep and we headed on up the road. Looking back, another jeep had managed to get through, but it would take a bit more work to allow cars or lorries to pass unimpeded.

There were more stones on the road to swerve around, more retaining walls, avalanche tunnels and sections where new walls were being built. Nassir continued to drive with one eye on the road and one on the slope above. I saw several photo opportunities but decided to get through this dangerous section before calling a halt, as I didn't want to stay around here longer than necessary.

The valley opened out where a tributary joined the main river. Here was the entrance to the Khunjerab National Park which was a ranger station and an office to collect entry fees, located at a place called Dhee (although I had also seen it called Dih, the local spelling was the same but obviously when translated into English, this place like many others and when reading dishes on a menu had multiple English spellings).

The price was advertised on a big board at the entrance. Nationals were charged 40 rupees, about US 40 cents, whilst foreigners were charged $8 dollars. This left me with mixed feelings, as I object to differential pricing and felt that I was being fleeced. On the other hand, I reasoned that I could afford more but thought that the differential was excessive and the government had already had £120 off me for my visa (foreigners coming across the border from China now don't even need to pay for a visa). I had made an effort to get here to an out of the way destination, despite security concerns and they wanted more from me. I paid up (but noticed that my driver and two guides were able to get in for free as they were with me).

Just 400 metres further on, around a corner, was a check point manned by police and the local militia, the Khunjerab Security Force or KSF. Apparently, there were new regulations as to who was allowed past this particular check point. Certain nationalities were barred from further progress, amongst them US, Canadians, British and French (coincidentally all large providers of troops for the International Security Assistance Force, ISAF in neighbouring Afghanistan).

On appeal to let me through, mobile phones were pulled out to refer to superiors to check whether I might be allowed through. A senior official in casual clothes, appeared as did another gentleman in a black leather jacket, giving the impression of a mobster or a Russian KGB agent. There were exchanges of mobile phones, to speak to superiors and to check orders and regulations. An American had recently walked around the post and carried on up into the mountains. A party of ten French mountaineers had been stopped but managed to persuade the authorities to allow them through the previous week.

Our appeals were all to no avail. The senior person was in casual dress, but obviously the man in charge, as everyone, except the man in the leather jacket, looked to him for orders. He apologised in English but re-confirmed that I could not go any further and when I queried why, the response was security, which I didn't believe. I couldn't see why it was safe for Etso (travelling on a Japanese passport) plus guides and driver, to be able to continue as I don't believe bandits or terrorists would distinguish by nationality. I discounted security from landslides as these are indiscriminate so it could only be political.

On pressing further, it was the Chinese who didn't want large numbers of tourists milling about at the border post which didn't cut any ice with me either, as there were so few tourists anyway and the Japanese are famous for taking photos whilst on holiday. Any ban on photography has been made pointless since search engine street view, bird's eye views and other satellite imagery have been readily available on line to the public for ages.

I was not going to get a proper and believable explanation, so I let it go. I was told I was welcome to stay this side of the barrier but not to go up the road. The new plan was for me to stay behind whilst the jeep would go on up to the border and would return to pick me up in three hours. I waved goodbye and wondered what I was going to do.

I walked back down the road for a couple of hundred meters and turned into the scrubland towards the river. I saw a footbridge and made my way across and headed up the side valley. I was walking through what looked like a deserted village, no glass in the windows, roofs collapsed into the buildings, no smoke from the few chimneys left standing and everywhere was overgrown. Out of nowhere, two armed civilians called me over and asked me where I was going. I wasn't concerned, as we were still close to the checkpoint and they didn't seem threatening.

I said I was going for a walk. I pretended not to understand all their questions, hoping that they would lose interest and would let me carry on. Then they asked whether I had permission to walk here and asked to see my police permit. After a further exchange of questions and answers, they escorted me back to the check point where a crowd of officials gathered and my escorts told their side of the story.

The same man, in casual clothes in charge, asked me what I was doing. I explained that I wanted to walk up the valley. Why did I want to walk up the valley? Because I like walking in the mountains. From the look on their faces, I guessed that they thought anyone voluntarily wanting to walk in the mountains must be mad. How far did I want to walk they asked. I explained that my plan was to walk for about an hour and a quarter up the valley, before turning round to retrace my steps and wait ready to meet up with my jeep and guides that had gone up the road.

I was given an apology and told this was not possible, but they reiterated their hospitality and that I was welcome to stay here. I pointed to the other side of the valley and asked if I could go for a walk on that side of the valley. But no, that was not possible either, as there were no paths and there was a lot of loose rock, but again, I was welcome to stay here. Staying in the same spot for three hours didn't appeal, especially for a person like myself, with itchy feet and a curious nature. As a last chance, I asked if I could walk back down the road. His faced brightened and I was told that if I stuck to the road they would not stop me but, and here his face became solemn again, added that there was a danger from falling rocks.

Well at least I could go somewhere, so I headed off back down the road. I passed the KNP compound and felt that I had been forced to part with my $8 entrance fee under false pretences. They must have known that certain foreigners were not allowed beyond the check point, just 400m up the road, but had still taken my money.

After about 500m, the sides of the valley closed in, as I walked back towards the narrow gorge that I had come up earlier, but still within eye sight of the checkpoint. There were large scree slopes up to my left and across the narrow raging river at the side of the road, there were more steep scree slopes on the other side. Standing there in the middle of the road, with no traffic and unlike my earlier experience here, in the jeep, there was no noise from the sound of the jeep's engine or the rush of air past its open windows.

The earlier clouds had been blown away and except for a few small puffy white clouds, the sky was blue. The sun shone and warmed the thin air. Up the slope, to my left, was a pair of mountain goats, making their way across the slope. Magpies swooped and squawked their raucous squawk. Other birds flew between the low branches of the scrubland around me.

It was wonderfully peaceful. Then, I noticed every now and again, a rock would roll down the slope. They were small but there was a constant although intermittent fall of rocks. Some of the rocks on the road had come down from the mountains above. One of these was half a meter across and as I ventured further down into the ever narrowing gorge, there were further examples of large rocks, littering the road.

Perhaps it wasn't so safe to walk along here, no one was about to provide any assistance and if I was hit, I could lie alone for ages before being found. Also, it wasn't a relaxing walk to walk forward, whilst continually looking up to see whether you might see the big one coming and jump out of the way. I turned round and headed back to the safety of the check point, in a broader section of the valley.

Passing the KNP compound, one of the rangers came out and invited me in for some tea. He introduced himself as Wali. Green tea came together with a packet of biscuits. We chatted about his job and his responsibilities to protect and monitor the wildlife in the park and to discourage poaching. He had a young family, a girl aged four and a boy aged one. They speak Burushaski at home and are fluent in Urdu. The eldest girl is just starting to learn English in school.

We touched on nationality and he was quite animated, saying that this area used to be independent and issued its own visas. The Hunza valley was a princely state that continued up to 1974, when it was dissolved and incorporated into Pakistan. They regard themselves as Hunza first, Kashmiri second and Pakistani in third position. There was a ground swell of public opinion for a resolution of the Jammu and Kashmir issue, where both Pakistan and India claim control and both occupy a part of the area. A return to peace and perhaps some autonomy seems out of reach, or at least a long way away.

His view on Chinese involvement was mixed. It was good to receive aid and he was thankful for that, although it would also mean that the KKH is likely to be widened and improved which would encourage more traffic along the KKH, through the length of their valley. He mentioned plans to build a railway which I had heard before, but wondered where they would lay the tracks, given the mountainous terrain and twisting valleys where any development may destroy the special nature of the area.

Development was not always a benefit to the local population but developing the KKH and a rail link would shrink the distance for Chinese exports, to the west and avoid the long sea passage south past Vietnam, around Singapore, the pirates in the Malacca Straits and the Indian Ocean.

There was significant international aid, provided to the Hunza Foundation from international charities which helped the displaced people from the landslide which formed the dam and Lake Attabad. People were resettled in Karimabad and other local towns and villages. People were not returning yet as it was unsure whether the lake level had stabilised and with the spring snow melt the level may yet increase again.

I thanked him for his time and the tea and left him to get on with his job. I paced the 400m between the KNP and the KSF and the 500m below the KNP. I reflected that the entrance fee to the national park of $8 for 400m, must make it the most expensive tolls I have ever paid for a stretch of road in the world. I made a point of looking at all the bushes, the flowers and stopping to look at the birds to help pass the time. The only traffic I saw, in all this time, was a bus full of Chinese workers heading for one of the construction sites along the road.

Time still passed slowly, but eventually the jeep returned. I eagerly climbed in and we headed back down the valley. Not far down the road was a boulder, the size of a mini bus, lying on the other side of the road. But on its way down from the slope, on our side of the road, it had hit the carriage way on our side and punched a big hole in the tarmac, before coming to rest on the other carriageway. Nassir slowed and bumped around the hole on the hard shoulder. I didn't remember this particular obstruction, on the way up and was glad that I hadn't gone for a walk down the road by myself earlier and equally glad to be heading back towards a slightly safer area.

We were approaching the avalanche tunnel, when the jeep lurched and Nassir braked hard. We had a puncture on a back tyre. The spare wheel didn't seem to fit the back axle. Nassir was unflustered and took the front wheel off and put it on the back and put the spare on the front. I wasn't sure how this worked from an engineering point of view, because surely a wheel would fit on the axle or wouldn't. All I could guess, was that the engineering tolerances were sufficiently wide to let this happen. I didn't like to think how we would have coped if it didn't work. In all this time, no traffic passed so we could have been marooned here for a while.

There hadn't been much that I could do to help, so I left Nassir to change wheels and spent some time investigating and relaxing by the river's edge, as far as possible from the steep valley sides and any falling rocks. When we reached the avalanche tunnel, the debris had been cleared away and we went straight through without slowing down.

In Sost, we stopped to get some engine oil. It was another visit to a garage and I was wondering whether the jeep was good enough to get back to the hotel, let alone for the next few days or further down valley, to Lake Attabad and back to Karimabad and a trusted jeep.

We were making good progress and the landscape was more open with fields here and there where there was water to irrigate the fields otherwise it was a rolling expanse of dusty rocky terrain of undulating countryside.

Just 10kms south out of Sost, we were going through a village and the jeep again lurched to the left and Nassir braked hard. Yet another puncture. There was a hole I could put my finger through and the tyre was as flat as a pancake. And we had already used the spare tyre.

There was a funeral ceremony underway across the road, with a lot of people milling around on the periphery. Nassir wandered over to the milling group and talked to some of the crowd. In less than five minutes, there was a group of 6 men who turned up in another jeep, with another wheel and gave Nassir their spare. It was duly fitted with lots of help from all those hanging about, as if this was the biggest show in town and everyone wanted some of the action. I realised that I had seen more tyre changes in three days in Pakistan than I had in 30 years of motoring back in the UK.

We got back to the Passu Ambassador where Mohammad Karim and I got out and we said our farewells to Judith, Etso and Karim, who were heading down the road to cross Lake Attabad, to spend that night in Karimabad, whilst I was to spend a few days with Mohammad Karim based at the Passu Ambassador and explore some of the local area.

I had some spare time so I headed off towards the local village. A short distance down the road, there was the local cricket ground. The pitch had been rolled flat but was largely bare sand with a few blades of grass and a scattering of weeds. A match had just finished. Passu had been playing Gulmit, the village further down the valley, near Lake Attabad and Passu had won. The crowd was spilling out of the ground and walking back to the village, with a trophy held high at the head of the crowd, with lots of waving of flags, chanting and singing.

I mingled with the crowd as they headed home. There were women in bright dresses, walking and talking in small groups and groups of raucous boys, some in shalwaar chemise and some in white shirts and black trousers. A few of the boys took time off from chanting for the opportunity to practise their English.

I had no idea what further celebrations were to take place, but where the road to the village turned away from the main road, I decided to turn around and head back to the hotel. Heading towards the hotel entrance, I noticed a Specialized mountain bike, resting against the wall outside the entrance, the same brand that I have myself at home.

It suddenly struck me that in all of the traffic in the towns that I had seen, and not just in Islamabad, there were colourful trucks, packed buses, cars of all makes, mopeds with multiple passengers, but there had been few, if any, bicycles. Sometimes when travelling, it is as much what you don't see, as much as what you do see. And I noticed that it was not padlocked.

It was a good quality bike with quality accessories, not a cheap brand and must have belonged to someone who obviously took his mountain biking seriously. Inside, Mohammad Karim was chatting to two men over a cup of tea. The bike's owner was Saijat Malik, an independent television programme producer, who was staying here overnight together with his cameraman. He was filming a series of programmes about himself mountain biking, through the three mountain ranges of the Himalayas, the Karakoram and the Hindu Kush. This was to be a thirteen part series, each programme being a half hour slot.

We had a long chat about mountain biking, the local area, his other projects and the ease or difficulties of making a programme. I was surprised that it wasn't scripted and that they rarely took retakes relying on having sufficient shots to create each block of 26 minutes of content for each half hour slot, the balance being for adverts and credits. It was quite an eye opener on how programmes are made.

Chapter 8

The Shimshal valley

Nassir picked myself and Mohammad Karim up, early the next morning and we headed northwards up the road. After a short distance, we turned right off the KKH and bumped along a rough track. There was a small monument to the opening of the Shimshal valley jeep road by Sheikh Ghazanfar Hussain in October 2003. It took nearly 20 years to build the track to reach the top of the valley and prior to this, it was only accessible on foot or horseback. This track would take us more than 55kms up the valley to the Shimshal village, high up the valley where it guards a pass above the village at over 4,735m.

I had asked the previous night what there was to know about Shimshal but the flow of conversation had drifted back and forth about mountain biking, northern Pakistan, the difficulty of boosting tourism, television programme making, why I wanted to visit this area and so on.

But I had learnt two interesting points. The first, was that the Mehtar of Karimabad had used Shimshal like a prison, banishing criminals here until they had completed their sentence. The second, was that there is an annual yak race where riders sit aside these animals and race them, apparently a unique event not repeated anywhere else in the world. Unfortunately, the race was a few weeks away so I would not get to see any yak riding.

We stopped at a police post, just in front of the bridge over the river. A flag was rustling in the light breeze but no smoke, no smell of any fire or cooking and there was no one about. It was just gone 7am and we had to rouse the police from their slumbers. They duly checked our passports, our local passes and took details of our names in a book. I took a quick look at the other entries in the book, I couldn't read the hand written names as the policeman entered our details, but judging by the dates and the large gaps in between those dates, it showed that few foreigners had come this way this season.

The track narrowed and dropped towards the edge of the river and we came to a suspension bridge across the Hunza River. The terrain was rocky but open, as we were still on the main valley floor, but as we crossed the Hunza River and headed towards the Shimshal valley, the valley sides closed in.

The track was cut into the mountain side, not too far above the water level. In places the valley sides closed right in against the river's edge and were so narrow and steep that the road was hacked out of the living rock. There was solid rock beneath us, to our left and overhanging the road above us. Around a corner there was a narrow strip between the road and the rock face where a spring seeped fresh water from the base of the cliff. Here was a sudden splash of green foliage before the road side returned to bare rock or scree as we bumped past.

The cliffs towered above us and often, they were so high above us and so close together, that we couldn't see the cliff tops. Here and there, were great boulders that had fallen from above, partially blocking the river that had not yet been eroded or pushed further downstream.

I was told that there were seven bridges across the river to take the track from one side to the other as the road builders struggled to push the route through less challenging terrain to avoid solid rock or keep away from dangerous scree slopes. I didn't keep a tally but each bridge was a suspension bridge, stretching high above a narrow gorge, often with an approach that required a tight 90 degree turn to get on and off the bridge itself. These bends and corners could only be negotiated by jeeps or similarly sized vehicles. No lorry could ever make its way up here.

The first bridge crossed a gorge, where there were hot water springs on the valley side. The air was laden with a strong smell of sulphur and the valley sides had streaks of yellow deposits from the sulphurous gases, escaping from the ground. The valley widened but not much further up the valley there was a deep narrow gorge. The road climbed high up the side of the valley to negotiate this gorge and we were now hundreds of metres above the river.

In cross section the upper part of the valley was a typical U shape created by a glacier cutting downwards. After the glacier had retreated, the river had subsequently cut its deep narrow gorge into the bottom of this U shaped valley. The road had to avoid the gorge and made its way across the upper part of the valley.

The track was just wide enough for one vehicle. There was a steep slope of scree falling down to the road on one side. On the other side, just inches from our tyres, the ground tumbled away steeply down to the vertical cliffs of the river gorge. We had been lucky not to meet another vehicle, as there was nowhere for two vehicles to pass.

I found myself holding my breath, partly at the spectacular scenery and partly from fear. We could hear the river thundering far below us but rarely caught a glimpse of the river itself. I was not reassured, as Nassir took one hand off the wheel, to fiddle with the radio to see whether he could get a signal even as he steered around a bend.

Nassir had noticed the dust on the road, ahead of another vehicle, several kilometres ahead of us. By some unknown agreement, the other car had pulled over, stopped and was waiting for us to pass. We had been travelling for nearly two hours and this was the first vehicle that we had encountered. We pulled alongside and exchanged pleasantries, none of which I understood as here, the local language that they speak is Wakhi. But asking Nassir for a translation, the conversation took the usual pattern between drivers on remote tracks consisting of some greetings, followed by questions on the state of the bridges and whether there were any rockslides or other dangers ahead.

We came across a shrine and stopped. The shrine consisted of a small plinth rectangle, less than 2m by 1.5m, about knee high with a metal offertory box on top. I looked around the plinth but there was no sign or writing. There was a number of poles randomly stuck in the ground around the plinth, none taller than a man each topped with a piece of square cloth like a flag which flapped in the breeze.

This was similar to the roadside box, opposite the Rakaposhi View Cafe that we had seen earlier. By putting money into the box, travellers hope to encourage the deities to whom the shrine is dedicated, to look after them and assist them to reach their destination safely. I couldn't see to which deity this shrine was dedicated to, but given the terrain, I was only too happy to call on any help available and slipped some notes through the slot in the top of the box.

There were several streams that flowed off the mountain pastures, high up beyond the valley sides that came tumbling down crossing the road and joining the river, somewhere to our left. These streams could turn into raging torrents, whenever the sky was clear and the sun shone strongly, melting the snow on the hills above. The torrent that is produced washes the track away or brings down big boulders, so the track can be rather indistinct whenever it crossed a stream and drivers were left to their own devices to pick a route avoiding big boulders which could ground a jeep and equally the deeper sections of the stream, which might flood the engine.

I had wanted to take a picture of the jeep negotiating one of these fords, so I made an arbitrary choice of one of the streams and got out. To get the right picture of the jeep, advancing towards me through the water, I had to walk through the stream to get into position. Then I would wave to Nassir to drive forward.

I found a place where the water looked shallow and took off my boots and socks, tying them around my neck. With one hand holding my trouser bottoms and hem of my shalwaar chemise out of the water and my left hand holding my camera, raised slightly above my head, but out to one side as extra balance, I waded into the water. The rocky stream bed was very uneven and I took every step carefully to ensure I didn't lose my balance. I sometimes used my left hand, still gripping the camera as a support against a boulder as I used a foot to probe the depth, but once the water was above my knee and I still hadn't touched the bottom, I would back off and try somewhere else.

The water was carrying a lot of silt so I could not judge how deep it was, without using a foot to probe the depth. Twice I had attempted a crossing at what looked like a likely place, only to be forced to turn around and find another place to cross, where the current was not too strong and where it was not too deep.

The water was snow melt, flowing straight off glaciers high above us and needless to say, it was freezing cold. After the initial shock, the crossing became easier, as the cold water took away some of the discomfort of the rough rocks on the soles of my feet, but I was across and waved to Nassir to follow in the jeep. I had stubbed a toe on a rock and blood was pooling around my toes, but I hardly noticed and took a step into the water for the cold water to stem the bleeding. The bottoms of my trousers were also wet, inevitable from the amount of splashing I had received, negotiating a path through rocks and water.

The resulting photograph was not the spectacular award winning photo that I had hoped to achieve. If the stream was passable for me, then it would be easy for the jeep to negotiate so the crossing was rather uneventful and unremarkable. I should have been on the lookout for a difficult section and made a note to take a photo at that point on the way back but my feet were wet and frozen.

I hopped back into the jeep and hoped that the frozen blocks of ice, that had once been my feet, would dry off quickly in the mountain air, so I could get my socks and boots back on. I was thankful for having made an offering at the shrine, as the clouds had cleared and the sun was shining, warming the thin mountain air but also melting some of the snow high up in the mountains, that would increase the water in the streams later in the day.

There are several glaciers in this particular area and we came across our first glacier in the Shimshal valley, the Mulungudhi glacier flowing down from Mulungudhi Sar 7,202m. We were going up the valley and on the left hand side, across the river, to our right, was the snout of a glacier that stretched away into the mountains out of sight. As the glacier advanced, it pushes its snout across a broad front along the rivers far edge as if to block the river and dam it completely.

In turn, the river constantly erodes the face of the glacier, either by melting it or undercutting its leading face. Debris from the glacier tumbles into the river and is washed downstream. This constant erosion always ensure that somewhere here, there is always a freshly exposed bank of glacial ice, some white, some a deep blue colour, but with a top covering of rock debris.

I got out to get a closer look and noticed there was a cold breeze that wafted down the glacier's valley and hit me full in the face. Despite the bright sunshine, this was distinctly cold for which I had not brought sufficient warm clothing and although my feet had dried and I was wearing walking boots, I was happy to take a few quick photos and hurry on.

Local legend has it that this particular glacier has never advanced and blocked the river completely. However, the Yazghail glacier further along the valley, has a much more dangerous history. The Mehtar posted a number of sentries at the snout of this glacier to watch and report on its progress. Glaciers are slow moving, but they can create enormous damage, especially for those communities downstream.

Should the glacier, coming down a side valley, reach the far side of the main valley, it creates an ice dam and as water cannot continue to flow downstream, it begins to back up in the main valley. There are various forces at work but simply put, there is a chance of a cataclysmic bursting of the dam known as a glacial lake outburst flood.

All the pent up water behind the ice dam escapes, causing a massive flood which can wipe out whole communities for large distances downstream. And the Yazghail glacier has a history of creating such devastating events which were known to the ancient local population. Hence, the Mehtar's stationing of sentries to give warning of such an event. These still happen regularly today but unless they are huge and particularly destructive, they rarely get international media attention or reported in the international press.

The road crosses the river and heads upwards, across a boulder strewn valley floor until the rate of ascent slows as the terrain flattens out and the valley floor widens. Now we were high enough into the mountains to see various peaks from the valley floor and many were clearly visible, including the dominant Destaghil Sar 7,885m, plus plenty of snow-capped majestic peaks.

This is a good mountaineering area and I saw a sign directing climbers up a side valley. Its mountains, not just Destaghil Sar but others such as Shimshal White Horn at 6,303m, Minglik Sar 6,150m, Lupghar Sar 7,200m, Yazghail Sar 6,000m, Kunjut Sar I at 7,760 and Kunjat Sar II at 6,831m plus several other peaks are all nearby and challenging peaks to climb and are a pull for mountaineers. Indeed, Samina Baig is a local woman and was the first Pakistani woman to scale the world's highest mountain, Everest and has also climbed the highest peaks of all seven continents.

The road crested a rise and followed a river cut terrace. In the distance, after more than three hours of travelling, I could see some human habitation that had also been built on the terrace, away from any potential flooding from the river, out of sight to our left. There were low squat buildings, stone walls and in contrast to most of the rest of the valley, some green foliage indicating that there must be a spring nearby to support the few farmsteads.

The fields around the houses were relatively small. These were for housing the animals in winter and to provide some protection against the icy wind. There was a little grass, a few scraggy shrubs and some shrubs that were tall but not quite what you might call a tree. The winters were too harsh and long for trees to grow well, but some stunted specimens did their best.

Below the terrace, on the wide flat expense of flood plain, adjacent to the distant river, were large enclosed square areas, bounded by stone walls. There was more rock than grass and only a few shrubs, struggling to put down roots into the rocks. There was a small irrigation ditch but little sign of any crops being grown. The irrigation water is used to water the fields for pasture to cut for fodder to store for the animals for winter.

After cutting fodder, the field may be used for rough grazing for the last green shoots before winter sets in and the animals are brought back to be near the farmhouse. The strong walls are as much to keep the animals inside in the autumn, when they are allowed in whilst they are there to keep them out whilst the pasture is growing ready to be cut for winter fodder.

There were no animals to be seen anywhere. As soon as winter gives way to spring and as weather permits, the animals are herded off to higher pastures, for the short summer high above the village, often accompanied by some men from the family. These pastures may be several days walk away from the village and the herders may be away for weeks at a time.

Autumn is always a critical time for herders this high up in the mountains. If the animals are brought down too early, they miss the last of the alpine pastures and will eat through their fodder, before the coming of spring. Leaving the animals for too long in the mountains and you may not be able to herd them home, through the snow and they may die of cold and starvation. Typically they go up in May and return in October.

The road was hemmed in closely between walls on either side and was only a little wider than the jeep and no place to pass. Luckily, there are only a few vehicles that ever come up here. For most of the year, they are superfluous, as the winter conditions are too harsh and farmers are too busy in summer to have the time to go anywhere, let alone have the money to afford a luxury such as a vehicle. The nearest petrol station is a round trip of more than 100kms, achievable in summer but the road is impassable in winter. The locals have no use for vehicles so don't see the point in making the road any wider.

The road left the village with the stone walls either side, giving way to a barren landscape. There was another similar small hamlet before we reached the centre of the main village of Shimshal. Between the small hamlets, the terrain was loose boulders and stones, an occasional plant struggling to grow and unlike the walled fields, it was bumpy, stony and inhospitable to any pasture or arable farming enterprise.

In contrast, around the main village the fields were larger with more trees and the soil was noticeably better with fields surrounded by neat stone walls. There were fields of potatoes, growing beneath ridges of earth and fields of wheat gently swaying in the breeze. Unlike everywhere else I had visited recently, where the harvest had finished, here the wheat was still green and was sometime away from harvest. It wasn't surprising, as the village is at an altitude of over 3,100m.

The potatoes grown here at altitude, are favoured by farmers in the lower valleys as seed potatoes. This is allegedly due to their greater resistance to disease, so are more highly prized and can command a premium price. Some are even exported overseas. It used to be a profitable business, until Lake Attabad was created. This caused an ongoing interruption to trade, making it both more difficult and expensive and this had an adverse affect on the farming community.

There was quite a lot of bird activity which was noteworthy, as there was so little birdlife on the journey here. The rough countryside outside the village provides little cover or food whereas the fields here provide rich pickings for small birds. And therefore, where there are a lot of small birds that in turn, attracts birds of prey. In the trees overlooking the fields was a type of falcon which waits in the trees for the small birds to break cover where upon they swoop down and attack. I watched for a while and saw several attempts but no successful attacks.

Driving through the village, there was a new community centre and a new school donated by Germany. This was a great advance as pupils up to the age of 15 years old can now be educated locally. Previously, they either stayed at home and received no education or if the family could afford it, the children would have to go away to a local larger town, such as Karimabad and board there to receive an education. Students over 15 years old still have to go elsewhere but there are several college and university faculties throughout the northern areas.

There is also hydroelectricity even this high up in the mountains. Water is taken from the river coming down from Odver

Sar 6,303m, high above the village. There is a problem, in that electricity can only be generated from June to October. For the rest of the year, the water flow is insufficient or non-existent, as it is frozen solid. Kerosene and gas is expensive so this puts a lot of pressure on local trees which provide firewood. Although trees can grow here, there are only a few, as the resource that they represent is in great demand. The leaves are used for fodder and the wood burnt to heat food and homes.

However, Shimshal is leading the way in solar energy. Virtually every house, plus the school, have some solar panels and can generate sufficient energy for their own needs. This is great when the sun shines, but if it is cloudy and in the depths of winter, then an alternative fuel supply is still needed.

I wanted to get a better view of the village, from a bird's point of view and conveniently for me, there was a bluff above the village. Nassir dropped us off and we started walking up a slope towards what looked like a good vantage point. We reached some trees but our path was blocked by a wall topped by thorns and a steeply sloping bank above. The well-trodden path had lead this way but seemed to peter out which didn't make sense. A women's voice greeted us from above, through thick foliage and Mohammad Karim explained where we were heading. She said we needed to back track five metres and head to our right and there we could climb over the wall.

We followed the directions and true enough, came to what I hesitate to describe as, a stile, but was more like a bit of the wall but without the thorns and a strategically placed rock, to assist those with shorter legs. We clambered over and were greeted by a lady with fine cheek bones, dressed plainly but wearing a big smile. We started chatting, but after the initial greetings and introductions in Urdu, she reverted to the local language Wakhi and Mohammad Karim translated into English for me.

She was a local farmer whose fields we were in. She took us around the farm and showed us the best view of the village from the bluff. There was a panoramic view, both down and up the valley. She was polite and civil, but very apologetic, as she did not have a fire lit to offer a hot drink and her husband was not at home so she could not invite us in. I was equally civil, but as we had to move on, I was disappointed not to have stayed longer or seen inside her compact farmhouse but I respected the local customs.

We headed back down the hill by a clearly recognisable track, to reach the valley floor again. There was a local hotel in the village and as I had had an early start, it felt like late afternoon, although it was only shortly after midday. The hotel was a newly built single storey building. I took off my shoes to leave them with a collection of other footwear outside and entered the building.

It was solidly built which had opened just a couple of months previously. It was run by Mizra, a former local guide who had built the hotel from scratch. There was a large central room, with a hole in the roof to allow smoke to escape from a fireplace in the centre of the room. This served as the main reception room, having both sitting and dining areas. It also doubled as a dormitory so although the hotel only had 6 individual guest rooms, it could sleep more than two dozen guests if you are willing to share. This might not suit everybody's tastes but at least the body heat would keep you warm and the price was very reasonable.

It was a family run hotel and there were several people sitting in the reception area, having a chat over some tea. I wasn't sure who was a guest, who was family and who was an employee. His eldest two sons were in higher education and boarded away from home, only coming home occasionally, although his younger children were being educated locally.

I had some green tea and biscuits, plus the chance to relax indoors with some protection from the wind and sun, plus a chance to sit down on comfortable rugs and carpets. I had a packed lunch with me from the hotel and had been assured that it was alright to eat it in the hotel but I resisted the temptation and restricted myself to an individually wrapped biscuit and a piece of fruit. The rest I would share with Nassir, or eat on the hoof in the jeep.

We started our journey back down the valley. The sun was warming the air, so we took the canvas top off the jeep. The sun was melting the snow higher up the valley sides and the streams were noticeably more swollen than when we had come up the valley in the morning.

After crossing one of the bridges, across the river we crested a bluff crossing one side of the valley and we were hit by a strong wind blowing straight down the valley. It was cold and it carried some fine particles that stung any exposed skin. We passed a sign announcing a re-forestation project and we could see the young saplings that had been planted which we had missed on the journey up the valley.

The area was fenced to protect it from animals and with the shade and water, there was a covering of grass under the trees. This would provide some fodder for animals during the winter for the local village, which also gave the village an incentive to look after the trees. A car was parked opposite the sign, with its engine running whilst the passengers read the sign. I would have liked to have had a closer look but it was unpleasant just here in the wind and the windblown sand, so we didn't hang around.

Another sight that we had missed on the way up, was a group of tents on the far river bank. This was a camp for itinerant miners, who panned the river gravels for gold. I had panned for gold at a claim in Dawson City in the Yukon, in Canada, so I was interested to compare notes. We crossed a rickety bridge and drew up at the edge of the camp.

The equipment that they used was the same as used by traditional miners in the Yukon. Gravel was shovelled into a shallow pan, suspended by ropes from a frame. Water is washed over the gravel as the pan is agitated, washing the lighter gravel over the edge and the heavier gold sinks to the bottom to be collected by hand.

I asked how successful they were and several of the men pulled out small zip lock plastic bags with a few flakes of gold. One man showed me a nugget the size of a tooth, which he was obviously very proud of having found, wrapped in cloth, inside a plastic bag inside a leather pouch that he kept in the chest pocket in his shirt.

They weren't working as the water level had risen too high and had totally immersed the gold bearing gravels. I looked around the camp and the tents were worn, the children were playing happily but their clothes were threadbare and torn and everyone was covered in grime. They have to earn enough during the summer so they can survive over the winter, before they come back for another season. I wondered how long that proud miner might be able to hang on to his precious nugget, before he had to sell it.

We crossed back over the bridge and headed down the valley. Around a bend, we came face to face with another vehicle, our third vehicle encounter of the day, heading up the valley. It was a Toyota pickup, packed with passengers. Here, the track was just a single car width and after some shouting at each other, Nassir reversed back up the road, round a corner and revved the engine to reverse the jeep up a steep slope, as far off the road as he could.

The Toyota crept forward and with a lot of helpful waving and shouting from the passengers, the driver inched past us, with only inches to spare from either scratching our paintwork or a precipitous drop down a sheer cliff to the raging river below. I was glad that I wasn't driving that pickup. Bur reflecting on our journey, I would describe this particular day's journey, as one of the top three day trips in the northern areas.

Mohammad Karim and I were the only guests in the hotel for breakfast in the morning but at least we had a great breakfast of scrambled eggs and green tea. Nassir picked us up shortly after breakfast and took us through Passu. He dropped us off a short distance beyond the village, at the side of the road and disappeared back up the road. This looked an unlikely place to start a trek and had I been on my own, I would have been concerned but I trusted both Mohammad Karim and Nassir.

Our trek today, was to see the Mehtar's horse stables at Yaskhandan on the far side of the river. Mohammad Karim, led me away from the road and down a boulder strewn slope. There was a little discernible path, as we hopped from boulder to boulder. We headed down the slope, towards the river and rounding a bend, I got my first view of the bridge that we were going to take.

The river here is about 330 meters wide and stretching from our side to the far side, was a rope suspension bridge just wide enough for two people to pass in opposite directions. The ropes (actually half inch thick steel cables) were tied into a great concrete and stone block, and looked solid enough. At the start of the bridge, we were over 25 meters above the river surface, but in the centre where the weight of the bridge caused it to dip, it was perhaps 15 meters above the river.

The bed of the bridge immediately caught my eye. It was made up of wooden slats, on average each one was about two inches wide, weaved alternately between the five steel cables taking the weight of the bridge and the load. The bed was not continuous as the slats were an adult pace apart and between the slats you could look through and see the surfacing of the water racing underneath. A walker could not look straight ahead and trust that your feet were in the right place. The gaps ensured that you had to look down all the time in order to place your feet centrally onto the slats.

There was a cable that might pass as a hand rail but at the beginning of the bridge, it was at head height so if you toppled sideways, there was nothing between you and the river below. I would find out later that as it dipped towards the centre of the bridge, it didn't keep its distance from the bed and so by the centre of the bridge it was below waist height so the reverse was the case that if you toppled sideways you would tumble over the top of the hand rail into the river.

Mohammad Karim set off first and after he was 20 meters across, I set out. I started out and tested the handrail … it swayed a lot. With two of us on the bridge and a breeze in the air, this caused the bridge to sway up and down and side to side. This was not a crossing for the faint hearted.

Mohammad Karim was not heavy, but I was not trusting the slats to support my weight, plus a day sack, a Camelbak full of water, lunch, waterproofs, plus warm clothes and as towel (having learnt a lesson from yesterday when I got wet feet). The slats were all weathered by wind and rain, they were warped, the creaking of the bridge had dislodged some of the slats and some were only weaved between two or three of the five cables.

Some had been replaced with whatever was available locally, such as fence posts or branches from a tree or shrub. It was hard to get a rhythm as the gaps between slats differed, some were short steps, and others were a bit of a stretch. I placed my feet firmly on the spot where the slat connected with the cable. I was hedging my bets and not trusting on just the strength of the wood.

It took over 15 minutes to cross but I did take time to look around and enjoy the moment. There was the constant noise of the river rushing underneath. Water washing past rocks on the river's edge echoed across the river, amplified and directed into the centre of the river by the steep banks. These sounds were augmented by water rushing around a gravel bank in the middle of the river. Looking down at the surface of the water, the heavy burden of slit that the river carried, created a patina beneath the surface of the water which glinted in the bright sunlight.

However good the view might have been and however exciting it was to experience swinging on a bridge, a long way above a raging river, where a fall would result in a long plunge into icy water, resulting in drowning, I was delighted to get back onto firm land.

We headed up the bank and veered to our left. There was an indistinct path weaving its way past boulders and down and up gullies that flowed from the higher ground down towards the river. The rocks gave way to pastures with long grass, thorn bushes with their long painful spines and meadow plants with bright flowers. There was plenty of water to feed these thirsty plants but no animals this side of the river, to graze the pastures so the green grass was high and lush.

The fields were hemmed in by low stone walls, protecting yet more pasture. There were fruit trees bearing apricots, walnuts and plums. Also, judging by the heavily leaden down boughs of the apple trees, there was going to be a bumper apple harvest this year.

There were several small buildings, making up a farmstead, but with their windows firmly shut and padlocks on the doors, there was no sign of life. As we crossed the meadows, there was a strong aromatic smell of herbs, nectar and pollen from all the different plants as they fought to attract birds and insects to pollinate themselves. There was thyme, lavender, borage and a host of others I recognised, but was unable to name. The apricots were a bit sour as they were not ready to harvest and the walnuts were soft and white, not brown and hard, ready to eat.

There was the sound of grasshoppers, rubbing their legs together, to announce their presence. Bees buzzed from flower to flower, busily collecting nectar and pollen. Magpies walked amongst the green pastures, feeding on insects and occasionally squawking at each other and at us, who were disturbing their otherwise deserted garden.

There was a small colourful mosque and what may have been a couple of shops in a square, but it didn't look like it had ever been a busy centre of a village and other than the mosque, there appeared to be no public buildings. As we ascended through the village and along the fields and pastures, the path gave way to rock and we had obviously left the village. If this area was where the Mehtar had kept his horses, there was no evidence of any buildings, although the land was productive so it would have been an ideal location.

This looked like an abandoned village, but observations can be misleading. This was an area used by local farmers in the autumn. It was free from animals so pasture and fruit trees could grow without interference. Villagers would live there for the autumn, cutting fodder, harvesting and preserving the fruits from the trees and collecting honey. Some animals would be carried across the rope bridge, to graze on the stalks of the pastures after winter fodder had been cut.

But this side of the valley relied on the foot bridge and was an uninviting place in the winter. Before the winter freeze came, the villagers would leave this area and move back to their villages on the other side of the river, for the winter. We headed back to the river and crossed the rope suspension bridge again. Having done it once, the second time was less daunting.

After crossing the bridge, we turned right and headed back towards Passu which was on our route back to the hotel. Walking through the village, there were the usual single storey farm buildings and houses, a single guest house, a shop next to the main road and a mosque and several small enclosed fields. For the first time, I saw crops other than wheat and potatoes. The soil in the fields, nearest the village had been nurtured by generations of farmers and the soil was thicker and richer. Over the wall of a small market garden, I could see carrots, onions, lettuce, pumpkins and tomatoes.

I had some spare time before dinner, so I decided to go for a short walk. I checked for local knowledge with the brothers who ran the hotel and told Mohammad Karim that I was walking up the road and would take a left hand turn to make an anti-clockwise circuit to bring me back to the road, adjacent to the hotel. I wanted to let someone know where I had planned to walk in case I got lost, had an injury or was kidnapped.

After leaving the road, I was walking through a recently created agricultural area. The terrain had been levelled by bulldozers and irrigation ditches had been dug and all the fields were of the same size. The farm houses were all of an identical modern concrete design set out at regular intervals along a dirt track leading from the main road. There was water and trees had grown tall, giving shade and fruit crops. However, as this was newly created agricultural land, the soil had not had time to develop and was thin and stony.

Walking along the track, some of the farms looked abandoned or perhaps they had never been occupied. This was not a prosperous area and as crops were struggling to grow in the stony soil, the harvests were probably below average. There were a few people about but not the numbers that would be milling about, compared to a similar density of farms in a more established village. Money had obviously been spent to assist the local community but I wondered whether this particular project had been a success or not.

I came to the end of the agricultural area and the track continued on up into the hills beyond. Just out of curiosity, I decided to carry on, but limit myself to walking for just half an hour into the hills, both to ensure I didn't get too far from territory that I recognised and so as not to be too late for dinner.

The terrain was rugged, there was little vegetation and I didn't know where I was going but the views from this far up the valley were interesting and worth the effort. I could see the road disappearing up the valley towards Sost and the Khunjerab Pass. The Hunza River was flowing in the bottom of the valley and I could see the entrance, off the main valley, up towards Shimshal and down towards Passu. Although, it was getting towards late afternoon and the light was fading, I saw no electric lights from any of the buildings, probably another power cut.

I had an unwelcome visitor during the night. I awoke during the night and couldn't get back to sleep and had to go to the bathroom. I fumbled around for the light switch and was mildly surprised when I flicked the switch and the light came on. That mild surprise transformed into a massive surprise when I entered the bathroom and there on the wall in front of me staying perfectly still was a giant reddish centipede the width of a man's hand with each of its individual body segments and associated pair of legs glistening and reflecting the light from the light bulb.

Sensing that this insect was unlikely to kill me with a single bite, I left it alone, I did my business and went back to bed. But the size of its jaws haunted me, and was I sure that Pakistani centipedes were not the most venomous insects known to man? I was never a good biologist at school and trying to get back to sleep was proving a Herculean task, so I decided to go back and remove it so that I could at least get some sleep.

I flicked the switch on and carefully checked the floor, before putting my bare feet on to the tiles. I headed to the bathroom, switched on the light and disaster. The wall upon which the centipede had stayed so still earlier, was now completely bare. I looked high and low, in the bath, under the basin, behind the door and around the window, but no results. I checked under the bed, on the bed, between the sheets, behind the chest of drawers, and everywhere else, but I could not find any sign of a centipede.

Was this good or bad? Had I checked sufficiently diligently, to ensure that it was not in my room. Or was it so well concealed that I had missed it and later that night, it would re-emerge and sting me to death? I did another thorough check and found nothing, I resigned myself to perhaps being killed in my sleep and not waking up in the morning. Needless to say, when the alarm went off in the morning, I wasn't feeling refreshed but relieved that I had managed to survive a vicious attack by perhaps, the world's most venomous centipede. I dressed and banged my shoes together, to ensure there were no unwanted visitors, hiding inside before putting them on.

Chapter 9

Return to Karimabad

Nassir drove into the hotel's car park and came to a halt. He got out and walked around to the front passenger's side and kicked the tyre. It was soft. It looked like there would be a delay, as the spare was put on the back and the back tyre transferred to the front. After this slight delay, we headed for Borit Lake. There were separate signs for both Borit Lake and Borag Lake using different names but pointing in the same direction.

Mohammad Karim confirmed that they were the same place but the lake had different names in different languages which can be very confusing for those not in the know. I had seen Borag Lake a few days earlier so I was a bit disappointed to discover that I was going back to the same place, rather than seeing another lake.

We turned off the main road and headed up the side of the valley. We had left the flat bottom valley and its green foliage and we were back amongst tumbled rocks, with little or no foliage. Higher up the valley side, we came across small flat fields but in a series of terraces, up the side of the valley, with green trees and wheat in the fields. It stood in stark contrast to its barren rocky surroundings. The plan for the day, was to walk from Borag Lake across the Ghulkin glacier, through the village of Ghulkin, to re-join the KKH at Gulmit and cross Lake Attabad back to Karimabad. As I had seen Borag Lake already, I opted for an alternative route to get to the glacier.

Just above the last of the terraced fields, we left Nassir and the jeep to set off across the barren landscape, following a footpath. Towards the top of a slope, we were climbing a narrow defile 2 metres wide with vertical walls, cut into the crest and up to 10 meters deep. Emerging from this defile, we were facing the expanse of the Ghulkin Glacier. The purpose of the defile was suddenly obvious. Melt water from the glacier that flowed down its edge between the ice and the glacier's lateral moraine was diverted through a rock built tunnel, built under the floor of the defile and channelled down towards the terraced fields that we had seen earlier.

The glacier was a mass of angular rocks, over laying the ice of the glacier. There were smooth slopes of ice with a jumble of rocks resting on the top. As the ice melted, the support that it gave to the rocks on top disappears, until the point where the rocks above succumb to gravity and roll down the slope to collect at the bottom. There, pools of icy water and small streams flow across the surface, only to disappear into the gaps between the rocks. Rocks glistened with water everywhere. Smaller stones lying in the streams that had been eroded by running water, were completely smooth. Some rocks that had yet to be subjected to erosion by water, had sharper edges.

Looking at a slope, it was difficult to tell whether it was ice with a covering of debris, or a scree slope. Walking in this terrain was challenging and tiring on the legs. Walking boots would slip on the ice or gain no purchase on scree and every step up, slipped half a step back. You had to pay attention to where you were putting your feet, to avoid both water and icy slopes. We avoided the areas where a stream disappeared beneath the surface. It might be just a small crack or it could be a large crevasse and the extra weight of a man could cause the edge to collapse.

At the same time you had to keep an eye on rocks at the tops of slopes. Small ones were not an issue, but the larger ones could break a leg or crush you to death. Falling rocks have distinctive noises. Higher pitched short sounds were small stones but longer deeper noises were the larger rocks. Often, we would hear a large rock start its descent, dislodging other rocks and we would quickly look up, to see whether it was coming our way. There was the constant noise of falling rocks interspersing the babbling of a dozen streams.

Using the larger stones on the ground, as stepping stones to avoid water and ice was not as fool proof as you might think. Some of them had not settled and would wobble as you placed your weight onto the stone.

Picking a safe route across the glacier was time consuming and tiring. Some of the gullies were so deep and the tops of slopes so high that we lost sight of the surrounding mountains and reference points. Moving forward and keeping the sun on our left, ensured that we continued according to plan to cross the glacier, but still we could walk three sides of a square to avoid some hazard only to have to walk another three sides of a square to avoid the next hazard.

I never asked whether it was safe, but I am sure that an English health and safety assessment would suggest that we should have turned around and found an alternative route but you didn't hire a local guide and totally disregard his advice. Although, once I saw Mohammad Karim, heading straight towards a steep icy slope, with a large rectangular rock more than 20 meters wide teetering on the edge of the top of the slope, with just about half of the rock jutting out into the air above the slope.

I did query our safety at this particular point and Mohammad Karim appreciated my concern and suggested an alternative route. The alternative route was over a stream, across a jumble of boulders and up a steep icy slope with more rocks teetering on top. I didn't like the alternative either and it was far from ideal but as the rocks above the slope were smaller, it looked like the better option.

We started heading downhill and soon came across more dams and irrigation ditches, diverting the glacial waters towards fields and the village buildings beyond. We had successfully negotiated our way across the Ghulkin Glacier, without injury. We walked through the village and followed a road downhill, towards the KKH. From our vantage point, high above the valley bottom, I had another view of the village and how it had been affected by the rising waters of Lake Attabad. It looked as devastating from up here as it had when we had passed it a few days earlier. The only difference was that today the weather was brighter.

We met Nassir on the road and headed down to the port to get a ferry. There was a long Chinese lorry with a cargo of cement bags that were being unloaded by hand and the bags carried across a gangplank onto a waiting boat. There were several other boats and after asking around, we loaded our bags onto the next boat that was due to leave and waited. A taxi arrived with four women and lots of baggage, as if they were moving house. Their baggage was loaded on the boat and they disappeared into one of the make shift cafes. I sat and waited.

The ferries don't have a timetable but the captain will set off when he has a full boat, typically 30 passengers. I walked around the small port, watching the porters carrying cement bags and looking in the small shops, no more than wooden sheds that had sprung up to serve the waiting passengers.

We waited for an hour but no more passengers arrived. Initially, I was unconcerned about a long wait, as we were ahead of schedule having not started our morning walk from Borag Lake, but from a spot further along the valley. But we couldn't wait all day and locals familiar with the ferries would not turn up late in the day and still expect to catch a ferry so the later it got, the less likely it became that there would be enough travellers.

There is an alternative way around to getting the captain to set off. If we buy all the remaining tickets, the captain will set off. Mohammad Karim didn't have sufficient money with him, so I dug deep and passed him a few notes. When it looked like our boat was about to set off, several more passengers appeared out of nowhere and clambered aboard. I suspect that they were waiting to see when the boat would go and at the first sign that the captain was preparing to go, they hurried out of the cafes.

We set off, but instead of heading downstream we turned upstream. First stop was the village on the opposite bank. The boat nosed its way towards the shore and a crew member jumped onto the rocks, pulling on a rope to moor the boat. A plank was pushed over the side onto the rocks, to serve as a gangway. A number of passengers got off the boat to be greeted by some of the waiting crowd. Their baggage was unloaded and then some of the waiting crowd peeled away and boarded the boat and we set off again, this time heading downstream.

We passed some large pontoons moored against the bank. These were used as ferries for heavy lorries to transport them up and down the lake. One was Chinese and the other was used by the Pakistani army. These were available for hire, but I was told they were expensive and it was much cheaper to hire labourers, to unload cargo from lorries onto the boats, to be ferried down the lake and then reloaded onto lorries at the other end of the lake.

There was another village further on, where we stopped and after the disembarking and embarking of several passengers and their luggage, we headed off down the lake. The trip was the same as the trip earlier in the week. And unlike my last trip which was in the rain, today, the sun was shining and it was warmer. Along the east bank there were clouds of dust, dislodged up by various groups of Chinese workers who were digging into the rock to build a new section of the KKH to bypass the lake, building tunnels, avalanche protection and retaining walls.

We reached the southern port on the lake and waiting on the dockside, beside the water, was a jeep and inside, was Karim and Koshal. I grabbed my bag and disembarked, walking carefully along the narrow plank that served as a gangway. As the weather was so much better than my first visit here, I took some time to look around the small port at the porters unloading goods, the waiting boats, the colourful trucks waiting for freight and the narrow channel that drained the lake. This was my primary interest and I scrambled across the rocks to look at the water flowing out of the lake.

It was a long narrow channel with steep sides and looking at its depth and length, it was no wonder it had taken nearly six months to shift enough rock rubble to create a viable channel. It really brought it home as to how big the landslide that created the dam and the lake must have been and how much work had been undertaken to drain the lake.

We retraced our route of a few days earlier, down the slope, past a row of giant mechanical diggers belonging to the FWO, past the abandoned Chinese brick works, past an old mine that a long time ago produced rubies, across a bridge with a stunning view of Altit Fort, high up on the cliff above the river and made our way back to the Hunza Embassy Hotel. I checked in and dropped my bags in my room. I flicked the light switch but there was no change in the gloom of my room, another power cut, no surprise there.

Karimabad is immediately recognisable by a fortress, set high above the valley, dominating the town below with a commanding view both up and down the Hunza valley, plus a view up the Nagar Hoper valley on the opposite side of the valley. There was a steep drop behind it that had been carved by a glacier that has since retreated back into the mountains. It was easy to see that this was an excellent defensive position. It was also an iconic symbol of the northern areas and a popular tourist attraction.

It was late afternoon but the fortress was still open so Koshal drove me up to the top of the town and pulled over at the local polo pitch which was being used as a football pitch by two local teams. I was introduced to Jahangir. He was a handsome man in his mid-twenties who lived in Gilgit. He was dressed in a light coloured shalwaar chemise. He spoke excellent English (and I was to find out later a number of the local languages used in the area) and was to be my guide for the rest of the trip. We walked up the narrow steep streets and came to the entrance to Baltit fort.

The fort is perched on top of a promontory and is about four storeys high. It sits on top of a plinth and the entrance is approached up a flight of 25 stone stairs that formed part of the plinth. It has a distinct architecture that originated in Tibet and the similarities were clear to see. The building is similar in style to the Potala Palace in Lhasa, whose historic rulers once had influence over this area of modern day Pakistan.

The front of the fort has been painted in whitewash but around the sides of the building, although largely built of stone there are intermittent courses of thick old juniper baulks of wood which are clear to the naked eye. This helps the building to flex without collapsing in the event of earthquakes and as the building is over 900 years old and still standing, it is a testament to the ingenuity of the builders of their day.

The building has not always looked this impressive. It was abandoned in 1945 when the mir moved out to another palace, lower down the side of the valley. It gradually decayed but was extensively repaired between 1990 and 1996 when it was handed over to a trust that continues to look after the fabric of the building and the contents on display inside.

Jahangir and I had a guide to take us round the inside of the fort and explain the exhibits, how the mir lived and ruled from this palace and some of the customs. The inside is not extensive but is well presented. There are carvings, carpets and furniture that represent how the rooms may have looked when in use, over a hundred years ago. Plus there are documents and photos of more recent events.

One striking feature, is one of the private rooms on the upper floor, with a large bay window with coloured glass looking out over the valley. This is also noticeable from the outside, as the bay window is on the fourth storey but supported by eight wooden columns, stretching from the ground up to the underside of the balcony. Adjacent to this balcony, is the summer throne room which also juts out beyond the walls into thin air and is similarly supported by a further four wooden columns.

I wanted a photo of the whole fort but was thwarted in that either I was too close or so far away that the fort was swallowed up by the mountains in the background. In an attempt to get a decent photo Jahangir suggested we head across the valley behind the fort. We had met Karim again outside the fort and the three of us walked down through the town past local shops and souvenir shops selling gems with lapis lazuli in abundance, carpets, cloth and a host of other trinkets for tourists.

Our route took us away from the main centre of town and downhill towards the stream that flowed from the glacier behind the fort. There was no bridge across the stream just here but the raging torrent in a deep canyon was crossed by an unusual and novel method.

There was a steel cable stretched from one side to the other on which was suspended a large wooden tray attached to a pulley. There were two long ropes attached to the tray stretching across the canyon to either side. In order to cross the chasm, the passenger would sit on the tray and pull themselves across the gap. If the tray was on the other side then pulling on the rope attached to the tray would bring it back ready to haul yourself across.

It was great fun for all of us and also for a number of children whose idea of fun was to travel back and forth across the canyon. There was a crossing some way down the valley but this was a great short cut for people on the far side of the valley to reach the centre of town without losing altitude, avoiding the time and effort of going down the hill to cross the stream and then up the other side.

We came to an organic chicken and duck farm where we waited for Koshal to arrive with the jeep. From this point I had a great view of the fort just as I wanted, it was a great view but unluckily the light was behind the fort so it was not a good photo. I waited as the sun moved around but as it got later, the sun edged ever lower towards the horizon and the shadows in the valley lengthened but it was too late in the day and I never got the shot of the fort that I wanted.

There are two forts in Karimabad that are both well worth a visit. On the first day back in Karimabad I had visited Baltit fort and today I was going to visit the Altit fort. This is also a very old fortification standing at the top of a cliff overlooking the river in a classic location for a fort with sheer cliffs on two sides and strong thick defensive walls on the other sides overlooking the village which was built just outside the walls.

I met my guide for the tour of the fort in the village outside one of the shops. He was a tall, slender, elderly gentleman who spoke excellent English and been a university history lecturer before retiring to Karimabad. Here he made pin money to augment his pension by taking tourists around various local sites and explaining some of the history.

On approaching the fort's entrance, there is a large public square and much of its area is taken up by a large square pool fed by one of the many irrigation channels that are built up and down the valley. It was the shape and size of a large swimming pool. There was some rubbish floating in one corner and the colour of the water which was heavily laden with silt was equally uninviting but this did not put off the local children who were having great fun jumping into its cooling waters to gain some relief from the scorching sun.

Just at the gate to the gardens of the fort was a small sawmill cutting wood into manageable lengths for construction or for basic wooden furniture. What made this particular sawmill unique was that it was a charitable foundation for the sole purpose of providing work for women.

Taking a glimpse through the works entrance, it was quite a sight to see women in their brightly coloured dresses deftly handling great baulks of timber through the various cutting and sawing machines. I had raised my camera to take a photo but in an instant there were hands waving in front of my raised camera and the gate was hastily slammed shut in my face. Needless to say, photography was not allowed.

The fort is similar in design and construction to the Baltit fort with courses of stonework interspersed with juniper wood layers for earthquake protection. The artefacts were of a similar vein as those in the Baltit fort and remarkably, there were several large cooking pots made from a single piece of stone. There were no barriers or guards and it looked as if everything was exactly as it would have been, hundreds of years ago. And the absence of other visitors reinforced the feeling that I was viewing something special and unique. I felt that I was having a personalised tour of the fort.

There was also the sheer cliff and a pinnacle of rock that was separated from the main cliff face by a couple of meters distance but with such a drop that it was certain death if you fell. Here young warriors would leap from the fort to the pinnacle to show off their bravery. The cliff was also used as an execution site with offending victims thrown to their deaths into the chasm below.

Looking from the parapets towards the town below the walls, I could see the pool in the main square and the single gate in the wall surrounding the village. There was a clear view of large wicker baskets on the roofs of the houses filled with apricots drying in the sun. The valley is known for its dried apricots and many of the roofs of houses, the tops of walls and any other flat surface have apricots drying in the sun.

I was back in the hotel for lunch and met Daniel and Nadia who worked for an English overlanding travel company. They were driving their expedition vehicle from Nepal to China and whilst the most direct route was through Tibet, the border was closed so they were making the long journey west through Pakistan to enter western China and then drive back eastwards to pick up their next group of travellers to make the return journey from Beijing back to London.

They were staying at the hotel and Karim was assisting them in getting their vehicle across Lake Attabad and across the border to Kashgar in China. There was a delay in getting the correct permits so they were kicking their heels waiting for the right papers to come through. I was due to visit the Eagles Nest that afternoon so it seemed quite normal to invite them along.

The Eagles Nest is a promontory set high in the mountains above Karimabad which gives a commanding view of the town, both of its iconic forts of Baltit and Altit plus a view both down and up the valley. It is also a local beauty spot where families and couples go to view the sunset. There is a hotel situated on the promontory with fine views of the valley.

After lunch we set off for the short drive from Karimabad to the Eagles Nest with Koshal driving, me in the front seat and Mohammad Karim, Daniel and Nadia in the back. Up twisting roads through fields and villages we headed up the side of the valley. There were several brightly decorated lorries, at the side of the road, picking up their loads of potatoes from local farmers which we had to swerve around.

We arrived at the hotel and settled down for some tea. The manager Ali was an elderly but irrepressible optimistic entrepreneur, who had started out renting floor space to backpackers in the 1970s from a small house on the high street but had moved upmarket. The hotel was clean, spacious and plenty of welcoming public spaces with soft comfortable seating. But its position high on the mountainside was its bestselling point. The view was as impressive as the guide books had suggested. Its height above the valley floor would also give some relief from the intense sun that bathed the whole area in the height of summer.

Koshal took Nadia and Daniel back to the hotel in the centre of town and I checked out my room for the night in the Eagles Nest. As with the rest of the hotel it was clean, tidy and had its own bathroom and television. Plus the hotel had its own generator so it had an uninterrupted power supply. It was up to international standards but with one drawback that I had got used to since travelling in this remote area. This was the intermittent nature of the electricity supply and how it affects television and despite the international channels that the hotel brochure in the room boasted that you could view, if the mains electricity wasn't working, the television relay aerial would not function and there was only static to view.

I decided to go for a walk and headed out of the hotel and along the approach road. People were still working hard in their fields with whole families pitching in to give a helping hand to pick crops, pull up weeds or irrigate crops. Heading towards the edge of the cultivated area, there were bare valley sides and barren rocky slopes. This was an area that had been set aside as a protected area. Here there were more great views and an open area where families and courting couples could come and watch the sunset.

Also, here on an area exposed to the strong winter winds were strange rock formations where the sand whipped up by the wind had carved strange shapes into the protruding rocks. Some of the formations might remind you of the inside of the alien's ship in the film, Alien and one particular formation was so clearly an eagle's head, I wondered whether this was the reason that this was called the Eagles's Nest.

That evening I dined in the hotel restaurant, not that there was much choice but I mention it as I had been intrigued that local menus included an item called apricot soup. Up to now, I had asked for it, wishing to try a local dish but had been told that it wasn't available. I had asked for it at lunch time and been told that it was not available, but the waiter had spoken to the chef in the afternoon, knowing that I was staying for the night and when he came to take my order for the evening meal he proudly announced that apricot soup was available.

How could I refuse … so I ordered the apricot soup, plus a main course. I was not sure what to expect until the soup arrived. It was exactly as described on the menu, being a warm soup made from local apricots. I was rather disappointed as I had expected something more exotic but it was just as described, as a soup made from apricots and with no other discernible ingredients it appeared to be literally warmed up apricots in water. All the other dishes that the hotel served that I tasted were great and I would thoroughly recommend the hotel to anyone as both the staff and the food were great but apricot soup would not be on my list of choices again.

The next morning, I left my bag at reception for Koshal to collect later that day and with Mohammad Karim I left the hotel for the two hour walk back to Karimabad. In cultivated areas, there were clear paths between the fields but in the more barren areas, there were no clear paths and I was very reliant on the local knowledge of my guide for the exact route but our general direction of travel was easy as there was the Baltit fort in the distance acting like a beacon. The easiest way of crossing this area is to find an irrigation channel and follow it towards your destination. This ensured a relatively level gradient that would lead to cultivated fields and therefore roads that would lead into the centre of town.

We reached the outskirts of Karimabad and made our way past fields into the more built up area of the town and finally into the main street. From here it was an easy route back to the hotel. Koshal was sitting in the jeep outside of the hotel waiting for us.

He had collected my bag from the Eagles Nest and had dropped it in my room and so I was ready for the next trip.

The plan was to go up the Nagar valley which is a tributary of the Hunza River which joins it opposite Karimabad. This was a separate state in ancient times and they were often at war with the mir in Karimabad. Having visited both the Baltit and Altit forts and having had some of the history explained, it was easy to see why these forts had been built here opposite the opening to the Nagar valley just metres away from the banks of the Hunza River.

We set off down the valley side towards the bridge over the Hunza River. Crossing the bridge, turning left would lead to Lake Attabad but we turned right off the tarmac road and immediately hit a rough track that followed the Hunza River until the road turned left it and headed up the Nagar valley. The terrain was rocky and dry and the river was constantly changing its course, as it meandered through the valley bottom before joining the Hunza River.

We crossed a concrete bridge and headed up the valley side which was farmed and obviously had irrigation water for the crops in the fields. There were also an increasing number of trees, almost exclusively poplar trees, some at the sides of the road or fields and others in small clumps surrounded by thorn fences to keep animals away and stop them from gnawing at the bark or eating the lower branches and leaves.

We passed through a village which was probably large enough to qualify as a town called Hopar Nagar. We headed for ever onwards and upwards and came to a bridge. There was an armed policeman standing there who waved us down. I didn't understand all of the conversation but it seemed that the bridge had been weakened and that we all had to get out and unload the jeep before it was allowed to cross the bridge. Koshal drove the empty jeep slowly across the bridge without incident and then we were allowed to cross carrying our bags and reload the jeep.

Finally, we came to the end of the road and parked the jeep. From here I set off on foot with Mohammad Karim and Koshal up towards the glacier. We crested a small rise and then descended down into the valley bottom. The snout of the glacier was out of sight down the valley to our left but we turned right to follow the glacier back towards its source high in the mountains.

The ice of the glacier was only visible in places as there was a lot of debris covering the ice itself. Only in places in the centre of the glacier or at the edges where the freezing cold water flowed down the side of the glacier and took away the debris was there any white ice visible. The rocks carried by the glacier were a varied range of colours from greys and blacks to also brightly coloured marbles.

The glacier had plucked all these rocks from the cliffs surrounding it to incorporate these chunks into the glacier and now as it slowly melted it was revealing all its hoard of rocks that it had carried down from the mountains over centuries. Judging by the height of moraine left by the glacier up the sides of the valley by earlier advances, it had obviously been much bigger in the recent past but as the world warms up and the summers are warmer, the glacier is gradually shrinking.

I wanted to press onwards into the mountains but I sensed that Mohammad Karim was tiring and I was aware, we had not brought any packed lunches with us. We were due to walk up another glacier later on the schedule, so I reluctantly turned around and headed back down the valley.

As we approached the village, we were surrounded by a fistful of vendors offering nuggets of brightly coloured rocks, some made into jewellery, plus an array of nuggets of iron pyrites which were claimed to be gold. They were sparklingly bright and very dense and so might appear to be gold and might fool unwary travellers but wouldn't tempt someone who knows the real thing.

I waved them away saying I was not interested and I was not molested anymore. I realise that they are trying to make a living and don't begrudge their entrepreneurial spirit but I am not in the market for trinkets. But I am surprised they feel it's worthwhile to hang about for the few travellers who do venture this far and that tells me that there must be a lot of gullible travellers, who do part with money on a whim, to make it worth their while hassling travellers into parting with their cash.

Koshal pulled up outside the first local restaurant that we came to as we headed down the valley and we entered and sat down to be served with green tea whilst we decided on what to order for a late lunch. We were the only guests and we ordered and then sat and chatted as we waited for our meal.

This was Ramadan which I was aware but it was only here that the implications were brought home to me. The owner and chef of the restaurant were observant but they also had a business to run so whilst they could not eat or drink during daylight hours, they would still be hospitable and serve their clients.

In retrospect, I was not too happy about ordering food and drink and causing them to be tempted to break their fast as they prepared the meal. Neither was I comfortable about me sitting in their home and eating in front of them, but I had ordered before I'd realised they were so observant. I made my apologies and silently vowed to be more sensitive in the future.

That evening, I had dinner in the hotel with Mohammad Karim and another local to whom he introduced to me as Churli who was the Director of Classical Music in Hunza. He had also originally used to own and run a souvenir shop in Karimabad. Needless to say that he spoke excellent English. He turned out to be quite a character as he related various stories of his life including being a film extra with a speaking part in a well-known English language film with more than a few behind the scenes stories to be told.

Our evening meal was interrupted by the hotel manager. There was a small party of Japanese tourists who were also staying in the hotel and there was going to be a concert of local musicians who were going to perform in the hotel recreation area whilst the guests were served an evening meal. I was interested in hearing the local musicians and seeing them in their traditional dress. I was less happy about joining a group of Japanese tourist for another meal with whom I had had no contact so I declined the invitation. However I did make the effort to sit on the public balcony overlooking the recreational area so that I could hear the music and at least get a glimpse of their traditional costumes.

Behind Karimabad, a few kilometres to the north, is a mountain called Ultar Sar. This peak remained unclimbed until quite recently in 1996 by a Japanese team. It was alleged to be the tallest unclimbed peak and several expeditions were launched to be the first to reach its peak. Although several attempts have been made to reach the summit, due to the difficulty of the climb, the peak has not been reached since. I use the phrase 'allegedly the tallest unclimbed peak' as this accolade is actually held by Gangkhar Puensum, 7,570m in Bhutan, the 40th highest mountain and likely to remain unclimbed as mountaineering in Bhutan of mountains above 6,000m has been banned out of respect for spiritual beliefs.

On the shoulder of Ultar Sar is a prominent rock spire rising more than 600m which dominates the view from Karimabad. This spire is called Bublimotin and its distinctive outline gives it a more commonly used name of Ladyfinger Peak. We were heading up the valley, behind the Baltit fort, to get a better view of this peak and one of the glaciers that flows from the massif beyond.

Mohammad Karim turned up at the hotel before breakfast and I knew that today's walk was going to be a challenge. On my previous walks with him, he had worn a shalwaar chemise and sandals, or sometimes ordinary black leather shoes. Today he was wearing a good pair of walking boots, a pair of walking trousers, an ordinary shirt and a backpack. He was obviously dressing for the terrain ahead.

We left the hotel and walked through the centre of town, passing Baltit fort on our right and headed upwards through tree lined fields, over irrigation channels and passing between walls surrounding fields and courtyards. There was a shout from above us and through the trees on the top of a small bank there was a group of men waving at us. These were friends of Mohammad Karim's. Although he worked as a guide, he also had some fields and some sheep and these were his friends and neighbours. We exchanged some pleasantries and explained that we were heading up the valley and would be heading back this way later that afternoon.

The fields gave way to barren hillside and the trees thinned out and there were none high up on the hillside as the soils were too thin and rocky and there was no water. But there was an irrigation channel stretching across the hillside taking water from the glacier to fields further down the valley. We turned right and followed the channel upstream. The path besides the channel was an easy gradient heading up the main Hunza valley and turned left into the side valley.

The terrain changed rapidly from the wide valley and gently sloping sides of the main river to a narrow steep sided canyon. The irrigation channel had been hacked out of the vertical walls of the gorge with rock beneath our feet, a rock wall to our left and a rock roof above our heads. The gradient was still gentle but walking along the edge of the channel had new challenges.

In places, the roof above the channel, was so low you had to walk bent doubled. This only brought the other challenge to the fore as there was a vertical drop to our right. I was trying to concentrate on the path and the route ahead to avoid staring into the chasm but as I walked bent doubled it is hard not to notice the precipitous drop just inches away from my right foot.

Looking up the valley, there was a clear line of the channel clinging to the side of the valley like a contour line on a map. Across the valley there were two more channels, one above the other, that had been cut into the vertical cliffs of the valley that took water away to water the fields further up the main valley.

We came across two workmen who were making repairs to the channel. Here there was a concrete tank with one inlet and two outlets. One outlet was directing water along the channel that we had been following. The other outlet diverted water down a crevasse into another channel tens of meters below us. By adjusting the gates on each outlet the amount of water going down each channel could be regulated.

Higher up the side valley, the valley floor flattened out and the walls of the valley retreated from the edge of the river and there was some rough pasture. At the downstream end of this alpine pasture was a small dam that diverted water into the irrigation channels on both sides of the valley.

At the top end of the pasture was a small shepherd's hut where a family looked after the animals and made a small living selling refreshments to walkers and climbers. I left my rucksack with Mohammed Karim, who was chatting with the family. The families who own the sheep take it in turns to stay up here in the shepherd's hut and they look after all the sheep on behalf of the community.

Dominating this scene was the snout of a glacier that tumbled down between two great cliffs. I walked across the pasture to get a better view. There was a great view of the Ladyfinger Peak, but standing at the snout of the glacier, there was a distinct cold breeze coming down the glacier from the massif high above us. I took a few photos and returned to the hut.

Some of Mohammad Karim's sheep were grazing here. At the end of the summer, the farmers all come up here and round up all the animals before sorting them according to which animal belongs to which farmer. The animals don't have any identification marks or badges but the farmers just know which are their own animals and will also recognise some of their neighbours animals so there are few disputes.

On our way back towards Karimabad, we came across a struggling party of Japanese tourists stretching along the path in ones and twos. Some were unfit, some were reacting badly to the altitude but many of them seemed to have backpacks that seemed to be bulging with equipment. Many of them had walking poles and as I have noticed many times in the past, people weren't using them as they were designed to be used, so the poles become just bulky extra weight, to be carried up the mountain and back again.

The expression 'all the gear and no idea' springs to mind. The guides with them who Mohammad knew, said that they had set off after breakfast, about the same time that we had. It was obviously going to be a long day for this group, unless they turned back before reaching the glacier.

We came across the concrete water tank where two workmen had been working that we had passed earlier in the day. One of the workers was still there and was known to my guide. They had a chat and he joined us in our descent back towards Karimabad. We headed back the way we had come, seeing all the sights in reverse order and from the other direction. We got back to the bank where we had been greeted by Mohammad Karim's friends and neighbours earlier that morning. They were still in the same place and I wondered whether they had moved at all.

They called us over and offered us a drink. This was the famous Hunza water that I had heard so much about. It was a local spirit distilled from fermented mulberry juice, made by one of the men that had called us over and he was very proud of his product despite it being an illicit product. There was little ceremony surrounding the drink. It was a clear liquid poured from a large plastic soft drink bottle. There were only two cups so sometimes we drank from a cup and sometimes from the bottle.

We sat and chatted for a while and the bottle was continually passed around the group. I felt it rude to decline but I drunk less and less each time the bottle came around. The spirit was quite strong stuff and the bottle was being passed around faster and faster. Mohammad Karim seemed to show no hint of returning to our track and ultimately to the hotel, so I took the initiative. I thanked my hosts for their hospitality and for their time, bid them all farewell and headed off by myself down the track towards the centre of town and the hotel.

I was familiar with the hotel menu, so I decided to check out the local stores and see whether I could buy my evening meal from what was on offer for the local city dwellers. I went past the centre of town with their souvenir shops selling carpets, local fabrics, gems from the hills and the like.

I soon came to an area away from the tourist area where there were some grocery shops. I took potluck and entered a store at random. There were tins of food, fresh local produce, bars of

Cadburys chocolate, stacks of soft drinks plus a host of other packets and tins that I was not sure exactly what they contained. Behind the counter, there was a cash register but no one was in sight. I wondered around the store and was mentally making a note of what I might buy.

After a while, I moved back towards the counter and then I noticed that the owner was asleep on the floor, hidden by the height of the counter until you got up close to its edge. He was in a deep sleep and despite my coming in and moving around, this did not disturb his sleep. As it was Ramadan, I guessed that he was observant and taking an afternoon nap and that he trusted the locals not to shop lift his goods or raid his cash register. I decided to leave him to his slumbers and left. I did however hover outside his shop just in case he woke up as I left but he didn't get up so I tried another shop.

The next shop I tried looked more promising and had someone behind the counter but I was struck that there seemed to be a lesser selection of soft drinks and no local produce, so under the gaze of the counter staff I beat a hasty retreat. I tried once more in another shop but had gone off the idea of getting my dinner so I bought some soft drink plus some chocolate. It seemed that I would be eating in the hotel restaurant again this evening after all.

On the way back to the hotel, I came across a cafe with a big sign outside advertising it as an internet cafe. I took a chance and entered. Although they had power for the screens and keyboards run off batteries, there was a power cut so there were no hot drinks or food. I decided to continue and tried signing into my internet account. Alas, to no effect; despite entering the right codes and passwords, my internet provider asked a few extra security questions and despite giving the correct answers, it decided that as contact was from an unusual source it denied me access to my own account and that was final. I was cut off from the internet until I returned home.

The schedule for the next day was pencilled in as a day off. Long trips need to have a few days off fitted into the schedule. Not necessarily just to allow a relaxing day doing nothing, but to be sacrificed if the need arises, to take account of delays in travel, local adverse weather, over runs and all sorts of other potential problems.

As it happened, there was no need to sacrifice this day, as things had panned out much as had been planned. Unfortunately, I had planned to visit most of the tourist sites so there was not much else that I could see to do that I had not planned to see.

I have an opinion of tourist sites and slot them into three categories. Primary sites are those iconic sites that if you are in the area, you just have to go and see. Secondary sites are those that are generally recommended but only if you have time to spare to go and visit. Lastly, I have found some great places to visit that appeal to me but don't appear on the generic tourist guides. These are the tertiary tourist sites that may often be personal favourites, local recommendations, spur of the moment finds or true hidden gems.

I had seen much of Karimabad up the valley to the east, northwards towards Ladyfinger Peak and southwards along and across the river and up the Hopper Nagar valley. It therefore seemed perfectly sensible to view the western part downstream. Therefore, I decided to head off down the valley to see what was there. I didn't have a guide or a map so I just followed my nose.

I walked up into town to a fork in the road. Right would take me up towards Baltit fort so I took the left hand fork to see where it might go. After passing a few hotels and phone shops I came across a grocer's shop and bought some bananas and yoghurt for lunch, which I stashed carefully in my backpack. I also came across several workshops, barbers and a chicken farm.

I had earlier bought some postcards and from reception in the hotel, I understood that there was a post office somewhere along this road leading out of town from which I could purchase postage stamps. The hotel had been happy to take my postcards and to buy the stamps on my behalf but this was part of the purpose of today's walk. I passed more shops selling what seemed like everything but finally on my right was the post office.

I entered through the main door and was confronted by two officials behind desks. I had not practiced my Urdu for buying stamps but they both spoke excellent English. I paid my money to the first man and took the receipt to the second man to exchange it for the stamps that I needed for my postcards. I stuck the stamps onto the postcards and posted them through the letterbox outside the post office. It was all rather functional and happened without incident or misunderstanding. I had hoped that there might be more of an encounter and a story about my brush with officialdom but it was not to be. The system was simple and worked very efficiently.

My plan was to walk for four hours on the outward trip, stop for lunch and then turn around and head back to the hotel. I wasn't trying anything too adventurous, I wasn't planning on heading into the hills but to just follow the road. Also, at the back of my mind was the experience that on straight walking routes out and back (as opposed to doing a circuit), the return journey was always quicker than the outward journey despite the distance being the same so I was factoring just three hours for the return journey.

It was a pleasant walk past fields, through hamlets, crossing irrigation ditches and sometimes enjoying the shade of trees planted beside the road. I felt relaxed and not threatened in the least from the locals or the environment. There was a group of youths filling in their time by playing cricket in the street, which I watched from a distance for a short while.

The only downside to playing in the street was not the traffic, there was very little all day, but whenever a badly bowled ball was hit for six, both sides would spend a long time hunting through the fields of potatoes or wheat trying to find the ball. I took one of these opportunities where the batsman had hit a six into the wheat to carry on my walk past both wickets in the road without interrupting their play.

I passed Haider Abad where I had been told that there was a mill weaving cloth operated as a charity providing work for disabled people which could be visited. This is a worthy cause but not a tourist site that appealed to me to visit. I identified the building in the village without difficulty, but passed it by without a visit.

From a promontory, high above the valley floor, I found a nice place to have lunch. There was a view of the river and across the river, I could see another road on which lorries were going up and down, seemingly like ants at this distance. And from my vantage point, I could gaze down and watch the traffic on the KKH as it snakes its way up the valley parallel to the river.

The return trip was uneventful and I got back to the hotel before dark. One thing I will mention about the hotel, was that it had a small library in various languages for their guests and I took a casual interest in looking through the available titles. Having nothing planned for the evening, I picked up a book, more out of curiosity than interest, just to pass some time. It was Mark Billingham's book titled, 'Sleepy Head' and from the cover, it didn't appeal to my literary tastes and was unlikely to get into my shopping basket, but I borrowed it anyway. I was amazed that within a few days, I had read it from cover to cover.

Chapter 10

Minapin glacier – Ice Station Cow

Today was a late start so there was no hurry. I was to transfer hotels to be taken to Minapin Nager village a few kilometres downstream westwards from Karimabad. The journey was unrushed and we stopped several times in villages along the way for some spare parts for the jeep and to buy some supplies. We also passed the spot where the cement mixer was about to fall into the gorge a few days earlier. This time there was no delay and we sailed through effortlessly.

Looking back at the progress they had made over the last few days, the concrete embankment was noticeably more advanced and perhaps in just a few more weeks, there would be nothing here to suggest that this had once been a major travel obstacle. In addition, there would be much improved access all year round with avalanche tunnels to protect traffic.

The sky was clear and I had a great view of Rakaposhi that had eluded me earlier on the trip. We stopped at the same cafe as we had earlier, but this time there was a great view of the mountain, towering above us as we drank tea. I wanted to take a closer look but Koshal had to pick up another guest and there was only time for a short walk up the valley and we would not get to the snout of the glacier, so I reluctantly agreed to head onwards. After a while, many mountains and glaciers begin to look like each other so I was not too disappointed.

I checked into the Diran Hotel in Minapin Nager. It was a modern built single storey building with a dozen rooms and a large garden with shrubs and flowers plus plenty of shade provided by rows of apple trees. The rooms were simply furnished with a double bed and a separate room serving as a bathroom with a toilet, a basin with a mirror above it and a washing area with a drain hole in the floor. There was a power cut but should I want some hot water to wash it was available from the kitchen (they would boil a large cauldron of water using gas) so I ordered this for the early evening.

I said goodbye to Mohammad Karim. Koshal took him back to Karimabad and I was left on my own. I went for a walk through the village past the mosque and back down towards the KKH and the bridge that we had crossed over the Hunza River. I soon reached the edge of the village and as I had been driven up this road and therefore felt that I knew it, I turned around and headed back through the village.

I was looking for a turning but there did not appear to be any main roads going up the valley side, only minor dirt tracks, so I stuck to the main road and headed out of the village in the opposite direction. I passed the Diran Hotel on the edge of the village and the road started climbing diagonally up the valley side. Fields and apricot trees soon gave way to barren mountain side but the track was definitely going somewhere even though there was no traffic.

The road took several hairpin bends as it rose up the side of the valley and in the far distance, further up the valley, I could make out some fields and farms, as if the next settlement was further up this track. Here and there, on the mountainside were the tell-tale marks of sulphur escaping from deep below the ground, leaving bright yellow streaks on the rocks and a whiff in the air. It was getting dark, the sun had set behind the mountains to the west so I turned around and headed back for that hot water.

Koshal had returned with Jahangir to the hotel before breakfast with a jeep full of bags and equipment and another fellow English traveller named Fran who would be joining me for a while. She was more than a decade younger than I and worked for a veterinary practice in Oxfordshire. Also in the hotel car park was a donkey for our journey. We were only due to be away for a few days so I repacked my bag, leaving behind things that I wouldn't need for a few days in the hotel to be picked up again on our return.

The bags were loaded onto the donkey and whilst its owner checked that the load was secure on the animals back, Jahangir, Koshal, Fran and myself set off on foot down the road through the village. We followed the road back towards the KKH but on reaching the first bridge across a small river the road turned right but we turned left to follow the river upstream towards the glacier. The track we were following started rising at a steep gradient.

Ahead of us there was a small bridge across the river heading back towards the village. From the bridge there was a marvellous view of some rapids with water crashing over the rocks. The bridge was so close to the base of the rapids that standing on the bridge, the water seemed to fall out of the sky. One disconcerting feature of this bridge was that there was no parapet or hand rail so I stayed as close to the centre as possible.

On our side of the river, there was a large hole dug into the side of the valley which hosted a construction site. A large hydroelectric plant was being built, probably half finished, to harness the power that could be generated from the drop in the river down the rapids. There were spillways, a turbine hall, a power house and a channel from the power house to take water back to the river but some months away from completion.

We continued up the track which hair pinned its way up the valley from which we had a good view of the construction site as we looked back. From high up the side of the valley we could also see our luggage on the back of the donkey being driven forward by the drover crossing the bridge just below the rapids.

It was still early in the day but the sky was clear and the sun shone strongly. There were few trees on this section of road and little shade so the rocks were already radiating heat back into our faces. Further up the valley, the valley floor widened and there was a small alpine meadow with a scattering of trees. We took a mid-morning break in a clearing next to a stream and it was here that the donkey caught us up.

We carried on up the valley and nearing the tree line, we stopped near a ruined shepherd's cottage for lunch. The donkey was left to graze and our lunch consisted of savoury biscuits, cheese, sweet biscuits and tinned fruit. Pineapple chunks are not my favourite but on a hot day the fruit and its juice was refreshing. The empty packets were put back into backpacks but the empty tin was placed out of sight, inside the ruined cottage. I expressed concern about littering but Jahangir said we would pick it up on the way back.

We started off again leaving the drover to go and find the donkey as we climbed a steep slope. The trees were thinning out until they disappeared completely and we were above the tree line. Around here, the donkey overtook us and carried on whilst we had another break. We were progressing well but the heat of the day and the thinning air was taking its toll and I noted that the breaks were becoming more frequent and my lungs were bursting. Minapin village is already over 2,000m and our target camp site is 3,261m so we were ascending over 1,200m in a day.

Cresting a ridge, we had a great view of the glacier spreading out in front of us and disappearing up the valley into the distance. This glacier had plenty of white ice showing but also some moraine on top. It was curiously streaked with bands of darker rocky surface interspersed with whiter streaks stretching along its length. Around a corner, we came across a gate in a fence stretching out either side of the path plus a sign welcoming us to the Minapin Nagar community camp site. We went through the gate, closing it behind us and we carried on. The track descended towards the campsite itself.

This is a flat meadow area in the shape of a crescent perhaps a kilometre long with a stream meandering through the centre. On our right hand side there was the high steep and in places vertical cliff face of the valley side whilst on the left hand side there was a jumble of moraine left by the glacier. There were a number of small buildings on one side of the meadow. There was a shepherds' cottage and a small storehouse and on the opposite side was a range of small stone built farm buildings.

There was a large tent set in a bend of the stream with a wire fence around it where the camp managers lived and provided meals and drinks. Scattered across the campsite were a number of cows and a couple of donkeys, one of them being the one that had carried our bags. And there were no other tents so it looked like we had the place to ourselves.

The cows were allowed to wander wherever they liked. The glacier had no grass, was very rocky and loads of crevasses so this acted as a barrier for the cows on one side of the camp area. The opposite side was the cliffs of the valley's side which hemmed in the animals. At the top end of the flat area there was more ice and a glacial coming down a side valley to join the main glacial, so only a short section of fence with a gate in it that we had come through earlier was needed to keep the animals within a manageable and defined area.

Fran and I walked around the campsite and we chose our respective sites and pitched our tents. These were simple tents consisting of an inner tent supported by a frame and an outer tent over the top. Camping shops would describe them as large enough for two people but in practice once you are lying down in your sleeping bag on your Thermorest mat with your bags next to you there is not enough spare space for another person and their kit.

Jahangir and Koshal would sleep in the camp manager's large tent which served as kitchen, restaurant and sleeping quarters. Inside this tent was a raised platform and carpets and although it might be cramped, it was comfortable. The raised floor kept the floor off the cold ground and the body heat from several people would make their tent warmer than our small tents.

I rolled out my Thermorest and plumped up my down filled sleeping bag. I changed from walking boots into sandals and left my socks to air on the ridge on top of the tent. Dinner was to be served on the ground between our two tents, and in the absence of furniture, I found a suitably sized flat topped rock nearby that would serve as my chair and I carried it back to place it in the space between the two tents.

Fran and I went for a walk before dinner to go up the jumble of moraine then along it to the far end of the campsite and generally get to know our surroundings. The light was fading and when dinner was ready, Jahangir brought it over to find me walking around my tent with my head bowed as if searching for something. He asked what the matter was and I explained that I had left my socks on top of the tent and they were no longer there and perhaps they had blown off.

Jahangir put the food down and straightened up. In a serious voice with a straight face but with a hint of a smile he said that you shouldn't leave any clothes out as the cows will eat them. As the socks were nowhere to be seen it was apparent that a cow had indeed eaten my socks whilst I had gone for a walk. I would normally describe myself as an animal lover but at that particular moment I felt an unusual antipathy towards the cows nearby.

I looked around at the nearest cows trying to pick out one with a guilty look but to no avail. My thoughts turned to why would a cow eat a pair of socks and later to whether the socks would pass through in one piece and therefore perhaps I could get them back. Over the next few days I found myself unable to pass a cowpat without having a closer inspection.

There was some time to kill between dinner and bed time but Jahangir brought over a Ludo set borrowed from the camp manager. The rules are slightly different from those that I remember from my childhood. Opposite players play as a team against the other two players, working together to get their pieces around the board and knocking off the opponents pieces making them start again from the beginning. Plus a few other rules around throwing sixes, three doubles in a row or touch and play (meaning that once you start to move a piece, you can't change your mind and move it back).

I played with Koshal and Fran partnered with Jahangir. It was great fun and we played several rounds and were oblivious to the chill in the air. I would not expect that a child's game could give so much fun to adults. Had I been asked to suggest a way to pass some time this would have been a long way down the list.

I didn't have a good night. It was cold and I envied my guides sleeping in the large tent as their collective body heat would help to maintain the temperature at a reasonable level. But that wasn't the worst aspect. There were two male donkeys who woke me up at 4am baying. And they didn't stop and they spent of what was left of the night baying at each other. I mentally added donkeys to my list, at probably first equal with cows, of animals against whom I now bore a grudge.

After breakfast which found us eating with our gloves on as protection against the cold we meet our guide outside the large tent for the walk up the glacier to Diran base camp. The elevation is only 400m higher than the camp but it does involve a 12km walk across the glacier and a lot of up and down. We headed up the steep moraine bank flanking the camp site and down again onto the glacier itself. The first section was a scramble across rough terrain. There is only rock here with no ice showing through as there is a lot of debris covering the ice core of the glacier.

As we progressed more ice started to show through and we came across the first of many streams to be crossed. The surface of the glacier is constantly changing so that there are no well-worn routes across it and you are dependent on the skill of the guide. When we get to a stream we had to walk up and down to find a suitable place to cross by jumping from one side to the other so both sides of the stream have to be just right.

In places there were mushroom like formations. These were large rocks balanced on a stem of ice. The rock would protect the ice beneath it from direct sunlight and therefore it melted more slowly. As the ice surrounding it melts and the ground level becomes lower it leaves a stem of ice topped by a rock that resembles a mushroom.

Towards the centre of the glacier the terrain changes again. There is still plenty of rock and ice but some of the streams run at the bottom of deep crevasses, some of which can be jumped but some are too wide and require a diversion to continue. It can be frustrating and tiring to walk three sides of a square to get around one crevasse only to be faced with another crevasse that needs a diversion of another three sides of a square.

We would carefully cross crevasses and occasionally we would drop a stone down into the depths to see how deep it was. Some were very deep and several seconds passed before a stone either fell into water with a plop or rattled on other stones at the bottom of the crevasse. The route also followed ridges with steep slippery icy slopes either side which we would avoid if we could but sometimes we would just have to inch our way along.

Finally we got to the far edge of the glacier and the walking became easier. We crossed the edge of the glacier and set foot on firm ground. Between the glacier and the sides of the valley was rolling alpine meadows where a number of cows were grazing. Here was base camp opposite the mighty peak of Diran 7,266m, a pyramid shaped mountain to the east of Rakaposhi first climbed in 1968 and from our position there were several other beautiful peaks. These may not be the highest peaks but they are renowned for their beauty.

There were several tents belonging to a mountaineering expedition and our guide sat down to chat with some friends who were working as guides or cooks for the expedition. Meanwhile, we sat down and had a picnic lunch, very much like the day before of savoury biscuits, sweet biscuits, some cheese and fruit juice. As the sun beat down and warmed the air the cold of the morning was far away.

The stream next to where we sat burbled quietly in the background and the cows chewed their cud in the background. It was very peaceful and relaxing but we couldn't stay forever as we had to get back so we when our guide returned from chatting with his friends in the mountaineering camp we set off back to our camp.

I had asked whether we could take a different route back, partly to avoid some of the more dangerous crevasses and partly to see another part of the glacier. The guide took us back a different route to start with but there were impossible crevasses to cross. So despite his best endeavours we ended up retracing our steps for part of the return trip.

However we did manage to traverse the glacier and from the peaks around us I guessed that we were heading straight across the glacier before turning and heading down the far side back to our camp. There were still crevasses to cross or avoid, streams to jump and rocky terrain to traverse.

Our guide was observing Ramadan and his lack of water was taking its effect in the high and dry atmosphere at this altitude. He called for more and more frequent halts. We had plenty of time so we sat and waited until he was ready to continue but eventually we got back to our camp.

Some other guests had arrived in camp during the day so there were several other tents dotted about. One pair of girls were from Germany. One was working locally and her friend had come to visit her and do some sightseeing including visiting the glacier. They had done some washing in the stream and had left their clothes to dry on some rocks not far from their tent. I thought nothing of it as there were no cows in view. We started to play Ludo which was fast becoming a gripping game as we learnt the tactics of the game and got better at playing so games were now much more competitive.

Fran noticed some cows passing us heading towards the German girl's tent and beyond it the clothes laid out to dry. Rather than let them learn the hard way she went over and warned them of the dangers of the cows eating their clothes. The clothes were duly collected and the cows dispersed and despite the animals not being able to express emotion, I am sure that they looked disappointed at losing their opportunity of eating something other than grass.

That evening we had our meal in the large tent followed by another session of Ludo where Jahangir and Fran maintained their lead in the number of games won but Koshal and I were closing the gap. Meanwhile that night the two male donkeys continued their baying at each other all night. I was in my sleeping bag wearing all my clothes in an attempt to stay warm and trying to get at least some sleep but a mixture of baying and cold kept me awake.

Our schedule suggested another day and night at the camp site but we had been lucky with the weather and we were ahead of schedule. We had explored up and down the glacier and had walked across it. The south side of the valley was an impenetrable cliff without any routes up so I was happy to head back to the village a day early.

During breakfast a cow had taken an unusual interest in Fran's tent and was working its head past the tent fly but with our knowledge of their dietary habits Fran lost no time in shooing the beast away. The donkey was loaded up and we headed back down the valley. We stopped at the same ruined shepherd's cottage. I was pleased to note that Jahangir without any reminding retrieved the empty pineapple tin that we had left a couple of days earlier putting in into his backpack to carry it down to the village.

We came to the hydroelectric construction site and this time crossed the bridge below the rapids to take a short cut through the village to get back to the hotel. Fran put up her tent in the garden in the shade of an apple tree whilst I upgraded to a room in the hotel. There was a power cut so no lights but a bucket of hot water was available on request from the kitchen. Although we had got back to civilisation the conditions were not that different from camping.

For the rest of the afternoon Fran and I walked around the village exploring back streets and following tracks past fields to outlying hamlets. There were fields of wheat, potatoes and maize with apricot trees growing at the borders, occasional tomato plants and to my surprise cannabis plants growing like weeds in the borders. I refrained from taking photos of scenes with villagers but Fran was bolder and being a woman was able to gain the locals trust and with permission from some of the ladies she was able to take a few photos of women and children in village scenes.

On our way back to the hotel there were some rocks at the side of the road covered in apricots drying in the sun. It is a sign of how trusting the community was as I am sure that had this been at home then they would either have been stolen or swept off the rocks and into the dust.

It was a bright warm morning and the hotel owner had suggested having breakfast outside. So Fran and I had a leisurely breakfast in the garden in the dappled shade of the trees. We loaded the jeep and the four of us headed down the road to cross the bridge over the Hunza River and follow the KKH for the hour and a half drive back to Gilgit and the PTDC hotel.

We headed into town to find a tailor for Fran. One of her shalwaar chemise dresses was rather too long and the low hem line too tight and was constricting her ability to move, most notably her ability to get into and out of the jeep. We were recommended a tailor and we found his shop open but no one was about so we wondered what to do. All of a sudden a man jumped up behind the counter and greeted us making all of us jump.

He had been asleep behind the counter on account of this being Ramadan (eating evening and morning meals during the dark hours of night which meant little sleep so people make up for it during the day). Jahangir said what was required and the tailor nodded and said the alterations would be ready the next day.

We headed out of town to see a carving of Buddha carved into a local cliff above the town that was created hundreds of years before when the area had a greater Buddhist influence from further east. On the return journey Koshal dropped us on the outskirts of town as I wanted to savour more of the town on foot rather than from the back of a jeep at speed.

The streets were busy with shops selling all sorts of goods. We passed a market and I wanted to check it out. There were stalls selling vegetables and fruit but many of the stalls were selling meat. There were sides of mutton and de-feathered chickens hanging from hooks. There were live chickens to buy housed in wire cages and plenty of butchers selling their wares and practising their trade at the side of the street. Associated with their trade was the blood from the animals but they merely allowed it to run down the gutters in the street. After seeing that I was much more careful where I put my feet.

The market was busy with buyers swelling the streets and delivery men taking halves of sheep or crates of chickens to their buyers. We were dressed in shalwaar chemise but I had no doubt for a moment that anyone thought that we were potential buyers but I sensed no stares or animosity. There were a few curious smiles that we returned but for the most part we were left alone to wander and we finally we returned to the main road.

There was a bridge over the Hunza River just wide enough for a single vehicle. This was a suspension bridge with the base constructed of wood but with the weight of the track bed taken by steel cables up to the suspension cables high above our heads. There was a sign saying that it had been built over a hundred years before by the British and judging by the rusty nature of the cables and the holes between boards of the track bed, I could well believe that this was the original bridge.

On the far side there were a few shops as the road made its way downstream towards the new concrete bridge across the river. Several of the shops advertised ice creams but as this was Ramadan and it was offensive to see people eating in public, there were no sellers prepared to sell ice creams to the public until after dusk.

In the hotel there was power and the television worked. This was when I discovered that the royal baby had been born the day before on 22 July 2013 and named as George Alexander Louis. Needless to say this was the main topic of conversation that evening and despite being in a remote area of a foreign country, several people in the hotel, once they knew we were English were obviously aware of the royal birth and came over and chatted to us and commented on the news. I would have happily celebrated and drunk a toast to the new baby at the bar but being a Muslim country there was no bar so a cup of green tea would have to do.

Chapter 11

Nanga Parbat

We had a long way to go so we set off early from the hotel heading south east. We passed the airport and Karim's offices as we headed out of town. I had asked to stop to pick up some local dried apricots. The area is renowned for them and allegedly are useful to combat altitude sickness. The first row of shops we came to had apricots but I didn't like the look of them as they appeared to be fairly dark and very wrinkled as if they were too desiccated. I wanted dried but still soft with at least some moisture left in the fruit.

The next stop was the bus station on the outskirts of town. This wasn't the local bus station but the terminus for long distance bus journeys for destinations throughout Pakistan. Koshal found a space to park the jeep and we entered a shop and found just what I wanted. I bought a couple of kilos in separate quarter kilo packs so that I would have some fresh in reserve in my main bag and a small quantity to carry in my day pack and ready to eat.

After leaving the bus station we headed southwards along the KKH and passed through the Gilgit welcome arch which was a huge arch straddling a dual carriage way and must be a great source of local pride but there was not enough traffic to justify construction of a dual carriage way just yet. Two way traffic went through one of the two arches and it would appear from the poor state of the road that it had not yet been finished.

A short distance beyond the arch there was a great cloud of dust wafting its way up the valley. We had not seen any traffic coming towards us for some time so it seemed likely that that had been a catastrophic event further along the road.

We pulled up on the side of the road and waited for some time. There was no traffic coming towards us but the cloud of dust continued to billow towards us. A few vehicles over took us but they slowed and pulled up on the side of the road before they were obscured by the advancing dust cloud. I got out of the jeep and walked away from the road towards the river on our left to see whether I could get a better view.

The dust cloud gradually cleared and traffic started coming towards us so I hurried back to the jeep. We pulled out on to the main road and drove slowly towards the problem area. It turned out that there were road improvements taking place and there had been some blasting. The cliff above the road had been blasted to reduce the risk of avalanche and the debris had been shovelled over the edge of the cliff below the road and both the blast and the shovelling of debris had produced the giant dust cloud that we had seen.

Just a short distance down the road was another construction site. A tunnel was being built through one of the promontories that cut across the road on its journey down the valley. There were a notable number of Chinese workers and several black shirted policemen guarding them. Until the tunnel was complete the road weaved its way around the promontory with tight turns and precipitous drops to our left.

We came to a tourist spot that had been built on top of a pointed rock beside the road. The sign painted boldly on the side of the edifice proudly claimed in capital letters in not quite correct English that it was the 'junction point of 3 heights of mountain ranges of the world'. This was the point where the Karakoram, the Hindu Kush and the Himalaya mountain ranges officially met. It was also the point where the Gilgit River from the west meets the Indus River that rises in the Himalayas and they join and flow southwards.

There was some flat land on the opposite bank and I expressed surprised that it had not been cultivated. There was a simple answer which was that this area was reserved for the army, hence no cultivation was permitted. We continued down the KKH but came across various check points where there were tail backs and congestion as traffic backed up as travellers papers were carefully checked.

The place which we were heading for is only 50kms from the disputed border between Pakistan and India. This is a tense border with frequent shelling and other military activity. This has been a source of potential conflict between the two nations for decades and both sides have an appreciable military presence in the area.

We turned left off the KKH and headed down the valley slope towards the river and a long bridge with supports driven deep into the bedrock of the fast flowing river. There was yet another check point and we passed through and crossed the bridge. We turned up the Indus valley for a kilometre and then right into the Astore river valley, a tributary of the Indus River.

The road narrowed to a single track in places and was hacked out of the vertical cliff faces. There was some traffic on the road and vehicles inched past each other on the wider sections of the road. There was a heavily laden lorry crawling its way up a steep gradient throwing out lots of thick black smoke as it toiled its way slowly upwards. I was glad when the road widened enough and we could overtake and we could get some fresh air.

Around a corner we came across another lorry that had pulled over to the edge of the road and the driver and another man were standing in front of the open bonnet from which a lot of steam was escaping. As we passed I noted that there were a number of passengers travelling on the roof of the lorry and noted that they were wearing army fatigues. Two cars both filled with passengers caught us up and at a wider section of road, Koshal pulled over and let them past before re-joining the road.

After just a few minutes he pulled over again. We had a puncture so there was an enforced break whilst the wheel was changed. The spare was on and the last nut and bolt was just being tightened when the lorry belching out clouds of black exhaust fumes that we had passed earlier came around the corner. We wasted no time and jumped back into the jeep and set off again before we got stuck behind the lorry.

We came to a police post and pulled over. This time there was a delay. Our permits and passports were inspected in depth by three policemen and details written into a book by a fourth. There was some radio traffic with their commanding officer during which I heard our names and nationalities mentioned. Eventually the radio traffic finished, there was a short exchange amongst the police until one of the policeman got into our jeep.

We had not been allowed to travel further without an armed guard and one of the policemen had been ordered to escort us and he didn't look pleased. After a few words exchanged in Urdu the atmosphere was tense but quiet as we resumed our journey.

But the atmosphere didn't stop me for asking for a stop to view one of the many foot bridges spanning the river. All these suspension bridges were sometimes just wide enough for foot traffic and others were wide enough for a vehicle. The bed of the bridges were wooden planks but on the wider bridges, one side of the planks had been broken so that only foot traffic could cross.

I was intrigued and queried this as the damage looked so carefully and selectively undertaken and for its repetition on bridge after bridge. The explanation was that the locals would overload their cars or carts and try to drive across and the wooden planks and that they or the steel cables would break and the vehicle and occupants would be thrown into the river below drowning the people and leaving the damaged bridge requiring expensive repair. Therefore this selective vandalism was to deter people from attempting to cross the bridge with heavy loads.

We caught up a convoy of buses filled with soldiers crawling up the road and throwing out clouds of black exhaust fumes. At the head of the column of buses was an army lorry and at the rear was a military ambulance. These were conscripts who were to replace soldiers at one of the many bases in the area. The area is in the disputed Jammu and Kashmir area and never far from the line of control with India.

Soldiers would take up their positions for a few weeks or months before being rotated and redeployed to another area.

We worked our way past each vehicle until we had open road ahead of us again.

After just a few kilometres we came across another military convoy halted at the side of the road. There had been a landslide that had partially blocked the road stopping the buses from passing. Several soldiers had evidently moved the smaller rocks aside but there was one large boulder the size of a Mini in the middle of the road that had defied the soldier's attempts to move it. It was surrounded by soldiers, with several officers looking on and a lone soldier with a small hammer was repeatedly hitting it with no effect other than making a noise. Our jeep was able to squeeze past and carry on but with another convoy heading up the valley I wondered what the army would do to clear their path.

We reached the town of Astore more than an hour and a half after leaving the police post and stopped at the police station to change guard and collected a new guard called Muzzarfar Ali who was due to be us for a few days. With our new guard we headed to a hotel for lunch. Muzzarfar Ali sat in a corner and read the paper and Koshal went to find a garage to repair the spare tyre whilst we ate.

Waiting for Koshal to return, I opened a local English language paper and scanned the contents. There was plenty of local news, advertisements, local and international sports reports and one article which caught my eye reporting news of two deaths on K2, an Iranian and a German from climbing accidents. It wasn't clear about what the accidents involved but I was going trekking up to K2 to base camp but I wasn't going to be doing any climbing. It is always sad when people are involved in accidents and lose their lives and it brings home the fact that the mountain is a killer.

The road out of town climbed upwards and the valley narrowed again so that there were few fields as the rocky valley sides plunged straight down into the river. By late afternoon we were nearing our destination and we turned off the main road up a side valley and the tarmac of the main road ended and we were on a rough track. The water in the river was suddenly very different. The confluence of the two rivers emphasised the differences.

The water in the main river was nearly blue with occasional white waves where the water crashed over and around rocks in the river. The water in the small river which we were to follow was a muddy brown colour. The river just below the point where the rivers met was blue one side and brown on the other until the muddy waters finally overwhelmed the clearer blue water changing all the water to brown.

The side valley was host to the Rupal River and the valley widened out and there were fields and greenery. Women working in the fields beside the road, had their heads uncovered, but they quickly pulled their scarves over their heads when they heard us coming. Further up the valley, we could see that there were snow-capped peaks.

We passed through the lower village which was more of a scattering of buildings rather than a village. Some farmers were unloading grain into a storage building with fellow villagers and children looking on. As we passed, some carried on with their work, some stared but only a few smiled. It was the picture of the many blank faces set against the few that did smile that emphasised we may not be welcome.

We arrived in Tareshing late in the afternoon and dropped Muzzarfar Ali at the police station. There was a sign requiring all visitors to check in with the police, although the translation in English called the police station a police chokey, which I was quite sure, was not the intended interpretation. Opposite the police station was the not very imaginatively named, the Nanga Parbat Hotel, where we would be staying.

The hotel had two court yards. On the downhill part of the site, there was a large square one with rooms on two sides with walls surrounding the other two sides. On the uphill side there was a smaller irregularly shaped walled courtyard with rooms on one side. This was a two storey building which overlooked both courtyards but due to the slope of the land, approaching it from the smaller courtyard it appeared to be only one storey approached up a short flight of steps. This upper storey was all built of wood and inside consisted of a large reception area with a bedroom on either side.

Up a couple of further steps there was a living area with comfortable chairs and a settee surrounding a coffee table and a large captain's window or bay window overlooking the larger courtyard. A corridor to the left led to another bedroom and to the right was yet another bedroom and through this room was the toilet and wash area. This sounds grander than the reality, as it consisted of one hole with a footprint either side and another hole with a bucket of water next to it. This whole upper floor was a self-contained suite and Fran and I had it to ourselves.

There was a mixture of wiring which looped across the upper walls and through doorways, hanging from nails with ancient switches, bare wires, and junction boxes with wires hanging out which would have been an electrician's nightmare. The lights didn't work but I wasn't sure that this was because there was a power cut or whether the system didn't work anyway.

The windows only had thin glass in them and there were a couple of cracks. Some of the windows didn't fit and there were gaps between the window and the frame through which sunlight could be seen. The floor was uneven and the planks that made up the walls were not aligned parallel to the floor but seemed to have warped or perhaps had never been laid straight and were irregular lengths and widths with gaps between them.

The curtains didn't actually cover the width of the windows so that there was a gap either at one side or in the middle. It was rustic and whilst it may not have even obtained a single star rating, it was quirky, quaint and clean, and in its own way, I would say it was charming in its simple functionality. I would recommend it for its sheer difference from the accepted or expected standard of a hotel, but with several provisos.

As at all new locations I wanted a walk to get to know my surroundings before dinner. Walking downhill the small row of shops that we had passed earlier all had their shutters up and their owners had gone home. There was another hotel where the mountaineers had stayed before heading up to Nanga Parbat base camp only to be murdered by the Taleban just a few weeks earlier. I wondered whether I could feel a ghostly chill as I looked through the gate to the compound but pushed the thought to the back of my mind.

Up the hill were a couple of grain mills that used the flow of water in the irrigation ditch to turn the stones to grind the wheat. Many of the trees had their lower trunks tightly swathed in random strips of cloth. This was to protect the bark from grazing animals who can strip a young sapling of bark in minutes and in so doing kill the tree. I noted a donkey tethered at the side of the road and wondered whether there would be baying tonight as there had been a few nights earlier on the Minapin Glacier.

Up a small incline there was an old wooden tower that had once acted as a lookout tower when the villages were under threat. It was quite old and not very substantial but given that wood here was valuable, it did make a statement that the local population had thought it worthwhile investing in this tower as part of their defence preparations. They were not many buildings, few were even two stories and the village wasn't very big although it was well spread out.

Our evening meal was brought to us and served on the coffee table of the communal room with the bay window overlooking the larger of the two courtyards. Our host asked if we wanted any light and although I had tried the switch again to no effect, I said yes and he disappeared and on his return my curiosity concerning the electrical system was resolved.

There was a separate new wiring system of small copper wires set in clear plastic that was put in on top of the old system which had been disconnected. They had solar power that charged a battery pack during the day and by plugging in the battery into the new system and by using the new switch that had escaped my notice earlier in the day we had sufficient light to see our food. But the new system was not throughout the whole suite. Some of the rooms and all of the bedrooms were still dark but I had had the foresight to pack a head torch so I was not concerned.

We had an early start the next day to reach base camp of Nanga Parbat so we went to bed early. As it happened I need not have worried about the lack of electricity as the moon rose and from a brilliantly bright moon shining through the clear mountain sky, it was nearly bright enough to read a book. Looking out of the window at the village there were very few artificial lights visible from the other buildings.

It was a cold night and a cold cloudy morning with damp in the air. I had got up in the night and put my thermals on but I was still cold so I was already awake when it was time for breakfast. We had packed our day packs with water, lunch, water proofs, extra fleeces etc. We waited for Muzzarfar Ali but there had been a change in the rota and we had another guard. This was a local policeman, with a long greying beard, dressed in casuals but wearing a beret which was the only sign that he was a member of the local militia. He was only a few inches over 5ft but carrying a machine gun with a large ammunition clip and a spare.

Judging by his wrinkled, leathery tanned face and grey beard I wondered how old he was and whether he was able to keep up with us. He was over an hour late from our planned departure time so it was after 7.30am when we left the hotel.

We headed up through the village and leaving the fields behind we crossed two steep ridges of jumbled boulders. Coming down the mountain were a number of mules. The mules were carrying ice that had been cut by hand out of the glacier high above the village and was destined to be carried down to Astore for sale in the market. On their return journey the donkeys would take wood for fuel up to the communities that live near the glacier and cut the ice.

It started to drizzle but we continued as it didn't seem too bad and not even bad enough to get our waterproofs out of our back packs. After a while the drizzle had turned into rain so we sheltered under a tree. This would have been fine for a quick shower but as the rain continued the leaves became so wet that it provided so little protection that we continued up the road looking for some better protection to wait to see whether the rain would blow over.

We came across a cluster of houses and a roadside shop in the last permanent community heading up the mountain and were about to enter when we realised that the shop was already a temporary refuge for a number of people. All was not lost as one of the people sheltering said that his house was nearby and we were all welcome to follow him. After a short walk up the road we came to a large stone built single storey farmhouse.

We left our shoes by the door and entered our host's house. We were ushered into the main reception room which had white-washed walls, a carpet on the floor and a low raised dais around the edge to sit on. We striped off our wet outer layers. There was a problem in that there was an absence of sufficient hooks, so we carefully folded our wet outer rain gear inwards so that the dry inside was not resting against the wet outer layers and would not drip on the carpet.

We sat around the edges of the room. Our host served green tea which was brought in to us on a tray by his wife who put the tray down and promptly and silently retreated to the back rooms. He didn't speak English but through our interpreters we expressed our appreciation of his hospitality and thanked him for it. It was a generous act of charity and he was appreciative of our thanks.

The room wasn't heated and it was a low ambient temperature but it was out of the rain and out of the wind and in no time at all our body heat had raised the temperature. I had been wearing my shalwaar chemise with the shirt tails falling below the knees. This had been below the bottom of my waterproof jacket so the lower part of the shirt was sodden which had also soaked through to my trousers.

I had waterproof trousers but had not chosen to wear them until it was too late not to mention the problem of how one wears water proof trousers and what to do with the extra material of the hem of the chemise. I had learnt a valuable lesson concerning shalwaar chemise that whilst they were great for blending in and great in hot environments they were useless in wet conditions.

After more than an hour we checked the weather and the rain seemed to be easing and it was more drizzle than rain. We said again our thanks for his hospitality and put on our waterproofs and boots and headed off up the valley. I noted that Jahangir had borrowed a better waterproof coat from our host than the one he had brought himself.

We came across what appeared to be a deserted village but all the windows were in good condition and the doors were solid and padlocked. This was a community that moved up and down the valley with the change in the seasons. They would spend the winter further down the valley. In spring they would move their livestock up to here and plant some crops in the local fields. In the summer they would move the animals up into the high pastures and live up there for several months.

As autumn approached and the snow started to fall they would head back down the valley. They would harvest grain in this alpine refuge and the animals would graze on the last green shoots. Late in late autumn the farmers would move their animals, the grain they had harvested and the hay that they could carry back down the valley to spend winter in the lower valley.

I had wanted to get to the base camp but there was always the nagging feeling (and the associated danger surrounding the death of 10 mountaineers at the hands of the Taliban) that there was a lot of bad karma around this site. The rain earlier that had fallen further down the valley had fallen as snow this high up the valley and the upper slopes within view from where we stood were clearly covered with a dusting of fresh snow. We had lost a lot of time in our late start and from sheltering from the rain and it was doubtful whether we could reach base camp and get back to the hotel in daylight hours.

We were wet through from the rain although the weather had brightened and the sun was peeking through scattered clouds gradually drying our clothes. So it was regretful but a necessary decision that since we were not equipped to stay overnight at these altitudes and that it was not possible to reach base camp and return within daylight hours that we should turn round and head back to the hotel. Also I was not over awed in viewing a site with such a recent macabre story.

On our way back Jahangir stopped off and exchanged his borrowed jacket for his not so well designed original jacket. We passed the small shop in which we had initially tried to shelter. There were small groups of school children in their uniforms walking up the road coming towards us as they returned to their homes further up the valley.

As we descended and the day got longer it got warmer and our clothes had finally dried out and the groups of school children coming up the valley were wearing T shirts with no regard to the temperature or the potential of rain. Many of them were carrying bags in addition to their school bags containing books and homework and it was easy to make out the shapes of cucumbers in plastic bags, small plants in flower pots with their top leaves pocking out of plastic carrier bags, packets of biscuits and tins in some of the bags. One lad that we chatted with had several axe heads that he proudly displayed and explained that he was taking them home for his father to fit shafts to the axe heads to sell locally.

One unusual sight that caught my attention that appeared coming up the valley was three teenagers, two in school uniform, heading across the two steep ridges that were near the village carrying toilets on their heads. There was no road for vehicles to deliver goods so these lads had been employed to carry the goods up to where they were required. It emphasized that these people walked over rough terrain up and down the valley every day without a second thought as it was just the way to get around whilst I was looking forward to a hot green tea and resting after a journey that they might think unchallenging.

It reminded me that earlier that morning I had questioned whether our guard might have been too old to keep up but even he had shown no trouble in keeping up with us all day and finished the trek as spritely as he had started as if he did it as an everyday event.

We got back to the hotel and dinner was served and the solar battery that had been charging all day plugged in to provide light. Muzzarfar Ali had seen the light and had come over with another colleague for a chat and I suspect to practice their English. We talked about our families, our jobs and Pakistani politics (although I was non-committal and changed the subject as soon as was decent as one should not discuss politics, religion or sex unless looking for confrontation). We also touched on sport, polo, the security situation and a host of other topics, too numerous to remember in detail.

Chapter 12

The Astore Valley

The next morning we picked up Muzzarfar Ali and headed down through the lower village and in some ways I was glad to be leaving Nanga Parbat even though we had not managed to achieve the desired original aim of reaching base camp. As is always the case with mountain weather it had suddenly changed and the clouds had dispersed and it promised to be a fine day with clear skies and brilliant sunshine, much like two days before and so unlike yesterday with its cold wet weather that had defeated us in our attempt to reach Nanga Parbat base camp. As travellers are often reminded, weather in the mountains can change very rapidly.

We followed the Rupal River back to the main Astore River and the confluence of the two rivers where the blue waters met the brown waters. We were due to head south across the Deosai Plains but in order to reach the road over the mountains we had to head north back down the Astore River valley before crossing and picking a road heading south east and then south to take us across the watershed.

This is an astonishingly pretty valley in my opinion helped no doubt by the good weather and the warming sunshine. Ignoring the HEP station near the bottom of the valley which is necessary to provide electricity to this remote community, this is an unspoilt valley that heads up to the high plateau of the Deosai Plains. There are hamlets along the route with a scattering of fields in the bottom of the valley. At one village we stopped at the police station and said goodbye to Muzzarfar Ali and picked up a new guard before crossing a small tributary stream on what looked suspiciously like a Second World War Bailey bridge and continuing our route up the valley.

On one stretch of road the pupils of a local secondary school had been lined up in rows and were doing exercises in the open on the tarmac of the road outside the school gates. They all grinned and a few waved as we passed by. They don't have a summer holiday as the winters are so fierce in the mountains that getting to school can be difficult so the school terms are compressed into the more benign month's weather wise from spring to autumn.

The fields and houses eventually gave way to barren rocky slopes falling directly into the river so there was no cultivatable land and no people. The river continued to weave its way down between these stark slopes until a section where trees had grown both sides of the road unmolested by man or animal creating a small patch of forest and shade from the sun for the occasional traveller passing through.

Moving above the tree line, the valley widened and become more like rolling open pasture and the road had gradual gradients both up and down as it weaved its way across the landscape. There were no trees but small hamlets could be seen on the far side of the river that had been built on the slopes of the valley sides.

These were carefully positioned to be above any flooding in the bottom of the valley but also away from danger areas where snow may build up high on the valley slope only to crash down in an avalanche and sweep away whole communities so these hamlets were often seen to be on the end of promontories projecting across the valley floor.

Despite being at quite a high elevation and the consequent bad winter weather the soil here was productive and farmers had taken advantage of the quality of the soil and there were great expanses of wheat, potatoes, tomatoes, maize, spinach and other crops and wherever water was available there were green fields. Farmers and their families were working their fields and paid us no attention as we sped by.

It was in this open countryside that we suffered another puncture and Koshal pulled over to the side of the road to change the wheel. I had seen enough tyres changes just recently and with little to catch my eye across a large and unchanging vista, and having a long drive ahead of us I opted to walk ahead down the road with the aim of getting back into the jeep when it caught us up after changing the wheel.

Fran and I were wearing walking boots but I noted that the guard was only wearing ordinary shoes. I checked that our guard was aware of what I intended and to see whether his job was to protect the vehicle or protect us foreigners. I wondered what his reaction would have been if one foreigner had walked off and the other had stayed put.

As it was Fran and I set off down the road and our guard followed. I could not judge from his expression whether he was delighted at the prospect of stretching his legs or whether he thought us mad to walk down the road when we could have sat at the side of the road and been driven after the tyre had been changed.

As we walked a couple of lorries passed us, the typical ordinary colourful lorries but these weren't carrying potatoes but carried army supplies for the many military bases in the area. After more than half an hour of walking, the jeep hove into view behind us and we all got back in. I'm sure as we clambered back into our seats, I caught a glimpse of relief from our new guard.

We reached Chilum camp which is a military base with an adjacent lorry park at an elevation of 3,498m. I was about to take a photo when I was reminded with a tap on the shoulder and a waving index finger that this was a military restricted area and photography was not allowed. We were now about 45kms from the disputed border with India but no one was allowed further down the road without the required pass.

Our journey was due to take us on a spur road on a left hand turning off the main road but first Koshal had to get the punctured tyre repaired. We were behind schedule but not too far so I had a green tea at a wayside cafe whilst waiting for the puncture to be repaired. Fran meanwhile was chatting to some of the drivers of the large colourful trucks that we had seen and there were plenty here in the lorry park. She wanted to get some photos of the trucks, not just from the outside but also from the inside. She got several of the drivers to pose in front of their trucks and a number of good shots of the insides of the cabs.

With our repaired tyre we turned out of the lorry park and stopped at a checkpoint. Our papers and permits were scrutinised and we were allowed to pass and as a large sign proclaimed, welcomed us into the Deosai National Park. A by-line on the sign also reminded us that we were only allowed to shoot the wildlife with a camera.

The park covers more than 3,000sqkms and at over an average of 4,000m, it is the second highest plateau after Tibet. Deosai means 'the land of giants' or in the local Balti language it is called Byarsa meaning 'summer place'. This is not hard to understand why it gained its name as summer place as it is a grassy but windswept expanse of rolling hills, good for grazing in the summer but inhospitable and bitterly cold in winter.

It is home to endangered brown bears, ibex, marmots and a host of birds including eagles. We stopped several times to observe the marmots but we saw no bears or ibex. It was disappointing to see that in many places the dirt track was being ungraded with large rocks acting as the foundations of a new road. Modernisation may often to be applauded but if it brings more tourists it may destroy the very fragile nature that everyone comes to visit. Hence my often repeated advice to get out and visit these places before they all become too commercialised.

We arrived at Deosai Lake which is about 2.3kms by 1.8kms and a depth of over 40m and at an elevation of 4,142m it is one of the highest lakes in the world. It was a lovely blue colour reflecting the bright blue sky overhead of that summer's day. It was after our normal lunch time but finally we stopped here for lunch. At this altitude, there should have been no mosquitoes but the illiterate little monsters had not read the guide books and as soon as we got out we were assaulted by biting insects. We ate our lunch literally on the hoof as we walked back and forth around the jeep so as to keep moving to avoid the mosquitoes from landing and biting. I was only too happy to finish lunch and get back into the jeep to get away from the mosquitoes.

After another 25kms we were approaching our campsite. It was reached after crossing an iconic rope suspension bridge that the jeep would have to negotiate which I was looking forward to experiencing. It was a big disappointment to discover that the suspension bridge had been closed and that there was a large new concrete bridge spanning the river just metres away upstream.

The camp site was rather basic with water pulled from the river, a long walk to the nearest dirt toilet (which had a broken door) and rather exposed to the wind blowing from the west and needless to say it would be cold overnight. It wasn't a difficult decision and despite being behind schedule we still had time to reach the next destination and the hotel in Skardu as long as there were no more delays.

It was a long shot but the campsite held no attraction so we headed on towards Skardu at an elevation of over 2,200m but a long way below the Deosai Plains at over 4,000m. We travelled across more of the plain until we reached a gap in the rolling hills and this was our route down off the plateau. The route descended and the sides of the valley grew taller and closer. The road followed a small stream down away from the plateau. The road started to zig zag down the ever steepening slope. We came across a herd of goats being taken down the valley. Our paths crossed several time as they took the direct route down the slope and we followed the road that hair pinned back and forth.

We followed the road which reached a flatter area and a number of fields. There was a vast hydroelectric dam that had created a large lake. Where the river flowed into the lake, it had caused the river to drop its load of sediment and create new flat land ready for cultivation.

The dam and its associated spillways and buildings housing dynamos and transformers took up a considerable amount of the valley bottom where the authorities had built the infrastructure to maximise the difference in water levels and therefore increase the electricity generation potential. It was awesome in the engineering achievement but I wondered what had been sacrificed beneath the waves to achieve electric power.

Shortly after coming out of the valley and entering the main Indus valley that played host to the city of Skardu we entered the outskirts of the city. We continued to descend until we reached the centre of the city and turned right towards our hotel situated slightly outside of the main centre but in a commanding position on a bluff high above the Indus River. There were lights everywhere and the electricity system was obviously working for a change.

The hotel was a modern multi storey concrete built structure with stunning views across the confluence of the Indus and another major tributary with an ancient fort perched high above the opposite cliff overlooking the junction. The rooms were spacious with western toilets, running water and showers with hot water. Although I noted that there was still a large bucket of water in the bathroom and an oil lamp in the bedroom just in case.

I was looking forward to a shower but I was also worried about my camera. The trip up to the Deosai plain, across it and down to Skardu was one of the top three journeys in northern Pakistan but somewhere across the Deosai Plain my camera had been affected by dust and would no longer open so I was unable to take any photos. I didn't have a second camera with me so I was desperate to get it fixed as soon as I could.

We were scheduled to meet with Ayas Shikri who was the manager and owner of the tour company who were going to manage my trek up to K2. The story of how this mountain came to be called K2 deserves a little space. Maps in India during its time as being part of the British Empire were rather imprecise and technology had advanced a lot alongside industrialisation. A great project called the Great Trigonometric Survey headed by Major William Lambton was started in April 1802 near Madras and would work its way across the area. The aim of the project was to produce accurate maps and measure the elevation of key peaks of the area. The East India Company had expected that it might take five years but in reality it took more than 60 years to complete.

The mountain now known as K2 was first surveyed by Thomas Montgomerie as part of the Survey. It was the practice to use local names but this mountain was so remote that it didn't have a local name. Therefore he used the abbreviation K for Karakoram and 2 as the number one had already been used for another unnamed peak now known as Masherbrum.

There was a proposal to name the peak after Henry Godwin-Austen in memory of an explorer but this was rejected by the Royal Geographical Society. Its then current practice was to use local names for peaks but the name appeared on maps and can still be found on some maps although now a days K2 is the favoured name. (But this ignores an inconvenient truth that the Society had named Everest after Colonel Sir George Everest, another surveyor for the Survey). It is also called the Savage Mountain as nearly a quarter of the climbers who have attempted to climb to the summit have been killed, the second most dangerous mountain in the world after Annapurna.

We climbed into the jeep and headed out into the city. After a number of turns by which time I had lost my sense of direction we slowed down outside a set of large gates protecting a large detached house and the surrounding walls enclosed a large compound. We pressed the buzzer to introduce ourselves and after a while when the buzzer sounded and we pushed the gates open to let ourselves in.

We were lead into the house to a spacious room dominated by a large desk at one end behind which sat the owner, Ayas Shikri. There were a couple of settees, a coffee table and a large flat screen television showing a tennis tournament from Australia with the sound turned down. We were served tea and apricots and introduced to Nadim, our mountain guide who was 21 years of age and had studied electronics at the local university.

Other members of the team were introduced, Hussain, our chef and Essan, assistant chef who both came from a village high up in the foothills of K2. After our initial meeting to explain how the system worked and what was expected of us, including having to sign some papers and an interview with the Ministry of

Tourism that afternoon (plus another interview on our return), we left the office and Nadeem joined us for the day.

As we walked back to the gate, there was a pile of camping equipment and a number of tents which was our equipment that was being checked out before being packed up ready for our trip.

We headed towards the bazaar partly to investigate the town centre but also to find a camera shop. We found a shop that sold phones, cameras and other small electrical items and I was told that he would fix my camera and to come back later to collect it.

We walked on through the town centre, along New Bazaar Road and College Road. The names of some of the streets made it feel like home but the shops were very different with open shop fronts and piles of wares stacked up on the pavement outside. We walked past a pharmacy well stocked with lots of prescription medicines, many whose names I recognised which appeared to be readily available over the counter rather than requiring a prescription. The prices also seemed cheap but they would still be regarded as expensive by local standards.

We walked through the women's bazaar selling ladies and children's clothing, both new and used. Over the road we walked through the old bazaar which was much more of a local food market with individual sellers with small shop fronts, a number of butchers with the meat on open display and piles of vegetables. Further on was a whole host of stall holders who were offering general goods and I had the impression that whatever you wanted you would be able to find it here.

We headed out of town past the local polo pitch towards the fort perched on the hill high above the town with commanding views of the town and along the Indus valley. This was the Kharpocho fort, over 500 years old built by a local powerful king named Ali Sher Khan Anchan. The fort surrounds an earlier and ancient mosque. The path up to the fort was a narrow winding track up the steep rocky slope and it was easy to see how just a few defenders could hold off an army.

The path skirted a long section of wall before reaching the gates. The walls were in good repair and inside the gate there was a janitor who had been asleep. He unlocked the inner gate and we could see a number of buildings to house soldiers and store-rooms backing onto the outer walls and the small mosque sitting in the centre. There were no exhibits, no leaflets and no information boards or signs. We were left to wander around at will.

The roofs were flat, made of branches, covered with twigs and finally mud. They were surprisingly strong and could take the weight of several people but there were holes in some of the roofs so we had to be careful where we walked. All morning whilst walking around the town and the fort, Nadeem was constantly checking his phone and texting as if his life depended on it.

Back in the hotel Nadeem produced some papers for me to sign in order to undertake the trek and obtain our permits. He appeared to be surprised when I started reading the document and I was about to put pen to paper to answer the first question. He said it was a formality, not to answer the questions and pressed me to just sign it.

I had spent thirty years in business and had often had to sign papers. I had got into the habit of actually reading whatever I had been asked to sign and to query anything that I didn't understand. It was a series of statements and questions with spaces for answers. It was a list of requirements concerning protecting the environment, not to pick and flowers, burn any wood or take any minerals. Rubbish had to be either burned, buried if it was bio degradable or carried off the mountain. No photos were to be taken of military installations, bridges and the like.

There were also questions on the guides, the trek and feedback on specific areas and that I understood the Ministry of Tourisms' requirements and that I was personally responsible to meet these requirements on behalf of the whole group including a dozen porters that I hadn't even met. I said that I couldn't answer some of the questions and sign it as I hadn't had my interview with the Ministry and hadn't completed the trek.

We were at an impasse as without my signature we would not get permits and we would not be able to go. I resolved the issue by signing but also adding in writing that I was signing under duress, that I had not had the promised Ministry of Tourism meeting that I had been promised and couldn't complete some of the questions as I had not started let alone completed the trek. Despite the provisos that I had added Nadeem seemed content as he had my signature and he returned to the office saying that he would come back shortly to take us to the Ministry.

We waited all afternoon in the garden drinking green tea, gazing out across the wide Indus as it flowed slowly past the hotel and turned a bend as it approached the Kharpocho fort off to our left. The only excitement was when some goats had wandered into the garden and had started eating the dahlias and the hotel staff rushed out to shoo them away.

It was late afternoon and we heard no more from Nadeem so I went to find Jahangir to find out what was happening. After some phone calls, it turned out that the meeting with the Ministry was now to be held that evening at Ayas Shikri's own home so after dinner Koshal drove us across town to a substantial carefully maintained home with its own enclosed garden. Jahangir, Fran and myself sat down opposite Ayas Shikri, and three men from the Ministry including a man introduced as Nassir who was also a guide who had completed the journey to K2 many times and knew all the regulations.

We were taken through all the rules, many of which I remember from the piece of paper that Nadeem had asked me to sign earlier that afternoon. Many times I had to rely on Ayas Shikri's organising ability and reliability to answer the Ministry's questions such as insurance for the porters and ensuring that we had enough kerosene for cooking. I was asked whether I was a vegetarian. Whilst not a vegetarian, I don't eat a lot of red meat so I mentioned this adding that at home I live on a diet of fruit, vegetables and fish.

The permits that we were about to be given only covered the route up the Baltoro glacier and back the same way. What I had asked for whilst planning the trip was the return trip to go via Gondogoro Pass to make a circular trek back to the start point. This was not possible was the reply so I pressed my point. Nassir chipped in and was clearer in his explanation that this pass is not open to trekkers this year.

The route involves a steep ascent and fixed ropes are required but these have not been erected and secondly there is no rescue team in place to cover this section so due to the lack of facilities this route it was not open this season. It was clear that I was trying to battle bureaucracy and I was not going to win but I had a plausible explanation and so I had to accept the situation.

I also had a special request. I had had such fun playing Ludo on the Minapin Glacier that I asked Ayas Shikri to add a Ludo set to our equipment list. I thanked our host and the men from the Ministry and we left. On the way back to the hotel we stopped off in town to collect my camera. The storekeeper proudly showed me that the camera now worked and relieved me of what I thought was a lot of money which I subsequently deeply regretted ever handing over.

I rather naively thought that he would use his skill to take the camera apart and clean the mechanism but on closer inspection he had used a sharp implement to prise open the lens mechanism loosening the dust to allow it to open whilst leaving a number of indentations in the chrome. I could have done that myself for nothing.

We were up at 6am and loaded our kit into a Toyota Land Cruiser. Nassir who we had met the night before was there as well to ensure that everything went according to plan. Stuff that we didn't need for the trek I repacked and left at the hotel. We headed into town for some last minute supplies and to pick up another member of the team. The sun had risen and was bathing the tops of the mountains around us in brilliant sunshine but the sun had not risen high enough yet to throw any sunlight onto the floor of the valley which remained in shade and cold.

We left town heading up the southern bank of the Indus and crossed a bridge into a desolate rocky empty plain with the road disappearing ahead of us where it reached some hills and was lost to view behind the rising topography. We went up and over these small hills and joined another valley with a wide river with sand or gravel bars, some breaking the surface of the water which were interrupting the rivers flow.

Along the banks there were green fields and farm houses. We stopped at the first village that we came to and found a garage and filled the tyres with air. There wasn't a puncture for a change but the soft tyres made for an uncomfortable journey for passengers. We followed the road up the valley passing fields, trees lining the edge of the road and the fields. Occasionally there were open stretches between fields where the ground was too rocky and uneven for cultivation where nothing grew.

By 10am we came to a bridge over the river to the north side of the river. This was a suspension bridge with a wooden road bed. But with our heavily laden vehicles, the bridge might not take the weight so the passengers got out to let the vehicles cross first. The bridge creaked and swayed and sagged as the first vehicle crossed. I was immensely glad that we had got out. When the last vehicle had crossed we followed on foot.

We had a break to have a respite from the rough track and the dust and had drinks in the shaded garden of a busy road side café. It appeared to be a popular place with trekkers and climbers. There were also numerous locals who frequented the place hoping to pick up work as porters or guides.

The valley now was devoid of fields and was just bare rock with an occasional shrub struggling to grow through the rocks. The road crested a rise and with a number of hair pin bends descended back towards the river. From our vantage point high above the valley bottom we could see up the valley. The river filled the bottom of the valley and tumbled and washed over the rocks in the river's path.

There was a significant feature here. There was a choke point in the path of the main river consisting of a very strong rock resistant to erosion but it had a fault line down the centre. The river had eroded this fault line following the weakness downwards. From upstream the river looked like it reached the rock and virtually disappears. It goes from a twenty metre wide, 3 metre deep river to a three metre wide, 20 metre deep river as it negotiates this constriction.

Further up the valley we came across a jeep heading down the valley. This section of road crosses a scree slope of loose rocks stretching high up the side of the valley with vertical cliffs above. Below the road the scree slope stretched down into the river with the foot of the slope was constantly being washed away by the river. We had to reverse back up the track until we found a stable and wide enough point to squeeze the two vehicles past each other.

Having found a place to let the jeep pass we carried on up the valley. We crossed a couple of streams by fords and worked our way around some avalanches that had cascaded down the valley side and across the road.

Just before reaching Askole, there are some hot springs above the road. The hot water bubbles out of the ground and trickles down the hill side and as it evaporates it leaves strange formation like stalagmites and weird shapes.

We reached the village and turned into the court yard of a large two storey hotel with the upper storey painted a distinctive red. This is the end of the road and the last village, set at an elevation of 3,050m. We were met by a group of porters and there was a lot of hand shaking and talking. I was introduced to one of them named Mansour who was the head porter for the village and who would organise our porters for us.

He was average height, a happy smiling face and liked to wear loud shirts. There was also another group who had arrived at the same time who had completed their climbing trips and were on their way down the valley. I was not sure who was part of our team of porters, who was with the other group and who were just visiting but I am sure it would all work out eventually. Some of what we had carried was for another group as I noticed several bottles of soft drinks being carried into the hotel. We set up our individual tents, the kitchen tent and the dining tent on the flat grassy lawn of the hotel.

There was talk of deaths on the mountain but it appeared that five Iranians, a German, a Pole and three Spanish mountaineers had recently lost their lives on the mountain, some in climbing accidents and some in avalanches. The exact numbers and nationalities varied according to who was telling the news but it emphasised the point that it could be dangerous. We said goodbye to our drivers and to Nassir who had been so helpful the night before who had accompanied us up the valley.

I had a short walk around the local village which didn't take long as there was not much to see, a small hostel, a couple of shops and a small museum detailing traditional life in the village. Although small it was fascinating. Amongst other exhibits it detailed traditional housing on three levels, the top for summer living, the middle for winter living and the ground floor used to house animals during the long cold winter months. Back in the dining tent Essan brought us some green tea and we sat down for a game of Ludo.

Chapter 13

Trek to Concordia K2

We were up at 5am for breakfast and to pack our tents away and to set off. There was lots of activity with mules and porters milling about, equipment left in piles and chickens pecking at the ground. Fran and I were ready and were hanging about as we had packed our personal stuff before breakfast and were waiting for the porters to get themselves sorted out. Eventually Nadeem was ready to lead myself and Fran up the valley ahead of the rest of the group who would follow and catch us up.

We put on our day packs and walked out of the hotel gates. At first it was easy walking on a wide farm track past fields where farmers were already at work. The fields quickly changed into rough pasture and finally there was just a rocky valley stretching away from us into the distance. There were other travellers on the road coming towards us. Firstly it was a porter or two who had walked faster or set off ahead of the main party heading back to Askole.

Later there were more porters, mules and trekkers making their way down in the valley. The porters struggled with their loads and greeted each other as most of them knew each other. The trekkers and climbers seemed to fall into two broad categories; either they had had a great time and were happy, smiling and content with their lot or they were exhausted and struggling with just a small day pack to make the last effort to reach Askole. I wondered which camp I would fall into in two weeks' time.

We were not alone in our ascent. There was a group of soldiers who were going up to a base high in the mountains. They were dressed in casual clothes, denims, branded tee shirts, caps, sweatshirts and the like and not a hint that they were soldiers but they carried guns. I would have easily have mistaken them for bandits or terrorists.

We came to a raging torrent of a small river rushing down to join the main river. There was a small foot suspension bridge crossing the raging torrent of muddy water. And the noise was surprisingly loud as the water crashed against the rocks in its path. We took turns to step onto it and pose for photos before carrying on.

At a flatter area with a few trees providing shade, we stopped for a break. The porters would stop here for a break and we could go on together. The soldiers passed us again and waved as they headed towards an army outpost a few hundred metres further on.

We were fully rested and the first members of our team eventually appeared. Hussain and Essan arrived first with backpacks but also carrying in their upturned hands the chickens that had been at the hotel. This was to be our fresh meat for the trip. The chickens seemed perfectly happy and didn't struggle at all at being carried and didn't run off when placed on the ground but perhaps they didn't know what fate awaited them.

The other porters were still somewhere behind but Hussain and Essan didn't stop for long and scooped up the chickens and carried on. There was still a long way to go and I was eager to avoid the heat of the day so before the other porters arrived we set off again.

Late afternoon we turned up a tributary away from the main river and on the far side we could see our camp but to reach it we had to head further up the valley before crossing a suspension bridge and heading back down the far bank. We arrived at the camp site run by the Mountain Guide and Porters Organisation, or MGPO for short that ran all the camps up the trail. This was Jhula Camp at an elevation of 3,150m.

There was a small stone built cottage for the staff and running water. The water came straight from streams further up the hillside and was cloudy and needed to be boiled and left to settle before drinking or using in cooking. Trekkers and their chefs camped in one area and there was a separate area for porters.

There were a collection of individual fibreglass cubicles that housed dirt toilets with holes to squat over or western style toilets, while other cubicles had a concrete floor with just a plug hole in one corner in which one could strip off and wash. There was no plumbing but there was a large bucket in each cubicle which you filled up with cold water from the tap. And I do mean cold as the water was melt water from the snow high above us and it seemed to be barely above freezing point.

Hussain and Essan had arrived some time before and had already set up the cooking and dining tents, getting a good position on some flat, sandy ground. The chickens that Hussian and Essan had carried up the valley were happy to peck around on the ground. Fran named them Ek, Doh and Teen in Urdu, translated as one, two and three. As the day wore on we would notice that only Ek and Doh were pecking around the tents and that Teen had seemingly mysteriously disappeared or had escaped.

That evening we would have chicken for dinner. We would know now for certain where Teen had gone. This scenario would be repeated as we ascended up the trail with another chicken disappearing until there were none left.

I had had a bad night as I was feeling sick and had an upset stomach so my sleep was disturbed as I made several trips in the dark but starlit night to use the facilities which were some way away from the tents. Returning towards my tent on one of these nocturnal trips I saw a bright torchlight being waved about up the valley at about where the bridge across the river was situated. I was in two minds as to what to do, either ignore it and go back to sleep or, fearing a terrorist attack, whether I should wake the others and take immediate flight.

My fear was beginning to win the battle but I didn't want to cry wolf so I walked along the track towards where I had seen the light and on a crest I left the track to sit down with a view of the track heading back towards the lights that I had seen earlier to wait to see what happened.

After an hour, there had been no more lights and no group of terrorists sneaking up on the sleeping camp and I was cold and stiff from inactivity. The need for a decision was more pressing as I needed to go to the toilet again so I decided that there was no danger and I headed back to the facilities and finally to my sleeping bag and I needed at least some rest as breakfast was 5am.

I could only face green tea for breakfast so without delay the guides lead us out of camp and the porters and chefs would catch us up. As we left the camp, the sun was already shining down on us warming the thin mountain air and the first section of the days walk was across sand. I was drinking plenty of water but with a disturbed night and empty stomach and following a sandy path, this was perhaps my worst day.

By the afternoon I was flagging and the stops were more frequent but Jahangir encouraged me to continue. Although we were heading along the valley there were still several gullies that crossed the path heading down to the main river. Some were dry whilst others had varying amounts of water flowing in the bottom. But each time we came to a gully there was the walk down to the edge of the water, walking up and down to find a place to cross where there was no bridge and the walk up the other side which was taking its toll on my progress.

Much of the valley side was barren but a long way up the main valley was an area with trees spreading up the valley side and this was where we were heading for. I am not sure whether knowing this helped me or not as after another hour of walking it didn't seem to be much closer. I had to dig deep into my reserves in order to continue.

In the end we successfully reached the next camp named Paiju at 3,480m. There were the now familiar fibreglass cubicles set 150m from the main camping area which was scattered over several terraces with our kitchen and dining tent on one level and I pitched my tent on the terrace above. The porters had their own camp area and facilities further down the valley side. The site had plenty of water and shade trees and other than the staff who looked after the camp over summer there were no other campers yet.

We had been at the camp and had settled in for some time but the porters had yet to arrive. When they did come into camp there was a reason for their delayed arrival. It turned out that one of the mules had fallen into one of the wet gullies and had been washed downstream.

The muleteer had to run downhill and wade into the water to pull the poor unfortunate animal out of the water. Luckily the mule wasn't injured and the load was still in place and thankfully nothing was lost. Equally lucky was the fact that the waterproof bags had lived up to their name and had not been torn on sharp rocks and the contents were still dry.

The next day was a rest day to get acclimatised to the altitude. Over a late breakfast I vowed to make any job last as long as possible as there was probably little else to do. I washed some clothes and hung them over some bushes to dry. Mules were left out to pasture higher up the valley and other than to load or unload, they were not allowed into the camp.

And thinking back to my experiences on the Minapin Glacier, there were no cows about so that my clothes were safe to be left on some bushes to dry and safe from being eaten. I wandered both up the trail and back the way we had come just to fill in time and we had a leisurely cooked lunch, drank a lot of green tea and played a lot of Ludo.

I watched as the camp staff tidied the camp in the morning. Litter in the main camping area was collected and the hard packed earth was watered to help keep the dust down. The cubicles were checked (I can't say washed, it was more of a hosing down with water if it looked like it needed it but no scrubbing or disinfectant).

It is a shame that not all areas received the same treatment. The porter's cubicles were not clean and there was a considerable accumulation of litter around their camp area and the track either side of the camp was also littered detracting from the beauty of the place. Not all groups took such an enlightened view about looking after the environment and taking their responsibilities seriously as had been explained to me by the Ministry so seriously.

As the afternoon drew on there were other groups that arrived on site. There were groups that were heading down the valley. There were also groups that were heading up the valley. The camp site filled up with small individual tents and larger kitchen and dining tents. The Ludo board was a great ice breaker as four people played on the dining table in the tent and were watched by another group of porters and chefs at the tent doorway. When a game finished some players would retreat to be replaced by others and another game started. The rules were universally known by all and since the majority of the conversation was suggesting how to use your dice throw or what number was the best to throw, I was soon fluent in counting in Urdu (even if it was only up to twelve, the maximum number possible from two dice).

Back in Skardu before setting off on the trek I noted that I was responsible for a party of twelve porters and that I had not counted anything like that number supporting us and since I had paid for twelve I had expected to see twelve so I challenged Jahangir. They are all here I was told but I still couldn't count twelve. So I listed out the staff that I had seen with us, two chefs, two guides and two muleteers is only six and Mansour, the head porter I had not seen since leaving Askole.

Then a big smile came across Jahangir's face as the penny dropped on the misunderstanding. Has no one told you, he said, each mule is the equivalent of three porters so the two mules are the same as six porters making twelve people. Mansour the head porter organises the porters from the village and the weight of their loads to ensure that the work is fairly parcelled out to all the villagers that want to work as porters. He doesn't accompany us on the actual trek. It was simple and obvious when you know. That might also explain why some of the porters supporting other groups looked a bit too old to be doing this type of heavy manual work but they needed the money.

The rest day was over and another walking day had arrived so it was up for breakfast at 5am after which we left the chefs and porters to pack camp and we headed up the valley with our two guides. One section of the route crossed a high bank which the river was eroding and under cutting. The ground had become unstable and there was a long crack that had formed in the ground running parallel to the river, a section of the bank up to 5 metres wide and 80 metres long that would soon collapse into the river. I made sure that I walked on the mountain side of the crack on what I hoped was the safer side.

Less than an hour up the track from the camp we came to the snout of the glacier. The river was pouring out from under the glacier but only near the river could the ice itself be seen as the overlying debris on top of the glacier covered much of the rest of the ice.

We started up the terminal moraine at the snout of the glacier and started to walk along the top of the glacier itself. There were many features that we had already seen on other glaciers but this one was the longest and I would be on it for several days.

We passed two camps on the rocky valley side above the glacier. These didn't have the same level of facilities as other camps but you could stop there if the weather turned bad or of course if you had all the time in the world and planned a long slow trek with short distances to cover each day. But they did have a small stone cottage for the staff who were only too happy to serve refreshments and we stopped for a break and to sip some hot freshly made green tea. At the next camp we stopped for hot soup for lunch which was a welcome break from the usual savoury biscuits and cheese.

There isn't a single route up the glacier as the mules can't cross some of the terrain and so may take a longer route to avoid obstacles such as very steep slopes or crevasses that we can jump but they must go around. Also the glacier moves albeit slowly but steadily, crumpling the surface, closing some crevasses and creating new ones and different parts of the glacier melt or flow at different rates.

At one point the track dipped and crossed a ridge of ice that was literally a knife edge, not even any space to put a foot down on a flat surface. There were steep and slippery sides with drops of tens of metres on both sides. On one side the slope finished in deep cold water flowing quickly past the ridge and the other side ending on a jumble of jagged boulders. Nadeem had no hesitation to walk across as this was where the track had led and he nimbly danced along the icy ridge to reach the far side. It was easy for him as he had given his backpack to Essan to carry and he waved at us to follow.

I was more respectful of the danger and suggested that we take an alternative route. We turned around and Nadeem reluctantly followed us complaining that we were going the wrong way. Jahangir found the mule track and we skirted the knife edge like ice ridge and followed a safer track up the glacier.

We reached our next planned camp, Urdugas at 4,130m which is set above the glacier on a rock promontory with great views down the valley with several terraces but no trees and so no shade. There was also a prayer area with three mats set out. There was no ornate mihrab showing the direction of Mecca but it was clear which direction the faithful needed to face. On the other side of the promontory was a small army outpost and weather station.

Some years ago a large section of the cliff collapsed and killed several people. There is a memorial to them with their names and a few details, where the metal plates just like the ones we were using for meals had had the letters formed by punching several lines of small holes with a small sharp point.

The cubicle toilets were all filthy and unhygienic and even our guides suggested that we might like to walk out of camp in the opposite direction to use the open valley side. The washing facility here was unique. A hose pipe run down from high up the valley side and provided a constant flow of water taken from a mountain stream. On the edge of a cliff where the rock jutted out was a small concrete square with a lip a couple of centimetres high and a plug hole that emptied straight out into the air to fall down to the base of the cliff a long way below.

There was no privacy whatsoever and it was useable only with swimming trunks but a marvellous view if you have a head for heights. I personally don't like heights without a hand rail but this was such a marvellous spot that I just had to brave the height and experience the position.

I also reflected on the fact that most of the group would help out with jobs but I never saw Nadeem do any work such as help with the tents or carry water as if it was beneath him. On arrival in camp he was first to wash and spent some time coiffuring his hair with the help of a small mirror whilst the rest of the group undertook the jobs that needed to be done. At least he wasn't on his phone as in Skardu as there was no reception up here in the mountains. But he showed no interest in helping out with the jobs that needed to be done.

There was a routine on walking days that we followed which rarely changed. An early start, up at 5am with breakfast at 5.30am often omelette with green tea and time to fill up our water bottles with boiled water that had cooled overnight. Then we packed our personal bags and took down our tents. Then we would set off with one or both guides and leaving the chefs and porters to pack away the kitchen and dining tents and load the mules. Then they would catch us up later but rarely did they arrive after we arrived at our camp for the evening.

During the day, Jahangir would point out the various peaks around us, naming them and giving their height or for the lesser peaks an approximation of their height. Hussain and Essan would overtake us during the day to set up the kitchen tent in a good spot at the next camp. We would stop a few times in the morning and afternoon for a quick rest with a longer stop for lunch which was usually savoury biscuits and cheese.

Arriving in camp in the late afternoon we would join Hussain and Essan who had reserved some space for our tents near the kitchen tent. When the mules arrived, we would unload them and put up our own tents. I would have a wander around to understand the immediate surroundings whilst the porters led the mules away to fend for themselves on whatever they could find to graze.

Water for drinking was collected and left to settle, then boiled to kill any germs and left to cool. We would chat over a game of Ludo taking turns to play and drink green tea whilst waiting for dinner. If there was time and enough light we might play some more Ludo but as dusk arrived we would retreat to our tents and sleeping bags.

We left Urdugas camp and passed the army outpost and headed down the valley slope and back onto the glacier. As we headed east there was the distinctive snow covered peak of Masherbrum to the south dominating the horizon. This was the first mountain to be discovered in the Karakoram without a local name so it was called K1.

Behind us on the track was a mule train heading our way with a few muleteers and a couple of dozen of mules. They were employed by the army to move supplies up to the camps along the valley. They caught us up and for a while we kept pace with them but we couldn't sustain the same pace and the mule train eventually disappeared out of sight ahead of us.

The terrain was rugged but the surface of the glacier was less undulating than the day before although there was a cooling breeze blowing down the valley. We kept to one side of the glacier to avoid the centre of the glacier that had more crevasses and streams. Nadeem and Essan were walking at a faster pace and pulled ahead and were a long way off. Due to the number of gullies crossing our path they were often out of sight although Jahangir, Fran and I stuck together. Nadeem was meant to be our mountain guide to base camp but he was conspicuous by his absence as he should have been within sight of his guests who were paying his fee ... basically Fran and myself.

Further up the glacier there were strange formations like pyramids of bare white ice sticking through the surface of the glacier that gave the scene an eerie feel. There was also a lot more snow lower down the valley slopes.

Goro camp is at 4,500m and situated on the glacier itself. Pitching a tent here is a challenge as the ground is uneven and stoney. An added issue was the ice that held some the of rocks firm in its grip and the usual method of moving a stone aside wouldn't work. Instead we moved handfuls of gravel to the chosen site to try to level it out enough to lay out flat in your sleeping bag.

There is no camp manager at this location and the facilities are more basic. Water was taken from a stream that flowed near the camp. The toilets deserve a special mention. There was a metal frame with steps going up to the cubicle which was covered in plastic sheeting on four sides with a slit in one side for a doorway. The floor was a metal mesh with a hole in the centre with a barrel underneath. And it wasn't clean to look at but at least in the cold temperatures there were no flies and no smell.

As a result of the rough ground and paucity of suitable flat sites our tents were well spread out across the area of the camp site. Despite the ground sheet and Thermorest it was still uncomfortable and lying on the frozen ground meant that it was cold inside the tent.

I was woken early in the depths of night by the tent shaking and the noise of crunching on the stones and ice just outside the tent. I had paid too much attention to the stones on the site rather than where the site was in relation to its environs. There was a mule train coming through the camp in the middle of the night and my guy ropes were too close the track. As the mules walked past on the same route that they had taken dozens of times before, they were tripping on the guy ropes shaking my tent.

By the time that I had got out of my sleeping bag and put my coat and boots on, the mule train had passed. We were moving on in the morning anyway but I made a mental note to be further away from the track in future. But on the bright side it was a clear night and I spent some time gazing at the stars trying to pick out constellations that were familiar. We were so remote here high in the mountains that there was no light pollution so the stars were all crystal clear. Being further east and south than at home, parts of the sky were unfamiliar and there were only a few stars and groups that I recognised.

I had changed from my shalwaar chemise to regular and warmer clothing now we were higher and it was colder. As I got dressed I noticed that there was some water inside the tent and the bottom of my sleeping bag was damp. It hadn't seeped through to the inside but I couldn't pack it away wet so I spread it out on top of the tent to air. Looking around the camp that morning, I noticed that the porters had moved their tent during the night.

The wind was a bit too cold and they had moved to a more sheltered site. Any surface water such as the puddle that had developed yesterday outside of the dining tent had frozen solid overnight. There was no forage up here for the mules so they were fed hay that they had been carrying.

We eagerly set about our tasks as the activity would help to keep us warm. It was only a short walk to the next camp but we were eager to get moving to get warm. Unlike the clear skies during the night there was low cloud and the air was damp and it smelled like rain or possibly snow. We hurried on to the next camp.

En-route we passed close to an army outpost on a small hill with signs directing us around the base of the hill. There was a noticeable amount of rubbish that had either blown down from the hill, or in the case of the empty large tins of meat and vegetables must have been thrown over the perimeter of the outpost. Some still had labels on proudly announcing that they contained meat produced on a particular specified army run farm.

The approach to Concordia camp at 4,650m was across a rocky barren landscape with ice poking through the debris in places, with the valley sides obscured by low cloud. It was cold and it had begun to drizzle. When we arrived in mid-afternoon the light was failing due to the cloud but we persevered and set up camp. The camp area was spread over several hectares as the number of flat tent pitches were few and far between. The local camp manager who was also a member of the rescue team came across to welcome us and I was immediately envious of his thick warm puffer jacket.

I had a wander around the local area. There was little to see in this bleak and barren place. There were some large tents belonging to the manager and the rescue team plus a large and unsightly pile of rubbish as large as one of the big tents that had been collected and bagged up which would be properly disposed of at the end of the season. There were a few tents belonging to other groups of trekkers or climbers.

By late afternoon the drizzle had eased off and there were small patches of blue in between the clouds and looking north we were eager to see the great peak of K2. We only seemed to see glimpses of it as the cloud was still too thick to reveal the whole mountain so we would have to be patient and hope for the best for tomorrow.

It was going to be a very long day for the round trip to base camp and back to Concordia. Breakfast was at 4.30am with the aim of leaving at 5am. We left camp heading north. Essan was leading us as he had been up here so many times as he was also a high altitude porter with Nadeem and Jahangir, Fran and myself. Our first obstacle was a steep icy slope where we had to exercise extreme care as we didn't want to lose our grip and slide down into the freezing stream below.

There was a rope to assist in walking down the steep slope backwards and with care and luck we should be alright. Nadeem thought we were being over cautious and slid down on his bum. Essan who was at the bottom looked horrified and shouted at him to grab the rope as Nadeem slide down towards him apparently out of control.

It was a tense moment but Nadeem slowed and Essan caught him before he plunged into the water below. I noticed that Nadeem didn't have a backpack and queried whether he had lost it on the descent but he had given it to Essan to carry his pack as well as his own. We walked upstream until we found a place to jump the stream and scrambled up the far bank.

We clambered over boulders and carried on up the glacier on a rather indistinct path. In the late morning we reached the Broad Peak climbers base camp at 5,100m. There was not much of a view as the clouds obscured any vista that there might have been. Besides being this low in the valley with the valley sides towering over us, the peaks are not at their grandest and the best views are to be had from Concordia camp.

Other than evidence that climbers had camped here there was little difference between this particular area and any other area of the valley with no sign of any memorial and no one there as the climbing season had finished and the trekking season had only just begun. I had expected something more and was somewhat disappointed.

K2 base camp is only a little higher at 5,135m but to reach it requires a trek up the valley side and down again as the direct route is too difficult and dangerous. This is similar to Broad Peak base camp but with many memorials to climbers lost, many made out of metal plates with lettering formed by punching small holes in the thin metal just like we has seen at Urdugas camp.

There are also bits of equipment left that had been found on the ice when searching for victims and brought back to base camp to act as a memorial. There seemed little point in going further if there was no view to be had and little to see so I turned around and headed back with Jahangir whilst Fran decided to head on up for an hour with Essan and Nadim to see whether there were any better views for herself.

The return trip was uneventful until Jahangir and I reached a stream that was too wide to jump but we needed to cross to get back to our camp. The water levels had risen since the morning as more melt water flowed down the streams as the day got warmer.

At the first stream we took off our boots, knotting the laces together and hanging them round our neck, we rolled up our trousers above our knees and holding hands we inched into the cloudy icy cold water, testing the depth until we found a fordable section and we had reached the far side.

The next obstacle was an even wider stream with no hope of wading due to its depth and the fast flowing current. We ended up walking several kilometres down the course of the river until we found somewhere to get across and then had to walk the same distance back up the river to the camp.

By the late afternoon the clouds finally cleared enough and eventually K2 could be seen clearly although I never got a totally uninterrupted view as there were still a few small clouds continually being blown across the vista.

Chapter 14

Return to Skardu

It was another cold night and I was eager to get going to get warm. We headed back down the glacier. We also had another mule with us. One of the muleteers had done a deal and bought another mule and judging by his broad beaming smile he was obviously pleased with his new purchase.

Hussain had over taken us but Nadeem spent a long time some way back up the trail talking with Essan which I took a poor view as he was our mountain guide and he had left Jahangir (who was our personal guide, not a mountain guide) to lead us down the glacier. The path was the same one that we had taken earlier and not too difficult to follow but I felt that Nadeem should at least be within sight and shouting distance of the clients who were paying him for his alleged expertise which I had serious doubts about.

We reached Goro and this time I made sure that my tent was pitched a little further back from the track as I didn't want night time trains of mules tripping over my guy ropes. I also used some empty feed bags for additional insulation against both the cold and any moisture from the ice seeping into the tent. We had some visitors from the nearby army outpost who wandered across to have a chat partly I felt just to relieve some of the boredom of such a remote posting.

After just a short walk we arrived at Urdugas mid-afternoon giving us plenty of time to relax. Another group turned up in the camp consisting of three people from Scotland and a host of porters. We chatted and compared experiences. They were also going down the glacier but we hadn't seen them at Concordia or Goro. They had taken a detour up a side valley before heading back to Askole.

My alarm clock had stopped working but camping conditions do not encourage lying 'in bed' till late. I heard people moving about and kitchen noises. I shaved, got dressed and got out of my tent only to find that the noises came from the other group who were getting up early. Now that I was up there was not much point in going back to bed but at least I was not going to be late for breakfast.

The sky was clear and it was nice to watch the sun rise and the sunlight creep down the sides of the valley as the sun rose above the mountain tops and chase the shadows away. It was a fine day as we walked down to the glacier.

On the trip down there was a group of Japanese tourists coming up the glacier. They were balancing on the backs of mules as the animals struggled over the rough ground, each guided by a muleteer. They didn't look at all comfortable and neither did they look like they were enjoying the trip. Perhaps it had looked good fun on paper back in the comfort of their own homes but the reality might not be matching their expectations.

We caught up the three Scottish trekkers and had a lunch of tinned sardines and lychees, a memorable lunch as it was a strange combination and perhaps my own fault as I had said during the planning that I ate fruit, vegetables and fish at home.

Essan tidied up and threw the empty tins into a gulley in a large arc that landed a long way from the path. A row immediately erupted as they were littering the environment and I was responsible to the Ministry and I had signed all the papers. Essan didn't want to go and retrieve the tins. Nadeem sided with Essan and didn't see the issue and seemed to be ignorant of the responsibilities that I had confirmed by signing the Ministry's permit request which he had insisted that I sign and which had been made so clear to us in our evening meeting with the Ministry officials.

Peace was restored when Jahangir clambered down the slope and retrieved the tins and put them in his backpack to be carried down to the camp for proper disposal. We went down the snout of the glacier and after more than another hour we were back in Paiju camp. The weather had been kind to us and we had not been delayed and there was some slack built into the schedule for bad weather but now there was a decision to be made.

I had a choice of either a rest day here or a rest day in Askole. There was little to do in Askole and I had already walked around the village and we would still have an evening there and I thought that the rest would do us all good so I opted for a rest day at Paiju camp and now that we were lower down the valley and it was warmer I changed back into my shalwaar chemise.

We met up again with the three Scottish walkers and had time to chat and time to people watch. There were several small groups that were also in the camp. There was a couple of Swiss walkers who had forgotten their tents in Skardu and would have to sleep in their dining tent. There was also a couple of Japanese walkers who constantly complained to their guide about the lack of hot water, no beds, the cold, the food, the hard ground and just about everything.

I was woken early as some of the other groups made a lot of noise as they got up early and packed their things so as to be ready to get off and head up the valley. Breakfast was porridge, paritha and omelette and of course green tea. I tried to make jobs last as long as possible to fill in the time. I washed myself, I washed my clothes, I went for a walk and joined in playing Ludo before lunch.

That afternoon I watched a large group of Japanese arrive and set up camp. Their dining tent was set up for them just below my tent on a lower terrace. They were having goat on their menu that evening and several of them screamed as their chefs butchered a goat beside the kitchen tent and carried the head past them up to their porters as a contribution towards the porter's evening meal.

Despite the horror expressed earlier evidenced by the screams, by the evening when the meal was served, they seemed to have a wonderful time chatting, laughing and eating a great buffet supper prepared by their chefs. I was on one hand envious and on the other hand astonished that their chefs could produce such a large banquet using just a camp stove. They were further entertained that evening by a lively display of local dancing and singing well into the night lit by bright lights, I wasn't sure whether it was gas or electric but it lasted way past my now usual bedtime of shortly after dusk.

We were due to set off early and despite the late night revelry that had kept me awake last night, I wasn't making extra noise on purpose but I had no guilty feelings and even took a certain malicious delight thinking that any noise that I was making may disturb those that had kept me awake the night before.

We took the same path as we had come up just a few days before. At mid-morning we arrived at one of the gullies that we had crossed by bridge a few days before but the bridge had been washed away and we would have to wade across. We walked along the stream's edge to find a suitable place to cross.

There was a choice of either protecting your feet from the cold water and the rough edges of rocks underfoot, but wearing wet socks and boots for the rest of the day or crossing barefoot with some discomfort from the cold water and rough rocks but at least being comfortable with dry socks for the rest of the day. Therefore I chose to wade bare foot.

A suitable place was found and I took off my boots and stuffed my socks inside. Pulling up my shalwaar chemise trousers up to my thighs I waded into the river. True to expectations the water was cold and the river bed uneven and rough and the water deeper than expected but I managed to get across as did the rest of the team. I dried my feet on the hem of my shirt and put my socks and boots back on. The bottoms of my trousers were wet but they would dry out and at least my feet were comfortable and dry.

Further down the valley there was a section which on our way up had been flat, easy walking amongst shrubs along the edge of the river. After the warmer weather and the increased snow melt, the river had risen and now this area was flooded and we had to jump from rock to rock using them as stepping stones to make progress. At other times we had to scramble across open scree slopes above the water line being careful to leave enough distance from the river to ensure that where the scree was unstable we didn't slide down the slope into the water.

After the barren rocky valley upper sections that we had recently seen, the lower sections after the flooded area seemed rather benign, with patches of scrubland, undulating terrain and the valley widening as we descended and helping the feeling of a good experience were the clear skies, bright sunlight and warming air. We came to a camp site that had no facilities but did have a manager who was happy to provide us with hot green tea so we had a break and basked in the sun drinking tea.

We reached Jhula camp and found a good position in the shade. We were the first to reach the site and had the choice of the best sites so we selected a little clearing surrounded by trees and I took one end and Fran took the other end. Our kitchen tent and dining tent were on the next terrace just above us through a thin stand of trees. Next to them was a Nepalese group of climbers with some well-known names who were known to our guides and porters but none of whom I recognised.

We were joined in our little clearing by a group of three Spaniards who squeezed their two tents into the small space between Fran's tent and mine. They were all from Madrid and as I had lived there for a while a few years earlier I was keen to catch up on developments. They knew some of the areas that I knew well but it seemed that some of the open spaces that I remembered had been built upon and were no longer the beautiful undeveloped open spaces that I had enjoyed jogging around.

We were up well before our Spanish neighbours and had set off before they had surfaced. We headed up the tributary, over the suspension bridge, down the sandy track and around the rocky cliff path to follow the path running parallel to the main river. Much of the scenery seemed oddly different now that I was seeing it from the reverse direction on my return journey but that may have been due to the bright sunshine and the fact that we subconsciously knew what to expect on our way home having meet and overcome the greater challenges of the upper valley.

The Nepalese party that had camped next to us the night before passed us in the morning at an amazing pace and we never saw them again. The route back to Askole was gentle in comparison to what we had encountered further up the valley and almost seemed like a Sunday afternoon stroll.

We got back to Askole and set up camp on the flat grassy lawns of the hotel that we had stopped at two weeks before. Mansour the head porter was there to greet us. We had green tea, cake, Mountain Dew which is the major local brand of lemonade plus yak curry which was somewhat disappointingly for me as it was almost indistinguishable from beef.

The owner of the hotel also came to greet us and welcome us to his hotel and to Askole in good English. We had a discussion ranging over a number of subjects and of course our experiences of the last few days. But it was also obvious that the lack of tourism was devastating to his business and only 5 % of his camp site was occupied and his hotel that evening was empty.

That evening we were told the news about our planned journey back down the valley tomorrow. There had been several landslides and the road was cut in three places and impassable to road vehicles. But they were passable by humans on foot inshallah. So just when you think you can sit in a jeep and relax there was to be more walking and depending on how big the landslides were, the journey back to Skardu was going to take much longer than the journey up. Which meant another and an unplanned early morning start plus that all uplifting optimism that I associate with the use of 'inshallah'.

We had an early breakfast that seemed to be an unusual mixture of eggs and porridge as if we were using up whatever was left from our stocks of food. I was packed but Mansour had arrived with some mules and porters and was ready to go. Hussain and Essan were not ready to go as they were still packing away the kitchen tent.

Therefore to assist in achieving our planned early departure time, we unpegged the tent and Jahangir, Fran, Mansour and I each took a corner of the kitchen tent and lifted the whole tent over the occupants and contents of the kitchen tent so that we could pack it away whilst the kitchen equipment was packed away in the open.

Some of the tents and kitchen equipment were loaded onto mules to be carried away to be stored for the next trip. Meanwhile our personal bags and the rest of the equipment were loaded onto mules and we set off on foot back down the road that previously we had been driven along in jeeps.

In under half an hour we came across our first obstacle, impassable for vehicles as the road had been washed away by the stream. There was a narrow path up the side of the valley across the stream and back down to the road on the other side. The humans managed this well enough but it was too difficult for the mules. The path was too narrow for them and their loads which scrapped against the cliff face as they tried to walk along the narrow steep rough path so despite enthusiastic encouragement from the muleteers with whips, the mules would not go forward.

They were forced to walk backwards until they reached a spot where their loads could be unloaded. Then the bags that the mules had been carrying had to be carried up and across the stream by hand. There were no mules on the far side but we had been joined by a couple of locals who wanted to travel down the valley and were hitching a lift with us. So between the assembled group, we carried all our bags down the road.

After twenty minutes we reached a farmhouse where there was a jeep parked on the drive. This was Mansour's house and we loaded the bags onto the roof off his vehicle and piled in. But there was not enough seats for one per person but the porters and locals were happy to make do with three bums on a pair of seats meant for two.

Mansour drove for a while but didn't seem confident in driving the jeep over the rougher terrain and soon swapped his driving role with another of our younger passengers. In total contrast he seemed to revel with the challenges of driving over rough roads and through streams. Perhaps it wasn't his vehicle and he wouldn't have to pay for any repairs that might be needed but he was evidently in his element and happy to drive.

After an hour of bumping along rough tracks and passing terraced fields of wheat and fruit trees we descended towards the main river and turned upstream to run parallel with the river until we reached a river crossing via a suspension bridge. But before we could reach the bridge there was a small rock fall that stopped us. It was walkable for people but too rough for the jeep.

Several of us jumped out and started to heave the larger lumps of rock into the river below on our right hand side. In what seemed like no time at all the driver hooted the horn to signal that he was happy to make an attempt and we watched as he negotiated the remains of the rock fall that we hadn't yet cleared.

We climbed back into the jeep and drove on and over the bridge. We took a right hand turn and then slammed to a stop. Whilst I had been helping to clear the road of rocks I had not noticed that on the opposite side of the valley, a long section of road after the bridge had been washed away by the river.

We were on the other side of the river but we were not going anywhere until we had negotiated this washout. Luckily there were a few locals hanging around who were offering their services as porters to hire. The way around the washout and landslide was to go up the steep valley side, walk parallel to the river and then go down until we reached the road again. We hired a few porters to help with the bags and followed a newly created path across the top of the obstacle.

On reaching a site after the landslide with some level ground adjacent to the remaining undamaged road, there was a jeep waiting for us from the local village arranged earlier by Mansour. We loaded our bags onto the roof and piled into the jeep and set off again.

The driver had thoughtfully brought along some bananas and offered them to the passengers. Nothing exceptional in that but it was what to occur afterwards that is memorable. We were travelling with some other villagers making the journey down the valley. I had finished my banana and had struggled in the confined space to get my back pack open and put the empty skin inside without too many elbow jabs and discomfort to my immediate neighbouring traveller.

One of our fellow porters behind the driver had finished his banana and had wound down the window next to him as if to throw the banana skin out of the window but he hesitated. From the anguish on his face it was not hard to tell that he had a dilemma whether to throw the skin out of the window or not and if not, what to do with it.

I like to think that the row on the trek a couple of days earlier above Paiju about throwing empty tin cans into the environment had been a big topic of conversation amongst the rest of the group behind our backs. And this was what had turned this particular fellow traveller to face a dichotomy. He had no bag into which to put his banana skin and he looked to be in a quandary. I leant back and stretched out on arm with an open palm and he was visibly relieved to place the banana skin in my hand. I put the skin into my backpack between my knees and wondered whether making such an issue out of environment protection might actually have had an effect.

We had been driving down the valley for half an hour when the jeep came to a stop where the road was wide enough to turn around. The road ahead was the same section of scree slope just above the choke point on the river where we had met a vehicle and had had to reverse during our trip up the valley. There had been a landslide where one section below the road had fallen into the river and another section where the slope above had slumped on to road.

This was a long way from any village so there were no porters looking for work. We grabbed our bags and started walking down what was left of the road. I was walking in a group and stopped to take a photo. On turning around I saw the rest of group a long way off running away from me. Then I noticed that there were a number of rocks rolling down the slope towards where we had all been standing, throwing up puffs of dust and setting off further stones rolling down.

I took to my heels and ran as fast as I could to follow the rest of the group. There were more trickles of rocks coming down but luckily no major landslide and we all managed to get past the landslide area without injury. Perhaps I meant without major injury as carrying our heavy bags and running along a rough path had left some of the group still panting even when I had caught them up and I had recovered. We loaded our baggage on to yet another waiting jeep. We headed up the hairpin bends above the choke point on the river and continued back to Skardu.

We stopped for refreshments at the same road side restaurant that we had stopped at on the journey up the valley. We sat under the apple trees in the garden waiting to be served lunch. There was a group sitting in front of us listening to a particularly expressive person who had his back to us, as if he was a preacher lecturing his listeners on a sermon. We ignored them and they ignored us until an apple fell on my head and I let out a cry of astonishment and pain.

This had not escaped the clutch of listeners who thought that this was extremely hilarious and they all laughed. The preacher carried on and his audience tried their best to listen to him but they were still distracted by the picture of me being assailed by an apple falling under gravity towards earth but hitting my head first. I had joined such other famous people as Sir Isaac Newton as being attacked with an apple but unlike Newton I didn't come up with any ground breaking physics as a result.

The rest of the return journey to Skardu was uneventful. It was relaxing after more than a dozen days of walking to just sit and watch the countryside pass by without the effort of actually having to walk and carry a backpack. We passed villages and features that I remembered well from my journey up the valley just a couple of weeks earlier.

We passed through the suburbs of Skardu heading for our hotel and turned off the main road. Immediately before turning into our hotel we passed a number of parked police vehicles with armed policemen milling about on the road. Inside the hotel's courtyard we saw two more armed policemen. Judging from the numbers of policemen and vehicles, security had been boosted considerably since we had previously visited this hotel. I did query this and there had been some indeterminate incident and so security had been strengthened. The details of the incident that had caused the beefing up of security were a little vague but I wasn't going to decline it.

I had hoped for a warm shower and going to bed early but it was clear that there was to be a final meeting of the expedition and for them to receive a 'thank you' or putting it more basically a gratuity for their services. I had not expected this as I thought that I had already paid a fair price but I didn't want to cause bad feelings as after all some of the team had been really good, whilst others had not lived up to my expectations. I worked out with Fran what we thought was an average reasonable amount given the different roles that they had undertaken. Then this was adjusted by what they had actually achieved against the expectations of fulfilling those roles.

I was not sure of the going rate but some were very pleased, almost overly pleased such as the muleteers with their tip and some were angry feeling that they had been unduly under tipped but then I doubted Nadeem's ability to be a mountain guide and both his recklessness and immaturity. I tried to explain that this was a tip, and not part of what they had already been paid and that what I had given them was a reflection of what I expected from them in their respective roles and whether they had fulfilled them satisfactory. It was not a pleasant experience to say some home truths but my philosophy is that hard truths must be faced and voiced, not swept under the carpet. The next group may get a better service.

Chapter 15

Jeep down the Indus

After a refreshing night in a soft bed with running hot and cold water, we were to return to Ayas Shikri's office where we are given green tea and apricots. He produced some questionnaires to complete. We answered a number of questions giving feedback on the trip. There were questions on whether the food was hot, well cooked, sufficient and varied. Did the chefs do a good job of looking after us? Did the guides do a good job? I give details of a few of the issues that had arisen.

I made a special point of mentioning littering of the environment as a general point although I doubted whether there would be any change. Finally I thanked him and his team for organising the details and generally I was very supportive and thankful and especially thanked him for the Ludo and for the fish.

We climbed back into the jeep with Ayas Shikri, and headed off for a debrief at the Ministry of Tourism's offices, on the other side of town. This ministry was housed in a large single storey building built of local dressed stone and relatively new judging by how clean the outside appeared. There was an adjacent building site where an extension was being built on one side. We walked in and we were ushered into a large office with a partner's desk with three chairs placed in front of it for the interviewees. The walls were smooth white plaster and on it were pictures of mountains, valleys and glaciers.

The man at the Ministry who we were meant to meet was not available but there was another feedback form that I had to fill in. Many of the questions were the same as Ayas Shikri had asked in his office and so my answers were largely the same. I expected to take Ayas Shikri back to his office but he seemed to expect to stay with us all day so I checked with Jahangir that I wouldn't have to pay him at the end of the day as an unwanted self-appointed guide. Having received an assurance that he was offering his services gratis, we headed out of town.

We were heading north west on the main road through the suburbs and I had a chance to see more of the town. There were groups of shops and walled compounds. These gave way to scattered houses interspersed with fields and orchards. The road was lined with trees on both sides for what seemed like kilometres as it headed out of town. We passed the airport on our right and the road reached and then followed the river.

Here the river was broad and calm as it flowed slowly past. Further down the river was a bridge over the valley where the river narrows significantly at a choke point. This restricted the river flow and water had backed up and had flooded some of the fields nearest the river. From a vantage point above the river we could look down at an area where trees had been planted in rows but their roots and the ground in between them were under water and only the trunk and branches poked out of the muddy waters. There were also three small islands that at normal water levels would be on dry land and reachable on foot.

We turned off the main road away from the river and headed up a small side valley. There were small fields, trees, little farmhouses and a stream running down the centre. At one point, across the stream was a small weir and a mill using the flow of the stream to turn its stones to mill grain.

We came to the Shangri-La Hotel, an up market hotel overlooking a little lake called Lower Kachura Lake. It had well-tended gardens and neat green lawns. There was another hotel overlooking the lake on the opposite shore, an exclusive holiday complex and an army rest house next door. The whole area was very green, scenic, and rustic and the reason why there had been so much holiday accommodation built around the lake.

We continued upwards and eventually the tarmac ran out but we carried on across a bridge over a raging torrent of a river, past a group of shops with women in their bright dresses and scarves and through a picturesque village centre. We parked the jeep in the shade of a large mulberry tree at the end of the track.

We walked past small neat fields surrounded by trees, walking on the raised footpaths between the fields and irrigation ditches. There were potatoes, lettuces, wheat, maize, marrows and small shoots of recently planted seeds which were still too small to be sure of what they may grow into. Chickens pecked between the neat straight rows of plants growing in the rich soil. There was a complete variety of crops and perhaps more than I had seen anywhere else in these northern areas.

We came to a small lake, named Upper Kachura Lake. This had been formed by a high glacial moraine that lay across the downhill section of what would have been the exit for water flowing down into valley into the lower lake. There is no discernible exit for the water and instead the water seeps through the rocks through underground passages and there had never been enough water for the lake to fill up and for the escaping water to cut a channel through the moraine. Consequently the water level rose and fell depending on how much water flowed into the lake in times of flood or as the water slowly seeped away and eventually lowered the water level.

There was a cafe on the edge of the lake and we stopped for a drink inside to get out of the sun. The lake had recently filled up with melt water and the recent rain. The lower terraces of the cafe had tables and chairs scattered underneath the shade of large trees but the whole area had been flooded so that only the tops of the tables and the backs of the chairs could be seen poking out of the surface of the water.

Dragonflies flew back and forth across the surface of the water looking for mates and for suitable places to land to lay eggs by reversing themselves into the water to lay the eggs under water. I watched them for a while and hoped that the eggs would develop into nymphs before the water level dropped exposing the eggs to air and therefore dry out and die. We sat by the lake for a while just watching the dragonflies and the occasional boat.

Rowing boats could be hired to row around the lake and a couple of families had hired boats and were making their way across the lake. A noisy group of youngsters were playing on the lake shore in swimming costumes to our left, standing knee deep in the lake splashing each other.

We walked back through the fields and made our way back down the track. We stopped at a hotel overlooking the lower lake for lunch. We had a look around at two of the four suites that the hotel had and they did look invitingly luxurious with bright decorations, western bathrooms, double beds, tables and chairs, a desk and lounge areas and a wonderful view of the lake and gardens through which we walked whilst waiting to be called for lunch.

We took Ayas Shikri back to his office in Skardu and were on our way back to the hotel. I had not had a haircut for several weeks and it was getting a bit long so I asked to stop off at a barbers. Koshal dropped us outside a barbers in a row of shops in the suburbs of Skardu and went off to find a parking spot. Fran came along to watch and take photos of me whilst I was in the chair. It was busy but I didn't have to wait too long and I settled down into the barber's chair.

I was to have my hair cut by a young chap with shiny greased back hair, a large moustache and generally rather camp. He also managed to smoke during the whole affair with his cigarette hanging out of one side of his mouth. To finish off he set a new razor blade on to the end of a cut throat razor and trimmed the hairline. Needless to say I didn't move a muscle.

I could observe out of the corner of my eye that Jahangir was also having a haircut and finished with some facial hair being removed by a process that I can only describe as two fine strands of cotton being crossed over each other to grip the offending hair and being pulled out by the roots. Koshal had joined us and he had his moustache trimmed and styled. We looked at each other and made complementary remarks on how well groomed we all looked.

We headed into the main street and I stopped for ice cream from a cafe. Fran had seen kebabs being grilled over a charcoal brazier in the street so she stopped and ate one of those as I tried to eat my ice cream faster than it melted. After a short walk around town to see what it looked like at night we walked up a stairway to a restaurant that looked out over the road and by co-incidence over the electronics shop that had 'fixed' my camera.

The restaurant was brightly lit with plastic table cloths but generally clean. There were three Europeans at another table but otherwise all the other diners were locals. And I noticed that there were a range of ages, some groups of similarly aged young men, whilst other groups were fathers and sons or grandfather, father and son but all of them were male. Fran was the only women in the restaurant.

We had a long all day trip ahead of us to get from Skardu down the Indus river valley for the 170kms drive and then pick up the KKH for 45kms to get back to Gilgit. It wasn't far in UK motorway terms but it would take us most of the day. We had packed our bags and loaded our stuff onto the jeep. Koshal and I were in the front, Fran and Jahangir in the back and the baggage tied to the back of the jeep and covered with a tarpaulin.

I knew the start of the route of by heart now, past the army post, the mosque, the polo ground, New Bazaar Road, College Road, the Ministry of Tourism, the tree lined road out past the airport, the view across the river where the road ran parallel for a while and then past the turning up to the Kachura Lakes that we had taken the day before and then we were on roads that were new to me.

We seemed to come to a rocky area without any farms, just barren rock. The road turned towards the river and approached the suspension bridge. We had a good view up the river and could see the wide expanse of the river and the flooded trees that we had seen yesterday morning a long way off in the distance up stream to our right. The river was calm up there but the bridge had been built across the narrowest crossing point possible and the river boiled as it rushed past the choke point and smashed into the rocks sitting on the river bed and the base of the cliffs of the narrow gorge below the choke point.

The road hugged the northern side of the valley all the way down to where it crosses the river to join the KKH and in all that way I only saw two minor crossings to the other side. These were narrow suspension bridges only wide enough for pedestrians. The road usually is quite high above the river with sheer cliffs dropping straight into the water's edge with cliffs above the road as well. There were spectacular views across the gorge to the other side and both up and down the valley.

The terrain is so rugged that even where the cliff doesn't plunge straight into the river, the slopes are too steep and rocky to allow vegetation to grow. There are only a few fields and farms scattered along the whole length of this part of the river. The road meanders across the valley slope with occasional parts that are wider to allow traffic to pass. The construction of this road reputedly cost more lives per kilometre than its more famous brother the KKH.

It has started to rain and we stopped to put the roof on. The cloud base had lowered but we could still see along the valley and the cliff tops. And looking down the valley we could see a small notch in the cliff face where the road was as it weaved its way down the valley. There wasn't much traffic on the road but we could see trucks slowly making their way along the road and with good judgement of speed and distance Koshal would find a place to pull up to let on coming trucks squeeze past without having to interrupt our journey for too long or reverse a long way.

I was very appreciative of his driving skills as I was in the passenger sit right next to the cliff edge all the way down the road and I had a particularly good view of the drops just inches to my left into the abyss sometimes hundreds of metres down to the river surface.

We passed through Dambugas, a lively little village opposite a minor crossing over the river. There were trucks and buses parked by the road side and a row of shops and cafes. It was a small but vibrant place but one of the few things of note on this section of road other than the scenery. Further down the road there were a series of caves dug into the mountain side on the opposite side of the valley with jumbles of loose rock falling down to the river below. These were actually where there had been several mines dug going straight into the valley slopes to mine for gemstones including rubies. Spoil from the mines had been thrown over the edge to create what looked like natural scree slopes but were in fact man made.

After more than five hours of travelling down the gorge the valley sides opened out and the tops of the cliffs retreated. There was more undulating valley floor and things looked better as the rain had eased off but there were still no fields or any cultivated land or any buildings.

The road headed down towards the confluence of the Indus and the Gilgit River. Just up from where the Gilgit River joins the Indus is a long suspension bridge that takes the road over the river and up the opposite valley side and joins the main KKH. It is only one vehicle wide and takes a few minutes to cross but luckily there was little traffic and we were able to drive straight across.

We were back to more open but barren and dusty valley scenery and very different from the gorge that we had just travelled down. The road was wide and with a good tarmac surface with barriers at certain critical paces where needed and now it was just 45kms on a good tarmac road back to Gilgit. It had been a great journey down the gorge but sometimes you just have to be there to experience the vistas, the perspectives and the drops off the side of the road. I would rate the gorge journey from Skardu to Gilgit as one of the top three must see journeys in the northern areas.

The KKH bypasses the centre of Gilgit, skirting it to the east to cross the Gilgit River and head up to the Hunza valley. We turned off left to get to the centre of town. We made our way towards town, through the Welcome Arch, past the bus station and the airport. We stopped at a row of local shops for an ice cream and a drink before continuing to the PTDC hotel.

We checked in but I wasn't one to sit around looking at the four walls of my room especially as I had been sitting in the jeep being thrown from side to side so I wanted to head into town to see what I could see. Jahangir came with me and I must apologise as I never thought to ask whether he wanted to do so as although he was thirty years my junior he might have been tired as well and his family lived just a few kilometres away and he had been away for several weeks. So please accept my belated apologies.

We turned out of the hotel and up the road. In order to get to the centre of town there were a number of small businesses to pass with their wares on display and actually working on making things. There were garages, tyre shops, motorbike part shops, sanitary ware supplies, blacksmiths, plastic bucket sellers, spade and axe head sellers, wood workers plus many more.

In a western economy like ours where we have one stop shops and everything is neatly packaged and wrapped up, I still find it fascinating that people elsewhere can make a living out of selling just one item or string of similar items without a load of fancy branding and packaging but also can have that 'can make do' or 'can repair that' attitude (but not when it comes to my digital camera).

We walked through the central market passing a load of shops with their wares on display, strong aromas coming out of cafes and spice shops, hawkers selling their wares and bright lights of fast food outlets Pakistani style selling their wares on the streets. We were heading through to the far side of town to try to find the British Cemetery, a little cemetery where some Englishmen had been buried who had died in the area in the late nineteenth and early twentieth century. It has formerly been called Hayward Gardens after George Hayward 1839–1870, a British explorer who had explored and mapped the area during the Great Game played between Russia and England in the late nineteenth century.

George Hayward was a Yorkshire man who in 1859 joined the British army and served in India for four years finally selling his commission and leaving the army in 1863. His first expedition to this northern area was funded by the Royal Geological Society to map the as yet unmapped Pamirs. Many of his trips were small affairs often just himself and a few porters. Several more expeditions followed with varying degrees of success until the summer of 1870 when he was at Darkot, now in the northern areas just 20kms from the Afghanistan border south of the Wakhan corridor where he was murdered on 18th July 1870.

There is speculation about who murdered him and why with some suggestion of him being involved in local political intrigues. His body was recovered and brought back to Gilgit and buried in an orchard which subsequently became Hayward Gardens and later the British Cemetery.

Taking a side street by an army base and coming to a high wall with a small door in it there was a sign outside proclaiming it to be the British Cemetery. Inside there was a jungle of trees with gravestones in neat lines in the shade of the trees. The garden was looked after by Kulan Ali, an elderly gentlemen with grey hair and a long beard who was proud of how clean and neat he kept the small space. The cemetery was cool and the high walls kept out the noise of the streets outside. Towards the far left hand side was George Hayward's plain headstone with a simple inscription.

Around him were headstones of other British soldiers, explorers and climbers stretching over several decades. I thought of Rupert Brooke's poem The Soldier and the opening lines, 'If I should die, think only this of me, that there's some corner of a foreign field that is forever England.' And here it was in reality, a small corner of a foreign city that was forever England.

We walked down to the river and along a quiet road to follow the river bank back towards the hotel. There were a few houses, an occasional shop, a house with a small courtyard with a saddled horse, tethered to a tree and a saw mill with workers manhandling great baulks of timber to be sawn to the desired size. It was getting dark and shutters were being put up, so it was time to get back to the hotel.

The next day was 14th August which is Pakistani Independence Day and a parade was planned with military bands and flags with a march past down the main street. The celebrations started with a 21 gun salute at 5am. Despite having been warned the night before about the 21 gun salute at the nearby army base, the first salvo still woke me up with a start. Heaven knows what

I would be thinking or doing at the sound of gunfire if I hadn't been warned.

It was also raining heavily and the rain hitting the tin roof of the hotel just added to the cacophony of noise. There were monsoons further south that was causing a lot of flooding with loss of life and we were getting the tail end of the rain as it headed northwards.

I would have liked to see the parade but given that it involved the military, large crowds plus some dignitaries to receive the salutes, this would seem to be a tempting potential terrorist target and therefore it seemed best to head out of town.

It was still raining and cold as we left town taking the Jinnah bridge over the Gilgit River and then onto the Nomal road. We passed the Karakoram International University and the last buildings on the outskirts of Gilgit and then up the Hunza river valley on the west side. On the opposite side of the valley we could make out traffic on the KKH along which I had travelled up to the Hunza valley a few weeks previously.

Our side of the valley was rocky and barren but further along the road the barren ground gave way to cultivated land, trees lined the road and around the edge of small fields. We passed through Nomal, a quiet village with a few shops and not much more. Despite being Independence Day and a bank holiday most of the shops were open. In the village centre there was a group of Boy Scouts in their uniforms preparing for a parade.

We passed the last fields and entered the Naltar valley. This has a steep road up a narrow valley, with the bottom of the valley taken up by the river and the road and no space for anything else. The road had a tarmac surface but in several places it had been washed away so we had to take a diversion or in other places so much debris had fallen onto the road that it was buried under a pile of debris from above. At a space in the valley that was wider we came across a HEP power station.

Above this site was a small dam and a bridge crossing over the river. The dam channelled the rivers force into pipes and ultimately into a turbine hall where the force of the water was converted into electricity. The turbines were generating electricity at full throttle and there was a hum from the transformers and power lines taking the electricity down to communities in the valley below. There had been so much rain that surplus water was still rushing over the spillway at one side of the dam, with its potential to generate electricity lost forever.

The valley above the dam widened out and there were fields and farmhouses. The road continued to climb upwards whilst the river was now out of sight in a deep gorge off to our left. On the steeper slopes that where unsuitable for cultivation there were forests of trees reminiscent of alpine valleys.

The road gradually reduced to just two worn tyre tracks as we climbed higher. It was still raining when we eventually reached the end of the road. This was Naltar Lake. The rain was still coming down like stair rods but even through the poor visibility I could see that here was a small lake, enclosed by gentle slopes with a scattering of trees with majestic mountains towering above us. It was very picturesque and I could understand why this was a renowned beauty spot.

At one side of the open space in front of us next to the lake was a small single storey stone built shepherd's cottage. Jahangir got out of the jeep and half ran to the building, beckoning to us to follow. I didn't know what to expect but followed anyway.

The former shepherd's building at such an advantageous position had cashed in on its location and was set up to sell refreshments. Outside, there was a sign proclaiming that the Naltar Lake Hotel was open. Inside the small stone building there was a single room with a hearth at waist height and a ledge at one end that served as a seating area. The cafe had been left in charge of Karim, a slim boy in traditional dress with bright intelligent eyes, just eight years old who was also in charge of his two younger brothers and had a couple of friends of his own age to keep him company.

Jahangir asked whether we could shelter a while from the rain and have a drink of green tea. Karim invited us to sit down and added some wood to the embers in the hearth and goaded them into a bright flame to heat the water in the kettle on the grid above the fire.

I was just happy to sit and not be bounced around in the jeep and enjoy the warmth inside the small building and to be out of the rain. But I noticed that the young Karim was very confident making the tea, serving us and also suggesting that we may like some biscuits to accompany our tea. We said yes and Karim took a key from his pocket and opened a chest under the ledge and took out a number of packets of biscuits to show to us so that we could select our preference. We made our selection and he closed the chest, locking it and spiriting the key away in a pocket somewhere within his shalwaar chemise.

At long last the rain eased off and we could walk around without getting wet to the skin. We thanked our hosts and went back to our jeep. I hadn't seen any money change hands and from the look on Karim's young face he hadn't been paid. I asked Jahangir whether he had paid and in our delight at the improving weather we had walked out and had forgotten to pay. Jahangir realised his error raising his hand to his mouth and opening his eyes wide. He turned around and paid the bill much to the obvious relief of Karim.

We walked around a knoll and up a path to another lake. This lake was an unnatural bright turquoise colour due to the chemicals washed into the lake. The lake didn't have a natural outlet so its level rose and fell according to how fast the water seeped through the rocks into and out of the lake.

We turned around and headed back down the valley. The road reached the river and turned right through the trees. There were clumps of trees interspersed with alpine pastures as the track wound its way back down the valley. On the valley floor where it widened out between the steep hillsides there were fields and farmhouses.

We turned right off the main road to go down towards the river and to cross a bridge to the far side. Here was an army camp and a few support buildings plus something I recognised instantly but was surprised to see. There was a long strip of grass that plunged down towards us from the hillside high above us. Along one side was a series of posts with a cable running down the length of the grass slope. This was a ski run without the snow, the piste being the grassy slope and the cable strung between the posts, being the drag lift to get skiers up to the top of the piste.

I am a keen skier and walker in the Alps and I like to see the difference in the environment on the slopes between skiing with the winter coverings of snow and walking the same alpine meadows in the summer with a carpet of flowers on slopes that I have skied in winter. Now that I have seen these particular slopes in summer, I feel compelled to return one day, to see the pistes in winter.

The return journey down the valley was the same route as the trip up but we saw the outcrops of rocks in reverse order. But the water level in the river was noticeably higher, and no more so than at one particular bend in the road around a protruding cliff where the road's edge was built up with a reinforced concrete wall that formed the bank of the river. The water was churning as it cascaded across rocks and there was so much water in the river that the spray was drenching the road. I was glad to get by fearing that the river might flood the road or worst still wash it away and we would be stranded up the valley and unable to get back to Gilgit.

On exiting the Naltar valley we didn't go back through Nomal and down the minor road back to Gilgit but took the bridge across the Hunza River and joined the KKH. We passed the cemetery with the yellow drill bit memorial for local workers killed during the construction of the KKH. Further down the road was the Chinese cemetery. Behind a stone wall with large metal gates for the main entrance was a quiet and well-tended area of about a hectare shaded by mature trees.

Here were the graves of dozens of Chinese workers who met their deaths whilst building the KKH. There were rows of identical stone tombs all with a short inscription on a separate stone in front of each tomb. There were tombs stretching away to left and right and off towards the back of the site with a central memorial to commemorate their efforts to build the KKH.

The high level bridge to carry the KKH across the Hunza River had not been completed so we had a rough track down the valley slope to a temporary Bailey bridge a few metres above the river. Then we had a rough track that lead up the bank on the far side and came out on the KKH. We followed this for a while and turned off to head into the south side of Gilgit.

We were met at the back at the hotel by Karim with some bad news. I was due to fly back to Islamabad and spend a few days there before leaving Pakistan for the flight home. There had been cloud cover for several days and there had been no flights arriving or departing from Gilgit airport for several days and the forecast was not looking good for the next few days.

Karim said that he would check again first thing in the morning to get me on aboard if there was a flight, and I suspected that this would be no mean feat as there would be a backlog of people all trying to do the same thing. Koshal drove Karim and Jahangir back to their respective homes and Fran and I were left at the hotel.

Chapter 16

The Swat Valley

We would be going our separate ways as Fran was heading off towards Chitral and the Kalash valleys to continue her travels and I wanted to see a few things in Islamabad. This was to be our last meal together so we had breakfast and sat and chatted as we waited for Karim.

It was late morning when a jeep and a mini bus pulled into the hotel's courtyard. There were still no flights so I would have to go by road so instead of a one hour flight it would be a nearly 600kms two day drive. I checked the map, knowing that the KKH went down the Swat valley which was a no go area for foreign travellers but I was relieved to note that there was an alternative route south out of Chilas to avoid the Swat valley.

I checked with Karim on which route I would be driven down and said that he would have a word with the driver. I was introduced to the driver but I must confess that I have forgotten his name for certain as I didn't write it down but it is a 50–50 bet that he was another Karim as it is a very popular name in the local area.

I said farewell to Fran who was going off in the jeep and I got into the minibus. It was a tarmac road all the way to Islamabad so four wheel drive wasn't needed and the minibus was air conditioned so it would be comfortable during the day. It seemed a bit excessive to have a minibus and driver to myself but I wasn't going to complain.

I waved a final goodbye as my driver drove out of the courtyard. He followed the now familiar roads out past the airport, past the bus station and under the Welcome Arch and headed for the KKH. He didn't speak English but we were able to get by but not to have a deep and meaningful conversation. Besides I don't like to talk to drivers whilst they are driving as the roads are so bad that the driver needs all their concentration for driving and should not be distracted by chatting to passengers.

We were driving along and I had noticed that there was no traffic coming in the opposite direction. That would not be unusual on some of the mountain roads that I had travelled over the last few weeks but was unusual on a main road. Then we came to a long line of stationary vehicles, largely coaches and buses but with a scattering of cars and lorries. We came to a halt behind the last vehicle in the line and the driver turned off his engine. He leant out of the window and had a conversation with another driver standing next to his vehicle immediately in front of us. He then told me that there would be a ten minute delay but I didn't understand the reason.

The ten minutes stretched into twenty and then thirty minutes with more vehicles pulling up behind us. I could see stationary vehicles stretching along the road both in front and behind as far as the eye could see until the road curved around a bluff in either direction and out of sight.

It seemed that we were not going anywhere soon. I walked up the line of traffic a few times but never too far from sight of the minibus and the driver. After nearly an hour I told the driver that I was going to front of the queue to have a look and walked up the road. People had got out of cars and off buses and there were groups of women chatting, groups of men smoking, families eating picnics and bored children standing on the edge of the cliff next to the road throwing stones into the river a long way below us.

Down the valley I caught sight of a line of traffic on the other side of the road facing towards me so the cause of the traffic jam would be revealed shortly. There was a Chinese road construction crew working on the road. There was a lorry mounted cement mixer pouring concrete into a large metal bucket that a mobile crane lifted and moved to a position above some shuttering where the contents would be poured into the shuttering and the process repeated.

The shuttering and the associated scaffolding was in the shape of a square pillar beside the road. As the level of the concrete neared the top of the shuttering, the scaffolding and the shuttering was extended upwards to contain and support the next bucketful. It seemed a straightforward process and I couldn't see why or how they could be so slow. But the cement mixer and the crane were both positioned across the road and only pedestrians or bikers could squeeze past.

After a while the last of the concrete was poured and the cement mixer moved off to get another load and drivers and passengers went back to their vehicles. The head of the line of traffic moved forward as soon as the mobile crane had lowered and secured its jib and moved out of the way. Our turn to set off came and we pulled forward through the road works and past the line of traffic facing the other way which backed up a long way before it thinned out and eventually there was just open road.

At the earliest opportunity my driver over took the bus in front. There was a lot of slower buses in front and at every opportunity he would accelerate, pull out and overtake. The road followed the river in a deep gorge and there were no trees or fields, just rocks and the road could be seen for some long stretches in front so sometimes we overtook several buses at once.

Only occasionally, there were those tense moments when a vehicle appeared around a corner and I wondered whether we would brake and pull in behind, but no, we just went faster and at times, seemingly only made it just in time. I was just a passenger but I did find myself involuntarily pushing my right foot down on some imaginary brake pedal. I left the driving to the driver and looked out of the window to distract myself from thinking too long about traffic accidents.

The scenery for the most part was barren and rocky. I could tell when we were nearing a village as there would be more fields and trees on the outskirts before seeing any buildings. At one village there was a checkpoint and all vehicles had to slow down and IDs and vehicle documents were being checked randomly, some vehicles being waved down to pull off the road but we were waved straight through.

At Chilas we were waved down and we started what was to become a familiar procedure for the next two days. Travel and security were dangerous so vehicles travelled in armed convoy with a four by four at the front and back of the convoy, manned by the army, with a heavy calibre mounted machine gun behind the cab. The lead vehicle would be waiting outside the village and the convoy would form up behind it. When the convoy was ready to go it would set off and drive at a fairly fast but constant pace with all drivers expected to keep up.

Reaching the next check point, usually the next village, the escort vehicles would peel off and get ready to take the next convoy back the way they had just come. The buses and other vehicles could stop to pick up and drop off passengers, refuel, take an opportunity to visit shops and take natural breaks. On the far side of the village there would be more escort vehicles waiting and the convoy would reform and when ready, it would set off again.

Each section was between one and three hours driving. Lorries didn't join the convoy as they were too slow but continued on their own at their own pace. Private cars could join if they wished but there were few cars on the road. But all mini buses, buses and coaches had to join a convoy.

Every time we set off in a new convoy, where ever we were at the start, my driver always drove faster overtaking the larger vehicles so we always ended up being one of the vehicles at the head of the convoy, often between third and fifth vehicle in the convoy. It was almost like Formula One racing with drivers jockeying for position, as the other drivers of the smaller faster mini buses were all doing the same thing and if we slowed for a corner and the road was clear, we would be over taken.

Similarly, if the vehicle in front just touched his brakes, the red tail lights were almost a sign to my driver to overtake, sometimes with a honk on the horn. If the driver in front was hogging the centre of the road he would get a longer honk to tell him to pull over to let us pass. Considering the conditions this was dangerous as there was often a cliff face one side and a steep drop on the other.

There was tarmac but the good surface was often only in the middle and the edges were broken and rough and bumpy. On the plus side there was the feeling that it was safer to be near the lead army vehicle and being at the front there was less dust disturbed by the few vehicles in front so visibility and breathing would be better.

We stopped in a village at 3pm for lunch in a restaurant. I ordered a vegetable curry and rice plus two bottles of water to take with me for the journey. We were soon back in the minibus and we stopped just outside of the village in number two position and waited for the next convoy to form up behind us.

Whilst waiting there were an ever increasing number of passengers and drivers mingling around at the side of the road. I pulled out my camera and I took a photo but before I lowered the camera an armed policeman shouted and pointed me out to his colleague. They advanced towards me menacingly.

I had had a look about before taking the camera out but must have missed them in the crowds. I had to show what photo I had just taken and delete it and only when they were satisfied that they and the army were not on any of the other pictures did they walk off but not before reminding me firmly but politely not to take photos of security personnel. I suppose they could have taken my camera or arrested me, so I think I had a close escape.

The rear army vehicle drove to the head of the convoy and the officers had a quick conversation and evidently concluded that it was time to set off … I never found out what the criteria was, but as the rear vehicle drove back down the line, there were a few shouts of encouragement at the passengers and drivers to get back into their vehicles and after a couple of minutes, the lead vehicle set off.

After two hours driving we came to another village with a long suspension bridge for foot traffic only across the wide muddy waters of the river below us. The convoy reformed on the far side of the village. It was evident that as we waited to set off on the next section of road that travel along this road was slow, not due to the speed you drove but due to the waiting to form into convoys.

Somehow the driver had collected two other people who had joined us in the mini bus. I wasn't introduced but he seemed to know them well and they looked friendly enough. My guide trusted my driver enough to employ him so in turn I trusted my driver. Although I was slightly surprised when the driver got into the back and had given one of my new travelling companions the keys to the vehicle.

It was after 7pm and usually, I had arrived at a hotel or campsite by this time. I queried my driver about where we were staying the night and was told Besham City. I suddenly realised that we weren't taking the route over the mountain south from Chilas but were in fact on the KKH going straight down the Swat valley, that no go area for British tourists as per the FCO. It was too late to do anything about it and thinking back, Karim was too busy getting me off in the mini bus and Fran off in the jeep to the Kalash valley that I don't think he actually did have that word with the driver to ensure that we took the alternative route.

My new driver was just as determined to maintain our position in the convoy and drove as aggressively as my original driver, who was now lying asleep in the back of the mini bus as if he was having a Sunday afternoon nap. Nightfall came and we were still hurtling through the night along the KKH. The scenery had been spectacular to see during the day but now that it was dark, I still had the danger but without the benefit of spectacular views.

From the tail lights of the lead vehicles, we were still negotiating winding mountain roads as they twisted left and right, up and down on the road ahead of us. Looking behind at the vehicles in the convoy, I could see that the road was still twisting up and down, around headlands and up sides of valleys to cross bridges over tributaries of the main river, lit by the lights of their headlights marking out where we had just travelled.

It was dark when we came to our meal stop. The whole convoy pulled off the road and stopped at a place where there were a number of restaurants, cafes, a mosque, shops plus a public toilet. Everyone got out as soon as the vehicles stopped and rushed off towards their preferred choice of establishment as if this was a motorway service station with just ten minutes before setting off again, which it probably was.

In the dark, it was hard to tell, but I don't think there was a village, just a number of businesses with the public spaces between the various cafes lit only be what light spilled out from the restaurants and cafes. I went to the shop and bought some food to eat in the mini bus.

This was a short stop and in no time at all, we pulled back onto the road and set off again. I saw a few more buildings of a village as if the stop was on the outskirts of a village and the rest of the village was further along the road. The new driver continued to overtake to get to the front of the convoy despite the dark and the pot holes in the road.

It was gone midnight and we still hadn't arrived at our destination. This was no surprise really, given that we had started late, had been held up by the Chinese road builders plus the delays every time the convoy stopped and reformed. I queried where we would stop and it was still Besham City, down the road somewhere off in the dark. We continued to follow the tail lights of the vehicle in front, over taking or being over taken as the vehicles and their drivers continued to jockey for position.

We passed a PTDC hotel on the side of the road but this wasn't Besham City and we drove straight past it. We came to a bridge over the river, crossed it and climbed up the opposite bank. Looking back there was a long line of headlights marking the road where it descended the bank, then a series of headlights in a straight line across the bridge and then a curving line of lights as the road wound its way up the slope. I couldn't make out the tail of the convoy as the line of lights stretched far away in the depth of the night.

Here and there, were lights of farms and houses, stretching up the valley sides on both sides of a dark strip, the black chasm that was the river, flowing at the bottom of the valley. We were obviously in a deep gorge and if only it was daylight, I am sure there would have been a spectacular view. If I had to travel down a no go area, I felt that at least I should have had some compensation in the form of spectacular views.

At 3am we arrived on the outskirts of Besham City and at the check point the lead vehicle peeled off and we made our own way into the city. There were concrete buildings, multi storied buildings, street lights and advertising hoardings none of which I had seen since leaving Gilgit. We stopped at a garage and our two passengers got out and walked away and my original driver filled up with petrol and got back into the driving seat. We headed out of the town and found the local PTDC hotel adjacent to an army post on the main road out of town.

We parked in the car park where there was only one other vehicle and walked into reception. There were a couple of low voltage energy saving lights that cast an eerie glow towards the more distant corners of the reception area and beyond, a seating area and the restaurant. The manager who greeted us, was a tall lean elderly man, wearing a shalwaar chemise, a long grey beard and no moustache and despite his obvious age, he still walked with a straight back.

I was not sure how to read the manager's face, and unsure whether he was expecting me and I was more than nine hours late, or whether late arrivals were quite normal and that he was awake anyway. I showed my passport and signed in. Then I was led along a labyrinth of paths through well-kept gardens lit by feeble lights on the corners of various accommodation blocks and finally to my room, with the usual simple double bed and a separate washing area with a bucket and a shower.

I might have just sat in the passenger seat for more than sixteen hours but just travelling can be tiring and this was the only night in all my time in northern Pakistan that I didn't check out the local environs for routes into and out of the hotel compound before going to bed. We had an early start at 6am in the morning and including washing and eating I would be lucky to get two hours sleep. I was grateful that my driver had had some sleep in the back of the mini-bus because at least he would be rested and therefore alert while he was driving the next day.

I had set my alarm but with little enthusiasm to actually get up early and equally doubtful whether it would work. Even so there was a knock at my door at 5.30am just to make sure that I was awake so I shaved and re-packed my bag and carried it towards the restaurant for breakfast. As it happened the alarm had decided to work so I was already awake when the knock came and I was in the bathroom.

In the dim light of dawn, I could tell that the hotel was on the river bank overlooking the Indus and on a bright sun lit afternoon there might have been a scenic view but in the damp cool of the early morning dawn gloom with mist rising from the river I hurried on to the restaurant rather than hover to absorb the atmosphere.

We were served omelette and green tea by the chef and I signed out at reception. I had seen no other guests and as we drove out of the hotel compound, there was still only one other vehicle in the car park. We made our way back to the main road and before the sun had risen we had turned south and were back on the KKH heading towards Islamabad.

There was little other traffic on the road and when we arrived at what would have been the convoy start point there was a police pickup waiting with a mounted heavy calibre machine and as they were ready to go and we were ready, rather than wait for a convoy to form, we set off straight away and we had our own lead vehicle to ourselves which we followed down the road.

The cliffs softened and the cliff tops receded away from the centre of the valley as we left the mountains and passed into the foothills. There were more fields, more pasture, more trees and more houses which meant more people and traffic. After two hours of driving we were in rolling countryside with fields stretching away across the landscape as far as the eye could see, dotted with trees and farms and frequent villages and towns. Late in the morning somewhere after Abbottabad the lead vehicle slowed and pulled over and waved us past. From here on there was less perceived danger so we lost our escort and were left to make our own way down the rest of the valley.

We had left the hills far behind and the road was crossing a fertile agricultural plain. After the dramatic scenery of the mountains and the way that the road weaved its way through the scenery, the flat straight road across the plain was rather unexciting. We hit the outskirts of Islamabad and took the motorway into the centre of the city.

We arrived and stopped outside a small hotel in the back streets of Islamabad but knowing where I was meant to be at the Hunza Embassy Lodge and knowing that this wasn't it, I queried the driver. I didn't understand his answer and I didn't want to get out of the vehicle for him to drive off and leave me marooned. But he asked me to go with him and speak to the manager of the hotel, and since he had driven me for two days and hadn't robbed me, poisoned me, murdered me or driven off the edge of the cliff, I gave him the benefit of the doubt and walked into reception (but carrying my bag just in case).

It all became clear when the manager introduced me to Rahim who was to be my guide in Islamabad. He worked in the hotel but juggled his time between the hotel work and his part time job as a tour guide and he confirmed that Karim had asked him to look after me for a few days. He was a youngish man with long black hair going slightly grey in places tied back in a ponytail. He spoke excellent English and had previously been a full time guide. However with the recent troubles and the drop in the number of tourists, he now had to take a job in a hotel to make ends meet. But his employer was understanding and allowed him generous time off whenever he could find work as a guide.

I was mollified and relaxed and the driver drove Rahim and myself to the Hunza Embassy hotel near the Faisal Mosque at the other end of town. Rahim would guide over the next few days as I wanted to visit the Rohtas Fort which I had expressed a specific interest in visiting being built between 1541–1549 AD enclosing five hectares and able to accommodate 30,000 troops and claimed to be one of the best examples of 16th century Muslim military architecture.

Another sight I wanted to see was Taxila, an ancient city nearby that was sacked by nomadic Huns in the fifth century BC, captured by Alexander the Great in 326 BC, captured by the Indo Greek Bactria empire in the 2nd century BC and each time rebuilding itself as it sat on important trade routes going north south and east west. It eventually fell into decline and was largely lost until re-discovered in the mid-19th century by the British archaeologist Sir Alexander Cunningham

But they were for the forthcoming week. I thanked my driver giving him a generous tip and settled into the hotel. It was late afternoon and having lived out of a bag for weeks, I was not about to unpack only to repack again later so I was happy to save on the effort and live out of a bag for a further couple of days. But having hot water and a shower I did take the opportunity to rinse out my clothes and leave them to dry in the room. I filled in the rest of the afternoon with a walk in the neighbourhood checking out the local shops.

I was surprised at how I had gone native. If I had been fresh out from England, I would be commenting on the beggars, the queues at the petrol station, the security guards on the shops and banks. I no longer gazed at exotic fruit at the greengrocers and marvelled at the cost per item for pence. There were western branded products of soaps, moisturisers, deodorants, biscuits, crisps, tinned fruit and breakfast cereals at prices that when compared to home prices were cheap but checking the prices of local equivalent brands, the local prices were half to a tenth of the price. And all this was now unremarkable and I just accepted as normal.

I picked up a local English language newspaper. There was only doom and gloom about political intrigues, mismanagement, assassinations, murders, floods due to the monsoons and further loss of life. Added to the current weather, it was not uplifting and I put the newspaper down and just looked at the rain.

I had some more time in Pakistan but my travels in the Karakoram and the northern Pakistan province of Gilgit Baltistan were over and I had time to reflect. After two months in northern Pakistan, I was still in one piece. I had completed a trip that I had wanted to do for ages and I was able to cross off some items on my bucket list to be replaced with loads of memories. In the relative comfort and security of the Hunza Embassy Hotel, I relaxed and fell asleep in no time.

Epilogue

My return journey retraced my steps to get to Pakistan, via a stopover in Dubai. Arriving back in London in September, on an English summer's day, it felt rather cool after the heat in Islamabad and Dubai. But at least it was home and there were plenty of familiar species of trees with hedges surrounding the fields. And everything was green without any grey rock showing through as I made my way homeward through gently rolling hills of south east England. I slept for two days and when I finally emerged I discovered that I had lost over 9kgs in weight during the course of the trip.

Over the next few months, I had some updates from people that I had met during my trip. The washed out road below Phander had eventually been repaired more than three weeks after I last walked around the washout on my way back to Gilgit from Chitral. It still did not have a tarmac surface, but vehicles could negotiate a rough track higher up the valley side above the washout itself.

The polo teams from Gilgit could eventually get their horses up the road to the polo grounds on top of Shandur Pass which I had so wanted to see, but had been postponed several times, due to the washout and I was unable to see any polo played whilst I was there. I might just have to go back on another visit.

There had been extensive flooding in Kalash village of Balanguru and the road up to the village had been washed away in three places and was now closed to all road vehicles for weeks. It required a six hour walk around the washouts and up the valley to reach the Kalash village. Several bridges across the river had been washed away and temporary bridges had been erected made of tree trunks lashed together.

The main modern suspension bridge built across the river to carry the heavy electrical equipment over the river to the HEP pant had also been washed away. Substantial damage had occurred to the water intake area from the river to the channel taking water to a point above the power house. Some of the channel walls had over flowed and had been washed away and water had cascaded through the turbine hall. One piece of good luck was that as it was still a concrete shell, so not too much damage had been done to the building. The turbines and transformers and other equipment had still not been delivered so despite being late, they were not damaged.

Repairs to the water channel and to the bridges did occur eventually but it was another year in the summer of 2014 before the HEP plant was commissioned and started to supply electricity to the village and the surplus was exported to Chitral. The electricity supply to Chitral increased but with increasing urbanisation and for ever increasing demand for electricity there are still power cuts.

The families that had left that side of the valley affected by the construction of the HEP plant have returned now that the irrigation channel feeding off the water channel funnelling water to the HEP station now has water in it again and would be harvesting their first crops during the summer of 2015. It will only be at harvest time, at the end of 2015, that it will be known whether the fruit trees have survived and are strong enough to produce a crop of fruit.

Reports from travellers in 2014, the year following my visit, didn't report seeing any World Wildlife project on the way to the Khunjerab Pass, so I hope that the snow leopard and lammergeyer that I saw, have been successfully released back into the wild.

Regrettably, the security situation is as troublesome as ever. It gives such heartbreak that political and religious differences should result in an inability to appreciate that people hold different opinions and that it spills over into such widespread violence, insecurity and loss of life. Especially in an area where the people are already challenged with harsh winters, earthquakes, floods, poor soils and creaking infrastructure. The stunning, breath-taking scenery is great for visitors but little compensation for those that have to live under such harsh conditions.

Karim didn't return to Gilgit the following year, as there were not enough tourists to provide enough work to keep him employed. Jahangir has a job in a coffee shop in Islamabad but still wants to work in the tourist industry and takes time off in the summer to guide tourists. The lack of tourists continues to leave hotels available but empty, especially above Lake Attabad. Five years after the catastrophic landside that created Lake Attabad, the first of two major tunnels high up the valley side above the lake is finished but it will be another two years before the road is open right up to the Khunjerab Pass. Meanwhile. the Chinese are busy building a motorway up to their side of the pass.

The visa issues to cross the border are as vague and as temperamental as ever. Some tourists are allowed through and others are denied visas for no known recognisable pattern. I wanted a visa to cross from China to visit Gilgit the following year but was denied it yet I met British passport holders in Kashgar that had come across the Khunjerab Pass.

Certain parts stand out as highly memorable but for different reasons. The Kalash valleys were especially memorable for their culture. The two week walk to Concordia to view K2 gave a great sense of personal achievement. I remember with fondness, some of the most spectacular scenery, such as the road along the Shimshal valley for its rugged scenery, the road from the village of Tareshing at the base of Nanga Parbat up to the Deosai plains, for its charm and alpine beauty, the road down from the Deosai plains to Skardu for its rocky, barren steep descent and the road from Skardu to Gilgit, for the breathtaking plunging cliffs of the gorge and the communities hugging those cliffs. I am hard pressed to pick out just one outstanding route to take.

Some of the less pleasant memories were fading, such as the freezing cold and uncomfortable ground under canvas on the glacier for night after night or the realisation that I was in a dangerous no go area as I was driven down the Swat valley. I think I have even forgiven the cow that ate my socks, leaving me with just a single pair of walking socks for the next four weeks and I can laugh at the incident now.

The author

Norman Handy was born in 1957 in Beckenham,
Kent in the south east of England. He went to
school in Beckenham and later went to boarding
school in Cranbrook, Kent. He studied Business
Economics and Accountancy plus Law for Account-
ants at Southampton University.

During his studies, he also travelled and after fin-
ishing university travelled and worked abroad. He
returned to the United Kingdom and after some
time working in a riding school, followed a career
for thirty years in the financial services sector in
London, including periods working overseas.

He has two children and is a keen horse rider,
walker and skier and of course writer! He spends
his time between his home in West Sussex and
travelling.

Norman Handy

Overlanding the Silk Road

ISBN 978-3-99048-708-2
354 Pages

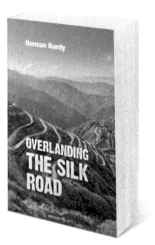

Overlanding the Silk Road is a real page turner, taking you on journeys you never thought you'd go on! From London to places like Kyrgyzstan, known as Asia's little Switzerland. Sit back and enjoy the beautiful scenery and experiences this book will take you on.

Norman Handy

The Klondikers

ISBN 978-3-99048-714-3
246 Pages

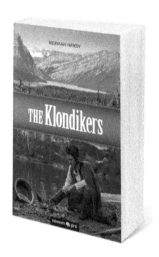

Have you ever wondered how gold is really found? Well you're about to find out as Norman Handy recreates the journey that one farmer from the wheat growing areas of the prairies around Calgary, may have experienced in his quest to find gold!

Lightning Source UK Ltd.
Milton Keynes UK
UKHW04f0631171018
330689UK00001B/5/P